WOOD

BY
HUGH WALPOLE

First Published 1909
Republished 2023

CONTENTS

CHAPTER I

CHAPTER II

CHAPTER III

CHAPTER IV

CHAPTER V

CHAPTER VI

CHAPTER VII

CHAPTER VIII

CHAPTER IX

CHAPTER X

CHAPTER XI

CHAPTER XII

CHAPTER XIII

CHAPTER XIV

CHAPTER XV

CHAPTER XVI

CHAPTER I

Robin Trojan was waiting for his father.

Through the open window of the drawing-room came, faintly, the cries of the town—the sound of some distant bell, the shout of fishermen on the quay, the muffled beat of the mining-stamps from Porth-Vennic, a village that lay two miles inland. There yet lingered in the air the faint afterglow of the sunset, and a few stars, twinkling faintly in the deep blue of the night sky, seemed reflections of the orange lights of the herring-boats, flashing far out to sea.

The great drawing-room, lighted by a cluster of electric lamps hanging from the ceiling, seemed to flaunt the dim twinkle of the stars contemptuously; the dark blue of the walls and thick Persian carpets sounded a quieter note, but the general effect was of something distantly, coldly superior, something indeed that was scarcely comfortable, but that was, nevertheless, fulfilling the exact purpose for which it had been intended.

And that purpose was, most certainly, not comfort. Robin himself would have smiled contemptuously if you had pleaded for something homely, something suggestive of roaring fires and cosy armchairs, instead of the stiff-backed, beautifully carved Louis XIV. furniture that stood, each chair and table rigidly in its appointed place, as though bidding defiance to any one bold enough to attempt alterations.

The golden light in the sky shone faintly in at the open window, as though longing to enter, but the dazzling brilliance of the room seemed to fling it back into the blue dome of sea and sky outside.

Robin was standing by a large looking-glass in the corner of the room trying to improve the shape of his tie; and it was characteristic of him that, although he had not seen his father for eighteen years, he was thinking a great deal more about his tie than about the approaching meeting.

He was, at this time, twenty years of age. Tall and dark, he had all the Trojan characteristics; small, delicately shaped ears; a mouth that gave signs of all the Trojan obstinacy, called by the Trojans themselves family pride; a high, well-shaped forehead with hair closely cut and of a dark brown. He was considered by most people handsome—but to some his eyes, of the real Trojan blue, were too cold and impassive. He gave you the impression of some one who watched, rather disdainfully, the ill-considered and impulsive actions of his fellow-men.

He was, however, exactly suited to his surroundings. He maintained the same position as the room with regard to the world in general—"We are Trojans; we are very old and very expensive and very, very good, and it behoves you to recognise this fact and give way with fitting deference."

He had not seen his father for eighteen years, and, as he had been separated from him at the unimpressionable age of two, he may be said never to have seen him at all. He had no recollection of him, and the picture that he had painted was constructed out of monthly rather uninteresting letters concerned, for the most part, with the care and maintenance of New Zealand sheep, and such meagre details as his Aunt Clare and Uncle Garrett had bestowed on him from time to time. From the latter he gathered that his father had been, in his youth, in some vague way, unsatisfactory, and had departed to Australia to seek his fortune, with a clear understanding from his father that he was not to return thence until he had found it.

Robin himself had been born in New Zealand, but his mother dying when he was two years old, he had been sent home to be brought up, in the proper Trojan manner, by his aunt and uncle.

On these things Robin reflected as he tried to twist his tie into a fitting Trojan shape; but it refused to behave as a well-educated tie should, and the obvious thing was to get another. Robin looked at his watch. It was really extremely provoking; the carriage had been timed to arrive at half-past six exactly; it was now a quarter to seven and no one had appeared. There was probably not time to search for another tie. His father would be certain to arrive at the very moment when one tie was on and the other not yet on, which meant that Robin would be late; and if there was one thing that a Trojan hated more than another it was being late. With many people unpunctuality was a fault, with a Trojan it was a crime; it was what was known as an "odds and ends"—one of those things, like untidiness, eating your fish with a steel knife and wearing a white tie with a short dinner-jacket, that marked a man, once and for all, as some one outside the pale, an impossible person.

Therefore Robin allowed his tie to remain and walked to the open window.

"At any rate," he said to himself, still thinking of his tie, "father won't probably notice it." He wondered how much his father *would* notice. "As he's a Trojan," he thought, "he'll know the sort of things that a fellow ought to do, even though he has been out in New Zealand all his life."

It would, Robin reflected, be a very pretty little scene. He liked scenes, and, if this one were properly manoeuvred, he ought to be its very interesting and satisfactory centre. That was why it was really a pity about the tie.

The door from the library swung slowly open, and Sir Jeremy Trojan, Robin's grandfather, was wheeled into the room.

He was very old indeed, and the only part of his face that seemed alive were his eyes; they were continually darting from one end of the room to the other, they were never still; but, for the rest, he scarcely moved. His skin was dried and brown like a mummy's, and even when he spoke, his lips hardly stirred. He was in evening dress, his legs wrapped tightly in rugs; his chair was wheeled by a servant who was evidently perfectly trained in all the Trojan ways of propriety and decorum.

"Well, grandfather," said Robin, turning back from the window with the look of annoyance still on his face, "how are you to-night?" Robin always shouted at his grandfather although he knew perfectly well that he was not deaf, but could, on the other hand, hear wonderfully well for his age. Nothing

4

annoyed his grandfather so much as being shouted at, and of this Robin was continually reminded.

"Tut, tut, boy," said Sir Jeremy testily, "one would think that I was deaf. Better? Yes, of course. Close the windows!"

"I'll ring for Marchant," said Robin, moving to the bell, "he ought to have done it before." Sir Jeremy said nothing—it was impossible to guess at his thoughts from his face; only his eyes moved uneasily round the room.

He was wheeled to his accustomed corner by the big open stone fireplace, and he lay there, motionless in his chair, without further remark.

Marchant came in a moment later.

"The windows, Marchant," said Robin, still twisting uneasily at his tie, "I think you had forgotten."

"I am sorry, sir," Marchant answered, "but Mr. Garrett had spoken this morning of the room being rather close. I had thought that perhaps———"

He moved silently across the room and shut the window, barring out the fluttering yellow light, the sparkling silver of the stars, the orange of the fishing-boats, the murmured distance of the town.

A few moments later Clare Trojan came in. Although she had never been beautiful she had always been interesting, and indeed she was (even when in the company of women far more beautiful than herself) always one of the first to whom men looked. This may have been partly accounted for by her very obvious pride, the quality that struck the most casual observer at once, but there was also an air of indifference, a look in the eyes that seemed to pique men's curiosity and stir their interest. It was not for lack of opportunity that she was still unmarried, but she had never discovered the man who had virtue and merit sufficient to cover the obvious disadvantages of his not having been born a Trojan. Middle age suited the air of almost regal dignity with which she moved, and people who had known her for many years said that she had never looked so well as now. To-night, in a closely-fitting dress of black silk relieved by a string of pearls round her neck, and a superb white rose at her breast, she was almost handsome. Robin watched her with satisfaction as she moved towards him.

"Ah, it's cold," she said. "I know Marchant left those windows open till the last moment. Robin, your tie is shocking. It looks as if it were made-up."

"I know," said Robin, still struggling with it; "but there isn't time to get another. Father will be here at any moment. It's late as it is. Yes, I told Marchant to shut the windows, he said something about Uncle Garrett's saying it was stuffy or something."

"Harry's late." Clare moved across to her father and bent down and kissed him.

"How are you to-night, father?" but she was arranging the rose at her breast and was obviously thinking more of its position than of the answer to her question.

"Hungry—damned hungry," said Sir Jeremy.

5

"Oh, we'll have to wait," said Clare. "Harry's got to dress. Anyhow you've got no right to be hungry at a quarter to seven. Nobody's ever hungry till half-past seven at the earliest."

It was evident that she was ill at ease. Perhaps it was the prospect of meeting her brother after a separation of eighteen years; perhaps it was anxiety as to how this reclaimed son of the house of Trojan would behave in the face of the world. It was so very important that the house should not be in any way let down, that the dignity with which it had invariably conducted its affairs for the last twenty years should be, in no way, impaired. Harry had been anything but dignified in his early days, and sheep-farming in New Zealand—well, of course, one knew what kind of life that was.

But, as she looked across at Robin, it was easy to see that her anxiety was, in some way, connected with him. How was this invasion to affect her nephew? For eighteen years she had been the only father and mother that he had known, for eighteen years she had educated him in all the Trojan laws and traditions, the things that a Trojan must speak and do and think, and he had faithfully responded to her instruction. He was in every way everything that a Trojan should be; but there had been moments, rare indeed and swiftly passing, when Clare had fancied that there were other impulses, other ideas at work. She was afraid of those impulses, and she was afraid of what Henry Trojan might do with regard to them.

It was, indeed, hard, after reigning absolutely for eighteen years, to yield her place to another, but perhaps, after all, Robin would be true to his early training and she would not be altogether supplanted.

"Randal comes to-morrow," said Robin suddenly, after a few minutes' silence. "Unfortunately he can only stop for a few days. His paper on 'Pater' has been taken by the *National*. He's very much pleased, of course."

Robin spoke coldly and without any enthusiasm. It was not considered quite good form to be enthusiastic; it was apt to lead you into rather uncertain company with such people as Socialists and the Salvation Army.

"I'm glad he's coming—quite a nice fellow," said Clare, looking at the gold clock on the mantelpiece. "The train is shockingly late. On 'Pater' you said! I must try and get the *National*—Miss Ponsonby takes it, I think. It's unusual for Garrett to be unpunctual."

He entered at the same moment—a tall, thin man of forty years of age, clean shaven and rather bald, with a very slight squint in the right eye. He walked slowly, and always gave the impression that he saw nothing of his surroundings. For the rest, he was said to be extremely cynical and had more than a fair share of the Trojan pride.

"The train is late," he said, addressing no one in particular. "Father, how are you this evening?"

This third attack on Sir Jeremy was repelled by a snort, which Garrett accepted as an answer. "Robin, your tie is atrocious," he continued, picking up the *Times* and opening it slowly; "you had better change it."

Robin was prevented from answering by the sound of carriage-wheels on the drive. Clare rose and stood by the fireplace near Sir Jeremy; Garrett read to the end of the paragraph and folded the paper on his knee; Robin fingered his watch-chain nervously and moved to his aunt's side—only Sir Jeremy remained motionless and gave no sign that he had heard.

Perhaps he was thinking of that day twenty years before when, after a very heated interview, he had forbidden his son to see his face again until he had done something that definitely justified his existence. Harry had certainly done several things since then that justified his existence; he had, for one thing, made a fortune, and that was not so easily done nowadays. Harry was five-and-forty now; he must be very much changed; he had steadied down, of course ... he would be well able to take his place as head of the family when Sir Jeremy himself....

But he gave no sign. You could not tell that he had heard the carriage-wheels at all; he lay motionless in his chair with his eyes half closed.

There were voices in the hall. Beldam's superlatively courteous tones as of one who is ready to die to serve you, and then another voice—rather loud and sharp, but pleasant, with the sound of a laugh in it.

"They are in the blue drawing-room, sir—Mr. Henry," Beldam's voice was heard on the stairs, and, in a moment, Beldam himself appeared—"Mr. Henry, Sir Jeremy." Then he stood aside, and Henry Trojan entered the room.

Clare made a step forward.

"Harry—old boy—at last———"

Both her hands were outstretched, but he disregarded them, and, stepping forward, crushed her in his arms, crushed her dress, crushed the beautiful rose at her breast, and, bending down, kissed her again and again.

"Clare—after twenty years!"

He let her go and she stepped back, still smiling, but she touched the rose for a moment and her hair. He was very strong.

And then there was a little pause. Harry Trojan turned and faced his father. The old man made no movement and gave no sign, but he said, his lips stirring very slightly, "I am glad to see you here again, Harry."

The man flushed, and with a little stammer answered, "I am gladder to be back than you can know, father."

Sir Jeremy's wrinkled hand appeared from behind the rugs, and the two men shook in silence.

Then Garrett came forward. "You're not much changed, Harry," he said with a laugh, "in spite of the twenty years."

"Why, Garrie!" His brother stepped towards him and laid a hand on his shoulder. "It's splendid to see you again. I'd almost forgotten what you were like—I only had that old photo, you know—of us both at Rugby."

Robin had stood aside, in a corner by the fireplace, watching his father. It was very much as he had expected, only he couldn't, try as he might, think of him as his father at all. The man there who had kissed Aunt Clare and shaken hands with Sir Jeremy was, in some unexplained way, a little odd and out of place. He was big and strong; his hair curled a little and was dark brown, like Robin's, and his eyes were blue, but, in other respects, there was very little of the Trojan about him. His mouth was large, and he had a brown, slightly curling moustache. Indeed the general impression was brown in spite of the blue, badly fitting suit. He was deeply tanned by the sun and was slightly freckled.

He would have looked splendid in New Zealand or Klondyke, or, indeed, anywhere where you worked with your coat off and your shirt open at the neck; but here, in that drawing-room, it was a pity, Robin thought, that his father had not stopped for two or three days in town and gone to a West End tailor.

But, after all, it was a very nice little scene. It really had been quite moving to see him kiss Clare like that, but, at the same time, for his part, kissing...!

"And Robin?" said Harry.

"Here's the son and heir," said Garrett, laughing, and pushing Robin forward.

Now that the moment had really come, Robin was most unpleasantly embarrassed. How foolish of Uncle Garrett to try and be funny at a time like that, and what a pity it was that his tie was sticking out at one end so much farther than at the other. He felt his hand seized and crushed in the grip of a giant; he murmured something about his being pleased, and then, suddenly, his father bent down and kissed him on the forehead.

They were both blushing, Robin furiously. How he hated sentiment! He felt sure that Uncle Garrett was laughing at him.

"By Jove, you're splendid!" said Harry, holding him back with both his hands on his shoulders. "Pretty different from the nipper that I sent over to England eighteen years ago. Oh, you'll do, Robin."

"And now, Harry," said Clare, laughing, "you'll go and dress, won't you? Father's terribly hungry and the train was late."

"Right," said Harry; "I won't be long. It's good to be back again."

When the door had closed behind him, there was silence. He gave the impression of some one filled with overwhelming, rapturous joy. There was a light in his eyes that told of dreams at length fulfilled, and hopes, long and wearily postponed, at last realised. He had filled that stiff, solemn room with a spirit of life and strength and sheer animal good health—it was even, as Clare afterwards privately confessed, a little exhausting.

Now she stood by the fireplace, smiling a little. "My poor rose," she said, looking at some of the petals that had fallen to the ground. "Harry is strong!"

"He is looking well," said Garrett. It sounded almost sarcastic.

Robin went up to his room to change his tie—he had said nothing about his father.

As Harry Trojan passed down the well-remembered passages where the pictures hung in the same odd familiar places, past staircases vanishing into dark abysses that had frightened him as a child, windows deep-set in the thick stone walls, corners round which he had crept in the dark on his way to his room, it seemed to him that those long, dreary years of patient waiting in New Zealand were as nothing, and that it was only yesterday that he had passed down that same way, his heart full of rage against his father, his one longing to get out and away to other countries where he should be his own master and win his own freedom. And now that he was back again, now that he had seen what that freedom meant, now that he had tasted that same will-o'-the-wisp liberty, how thankful he was to rest here quietly, peacefully, for the remainder of his days; at last he knew what were the things that were alone, in this world, worth striving for—not money, ambition, success, but love for one's own little bit of country that one called home, the patient resting in the heritage of all those accumulating traditions that ancestors had been making, slowly, gradually, for centuries of years.

He had hoped that he would have the same old rooms at the top of the West Towers that he had had when a boy; he remembered the view of the sea from their windows—the great sweep of the Cornish coast far out to Land's End itself, and the gulls whirring with hoarse cries over his head as he leant out to view the little cove nestling at the foot of the Hall. That view, then, had meant to him distant wonderful lands in which he was to make his name and his fortune: now it spoke of home and peace, and, beyond all, of Cornwall.

They had put him in one of the big spare rooms that faced inland. As he entered the sense of its luxury filled him with a delicious feeling of comfort: the log-fire burning in the open brown-tiled fireplace, the softness of the carpets, the electric light, shaded to a soft glow—ah! these were the things for which he had waited, and they had, indeed, been worth waiting for.

His man was laying his dress-clothes on his bed.

"What is your name?" he said, feeling almost a little shy; it was so long since he had had things done for him.

"James Treduggan, sir," the man answered, smiling. "You won't remember me, sir, I expect. I was quite a youngster when you went away. But I've been in service here ever since I was ten."

When Harry was left alone, he stood by the fire, thinking. He had been preparing for this moment for so long that now that it was actually here he was frightened, nervous. He had so often imagined that first arrival in England, the first glimpse of London; then the first meeting and the first evening at home. Of course, all his thoughts had centred on Robin—everything else had been secondary, but he had, in some unaccountable way, never been able to realise exactly what Robin would be. He had had photographs, but they had been unsatisfactory and had told him nothing; and now that he had seen him, he was at rest; he was all that he had hoped—straight, strong, manly, with that clear steady look in the eyes that meant so much; yes, there was no doubt about his son. He remembered Robin's mother with affectionate tenderness; she had been the daughter of a doctor in Auckland—he had fallen in love with her at once and married her, although his prospects had been so bad. They had been very happy, and then, when Robin was two years old, she had died; the boy had been sent home, and he had been alone again—for eighteen years he had been alone. There had been other women, of course; he did not pretend to have been a saint, and women had liked him and been rather sorry for him in those early years; but they had none of them been very much to him, only episodes—the central fact of his existence had always been his son. He had had a friend there, a Colonel Durand, who had three sons of his own, and had given him much advice as to his treatment of Robin. He had talked a great deal about the young generation, about its impatience of older theories and manners, its dislike of authority and restraint; and Harry, remembering his own early hatred of restriction and longing for freedom, was determined that he would be no fetter on his son's liberty, that he would be to him a friend, a companion rather than a father. After all, he felt no more than twenty-five—there was really no space of years between them—he was as young to-day as he had been twenty years ago.

As to the others, he had never cared very much for Clare and Garrett in the old days; they had been stiff, cold, lacking all sense of family affection. But that had been twenty years ago. There had been a time, in New Zealand, when he had hated Garrett. When he had been away from home for some ten years, the longing to see his boy had grown too strong to be resisted, and he had written to his father asking for permission to return. He had received a cold answer from Garrett, saying that Sir Jeremy thought that, as he was so successful there, it would be perhaps better if he remained there a little while longer; that he would find little to do at home and would only weary of the monotony—four closely written pages to the same effect. So Harry had remained.

But that was ten years ago. At last, a letter had come, saying that Sir Jeremy was now very old and feeble, that he desired to see his son before he died, and that all the past was forgotten and forgiven. And now there was but one thought in his heart—love for all the world, one overwhelming desire to take his place amongst them decently, worthily, so that they might see that the wastrel of twenty years ago had developed into a man, able to take his place, in due time, at the head of the Trojan family. Oh! how he would try to please them all! how he would watch and study and work so that that long twenty years' exile might be forgotten both by himself and by them.

He bathed and dressed slowly by the fire. As he saw his clothes on the bed he fancied, for a moment, that they might be a little worn, a little old. They had seemed very good and smart in Auckland, but in England it was rather different. He almost wished that he had stayed in London for two days and been properly fitted by a tailor. But then he had been so eager to arrive, he had not thought of clothes; his one idea had been to rush down as soon as possible and see them all, and the place, and the town.

Then he remembered that Clare had asked him to be quick. He finished his dressing hurriedly, turned out the electric light, and left the room.

He was pleased to find that he had not forgotten the turns and twists of the house. He threaded the dark passages easily, humming a little tune, and smelling that same sweet scent of dried rose leaves that he had known so well when he was a small boy. He could see, in imagination, the great white-and-pink china pot-pourri bowls standing at the corner of the stairs—nothing was changed.

The blue drawing-room was deserted when he entered it—only the blaze of the electric light, the golden flame of the log-fire in the great open fireplace, and the solemn ticking of the gold clock that had stood there, in the same place of honour, for the last hundred years. He passed over to the windows and flung them open; the hum of the town came, with the cold night air, into the room. The stars were brilliant to-night and the golden haze of the lamplight hung over the streets like a magic curtain. Ah! how good it was! The peace of it, the comfort, the homeliness!

Above all, it was Cornwall—the lights of the herring fleet, the distant rhythmical beat of the mining-stamps, that peculiar scent as of precious spices coming with the wind of the sea, as though borne from distant magical lands, all told him that he was, at last, again in Cornwall.

He drank in the night air, bending his eyes on the town as though he were saluting it again, tenderly, joyously, with the greeting of an old familiar friend.

Robin closed the door behind him and shivered a little. The windows were open—how annoying when Aunt Clare had especially asked that they should be closed. Oh! it was his father! Of course, he did not know!

He had not been noticed, so he coughed. Harry turned round.

"Hullo, Robin, my boy!" He passed his arm through his son's and drew him to the window. "Isn't it splendid?" he said. "Oh! I don't suppose you see it now, after having been here all this time; you want to go away for twenty years, then you'd know how much it's worth. Oh! it's splendid—what times we'll have here, you and I!"

"Yes," said Robin, a little coldly. It was very chilly with the window open, and there was something in all that enthusiasm that was almost a little vulgar. Of course, it was natural, after being away so long ... but still.... Also his father's clothes were really very old—the back of the coat was quite shiny.

Sir Jeremy entered in his chair, followed by Clare and Garrett.

Clare gave a little scream.

"Oh! How cold!" she cried. "Now whoever——!"

"I'm afraid I was guilty," said Harry, laughing. "The town looked so splendid and I hadn't seen it for so long. I——"

"Of course, I forgot," said Clare. "I don't suppose you notice open windows in New Zealand, because you're always outside in the Bush or something. But here we're as shivery as you make them. Dinner's getting shivery too. The sooner we go down the better."

She passed back through the door and down the hall. There was no doubt that she was a magnificent woman.

As Sir Jeremy was wheeled through the doors he gripped Harry's hand. "I'm damned glad that you're back," he whispered.

Robin, who was the last to leave the room, closed the windows and turned out the lights. The room was in darkness save for the golden light of the leaping fire.

CHAPTER II

It had been called the "House of the Flutes" since the beginning of time. People had said that the name was absurd, and Harry's grandfather, a prosaic gentleman of rather violent radical opinions, had made a definite attempt at a change—but he had failed. Trojans had appeared from every part of the country, angry Trojans, tearful Trojans, indignant Trojans, important Trojans, poor-relation Trojans, and had, one and all, demanded that the name should remain, and that the headquarters of the Trojan tradition, of the Trojan power, should continue to be the "House of the Flutes."

Of course, it had its origin in tradition. In the early days when might was right, and the stronger seized the worldly goods of the weaker and nobody said him nay, there had been a Sir Jeremy Trojan whose wife had been the talk of the country-side both because of her beauty and also because of her easy morals. Sir Jeremy having departed on a journey, the lovely Lady Clare entertained a neighbouring baron at her husband's bed and board, and for two days all was well. But Sir Jeremy unexpectedly returned, and, being a gentleman of a pleasant fancy, walled up the room in which he had found the erring couple and left them inside. He then sat outside, and listened with a gentle pleasure to their cries, and, being a musician of no mean quality, played on the flute from time to time to prevent the hours from being wearisome. For three days he sat there, until there came no more sounds from that room; then he pursued his ordinary affairs, but sought no other wife—a grim little man with a certain sense of humour.

There are many other legends connected with the house; you will find them in Baedeker, where it also says: "Kind permission is accorded by Sir Henry Trojan to visitors who desire to see the rooms during the residence of the family in London. Special attention should be paid to the gold Drawing-room with its magnificent carving, the Library with its fine collection of old prints, and the Long Gallery with the family portraits, noticing especially the Vandyke of Sir Hilary Trojan (*temp*. Ch. I.), and a little sketch by Turner of the view from the West Tower. The gardens, too, are well worth a short inspection, special mention being made of the Long Terrace with its magnificent sea-view.

"A small charge is made by Sir Henry for admittance (adults sixpence, children half-price), with a view to benefiting the church, a building recently restored and sadly in need of funds."

So far Baedeker (Cornwall, new ed., 1908). The house is astonishingly beautiful, seen from any point of view. Added to from time to time, it has that air of surprise, as of a building containing endless secrets, only some of which it intends to reveal. It is full of corners and angles, and at the same time preserves a symmetry and grandeur of style that is surprising, if one considers its haphazard construction and random additions.

Part of its beauty is undoubtedly owing to its superb position. It rises from the rock, over the grey town at its feet, like a protecting deity, its two towers to west and east, raised like giant hands, its grey walls rising sheer from the steep, shelving rock; behind it the gentle rise of hills, bending towards the inland valleys; in front of it an unbroken stretch of sea.

It strikes the exact note that is in harmony with its colour and surroundings: the emblem of some wild survival from dark ages when that spot had been one of the most uncivilised in the whole of Britain—a land of wild, uncouth people, living in a state of perpetual watch and guard, fearing the sea, fearing the land, cringingly superstitious because of their crying need of supernatural defence; and, indeed, there is nothing more curious in the Cornwall of to-day than this perpetual reminder of past superstitions, dead gods, strange pathetic survival of heathen ancestry.

The town of Pendragon, lying at the foot of the "House of the Flutes," had little of this survival of former custom about it; it was rapidly developing into that temple of British middle-class mediocrity, a modern watering-place. It had, in the months of June, July, and August, nigger minstrels, a café chantant, and a promenade, with six bathing-machines and two donkeys; two new hotels had sprung up within the last two years, a sufficient sign of its prosperity. No, Pendragon was doing its best to forget its ancient superstitions, and even seemed to regard the "House of the Flutes" a little resentfully because of its reminder of a time when men scaled the rocks and stormed the walls, and fell back dying and cursing into their ships riding at anchor in the little bay.

Very different was Cullin's Cove, the little fishing-village that lay slightly to the right of the town. Here traditions were carefully guarded; a strict watch was kept on the outside world, and strangers were none too cheerfully received. Here, "down-along," was the old, the true Cornwall—a land that had changed scarcely at all since those early heathen days that to the rest of the world are dim, mysterious, mythological, but to a Cornishman are as the events of yesterday. High on the moor behind the Cove stand four great rocks—wild, wind-beaten, grimly permanent. It is under their guardianship that the Cove lies, and it is something more than a mere superstitious reverence that those inhabitants of "down-along" pay to those darkly mysterious figures. Seen in the fading light of the dying day, when Cornish mists are winding and twisting over the breast of the moor, these four rocks seem to take a living shape, to grow in size, and to whisper to those that care to hear old stories of the slaughter that had stained the soil at their feet on an earlier day.

From Harry's windows the town and the sea were hidden. Immediately below him lay the tennis-lawns and the rose-garden, and, gleaming in the distance, at the end of the Long Walk, two white statues that had fascinated him in his boyhood.

His first waking thought on the morning after his arrival was to look for those statues, and when he saw them gleaming in the sun just as they used to do, there swept over him a feeling of youth and vigour such as he had never known before. Those twenty years in New Zealand were, after all, to go for nothing; they were to be as though they had had no existence, and he was to be the young energetic man of twenty-five, able to enter into his son's point of view, able to share his life and vitality, and, at the same time, to give him the benefit of his riper experience.

Through his open window came the faint, distant beating of the sea; a bird flew past him, a white flash of light; some one was singing the refrain of a Cornish "chanty"—the swing of the tune came up to him from the garden, and some of the words beat like little bells upon his brain, calling up endless memories of his boyhood.

He looked at his watch and found that it was nine o'clock. He had no idea that it was so late; he had asked to be called at seven, but he had slept so soundly that he had not heard his man enter with his shaving water; it was quite cold now, and his razors were terribly blunt. He cut himself badly, a thing that he scarcely ever did. But it was really unfortunate, on this first morning when he had wanted everything to be at its best.

He came down to the breakfast-room humming. The house seemed a palace of gold on this wonderful September morning; the light came in floods through the great windows at the head of the stairs, and shafts of golden light struck the walls and the china potpourri bowls and flashed wonderful colours out of a great Venetian vase that stood by the hall door.

He found Garrett and Robin breakfasting alone; Clare and Sir Jeremy always had breakfast in their own rooms.

"I'm afraid I'm awfully late," said Harry cheerfully, clapping his brother on the back and putting his hand for a minute on Robin's shoulder; "things all cold?"

"Oh no," said Garrett, scarcely looking up from his morning paper. "Damned good kidneys!"

Robin said nothing. He was watching his father curiously. It was one of the Trojan rules that you never talked at breakfast; it was such an impossible meal altogether, and one was always at one's worst at that time of the morning. Robin wondered whether his father would recognise this elementary rule or whether he would talk, talk, talk, as he had done last night. They had had rather a bad time last night; Aunt Clare had had a headache, but his father had talked continuously—about sheep and Maories and the Pink Terraces. It had been just like a parish-room magic-lantern lecture—"Some hours with our friends the Maories"—it had been very tiring; poor Aunt Clare had grown whiter and whiter; it was quite a relief when dinner had come to an end.

Harry helped himself to kidneys and sat down by Robin, still humming the refrain of the Cornish song he had heard at his window. "By Jove, I'm late—mustard, Robin, my boy—can't think how I slept like that. Why, in New Zealand I was always up with the lark—had to be, you know, there was always such heaps to do—the bread, old boy, if you can get hold of it. I remember once getting up at three in the morning to go and play cricket somewhere—fearful hot day it was, but I knocked up fifty, I remember. Probably the bowling was awfully soft, although I remember one chap—Pulling, friend of Durand's—could fairly twist 'em down the pitch—made you damned well jump. Talking of cricket, I suppose you play, Robin? Did you get your cap or whatever they call it—College colours, you know?"

"Oh, cricket!" said Robin indifferently. "No, I didn't play. The chaps at King's who ran the games were rather outers—pretty thoroughly barred by the decent men. None of the 'Gracchi' went in for the sports."

"Oh!" said Harry, considerably surprised. "And who the deuce are the 'Gracchi'?"

"A society I was on," said Robin, a little wearily—it was so annoying to be forced to talk at breakfast. "A literary society—essays, with especial attention paid to the New Literature. We made it our boast that we never went back further than Meredith, except, of course, when one had to, for origins and comparisons. Randal, who's coming to stop for a few days, was president last year and read some awfully good papers."

Harry stared blankly. He had thought that every one played cricket and football, especially when they were strong and healthy like Robin. He had not quite understood about the society—and who was Meredith? "I shall be glad to meet your friend," he said. "Is he still at Cambridge?"

"Oh, Randal!" said Robin. "No, he came down the same time as I did. He only got a second in History, although he was worth a first any day of the week. But he had such lots of other things to do—his papers for the 'Gracchi' took up any amount of time—and then history rather bored him. He's very popular here, especially with all Fallacy Street people."

"The Fallacy Street people!" repeated Harry, still more bewildered. "Who are they?"

"Oh! I suppose you've forgotten," said Robin, mildly surprised. "They're all the people who're intellectual in Pendragon. If you live in Fallacy Street you're one of the wits. It's like belonging to the 'Mermaid' used to be, you know, in Shakespeare's time. They're really awfully clever—some of them—the Miss Ponsonbys and Mrs. le Terry—Aunt Clare thinks no end of Mrs. le Terry."

Robin's voice sounded a little awed. He had a great respect for Fallacy Street. "Oh, they won't have any room for me," said Harry, laughing. "I'm an awfully stupid old duffer. I haven't read anything at all, except a bit of Kipling—'Barrack-room Ballads'—seems a waste of time to read somehow."

That his father had very little interest in literature Robin had discovered some time before, but that he should boast of it—openly, laughingly—was really rather terrible.

Harry was silent for a few minutes; he had evidently made a blunder in his choice of a subject, but it was really difficult.

"Where are we going this morning, Robin?" he said at last.

"Oh! I say!" Robin looked a little unhappy. "I'm awfully sorry, father. I'm really afraid I can't come out this morning. There's a box of books that have positively got to get off to Randal's place to-night. I daren't keep them any longer. I'd do it this afternoon, only it's Aunt Clare's at-home day and she always likes me to help her. I'm really awfully sorry, but there are lots of other mornings, aren't there? I simply must get those books off this morning."

"Why, of course," said Harry cheerfully; "there's plenty of time."

He was dreadfully disappointed. He had often thought of that first stroll with Robin. They would discuss the changes since Harry's day; Robin would point out the new points of interest, and, perhaps, introduce him to some of his friends—it had been a favourite picture of his during some of those lonely days in New Zealand. And now Robin's aunt and college friend were to come before his father—it was rather hard.

But, then, on second thoughts, how unreasonable it was of him to expect to take up Robin's time like that. He must fall into the ways of the house, quietly, unobtrusively, with none of that jolting of other people's habits and regular customs; it had been thoughtless, of him and ridiculous. He must be more careful.

Breakfast ended, he found himself alone. Robin left the room with the preoccupied air of a man of fifty; the difficulty of choosing between Jefferies' "Story of my Heart" and Walt Whitman's "Leaves of Grass," if there wasn't room in the box for both, was terrible! Of course Randal was coming himself in a few days, and it would have been simpler to let him choose for himself; but he had particularly asked for them to be sent by the fourth, and to-day was the third. Robin had quite forgotten his father.

Harry was alone. From the garden came the sound of doves, and, through the window that overlooked the lawn, the sun shone into the room. Harry lit a cigarette and went out. The garden was changed; there was a feeling of order and authority about it that it had never had before. Not a weed was to be seen on the paths: flowers stretched in perfect order and discipline; colours in harmony, shapes and patterns of a tutored symmetry—it was the perfection of a modern gardener's art. He passed gardeners, grave, serious men with eyes intent on their work, and he remembered the strange old man who had watched over the garden when he had been a boy; an old man with a wild ragged beard and a skinny hand like the Ancient Mariner's. The garden had not prospered under his care—it had been wild, undisciplined, tangled; but he had been a teller of wonderful tales, a seer of visions—it was to him that Harry had owed all the intimate knowledge of Cornish lore and mystery that he possessed.

The gardeners that were there now were probably not Cornishmen at all—strangers, Londoners perhaps. They could watch that wonderful, ever-changing view of sea and cliff and moor without any beating of the heart; to them the crooked, dusky windings of the Cove, the mighty grey rocks of Trelennan's Jump, the strange, solemn permanency of the four grey stones on the moor, were as nothing; their hearts were probably in Peckham.

He turned a little sadly from the ordered discipline of the garden; the shining green of the lawns, the blazing red and gold of its flowers almost annoyed him—it was not what he had expected. Then, suddenly, he came upon a little tangled wood—a strange, deserted place, with tall grasses and wild ferns and a little brook bubbling noisily over shining white and grey pebbles. He remembered it; how well he remembered it. He had often been there in those early days. He had tried to make a little mill in the brook. He had searched there for some of those strange creatures about whom Tony Tregoth, the old gardener, had told him—fauns and nymphs and the wild god Pan. He had never found anything; but its wild, disordered beauty had made a fitting setting for Tony's wild, disordered legends.

It was still almost exactly as it had been twenty years before; no one had attempted improvement. He stayed there for some time, thinking, regretting, dreaming—it was the only part of the garden that was real to him.

He passed down the avenue and out through the white stone gates as one in a dream. Something was stirring within him. It was not that during those years in New Zealand he had forgotten. He had longed again and again with a passionate, burning longing for the grey cliffs and the sea and the haunting loneliness of the moor; for the Cornwall that he had loved from the moment of his birth—no, he had never forgotten. But there was waking in him again that strange, half-inherited sense of the eternal presence of ancient days and old heathen ceremonies, and the manners of men who had lived in that place a thousand years before. He had known it when he was a boy; when he had chased rabbits over the moor, when he had seen the mist curling mysteriously from the sea and wrapping land and sky in a blinding curtain of grey, when he had stood on Trelennan's Jump and watched the white, savage tossing of the foam hundreds of feet below; he had sometimes fancied that he saw them, those wild bearded priests of cruelty, waiting smilingly on the silent twilit moor for victims—they had always been cruel; something terrible in the very vagueness of their outline.

Now the old thoughts came back to him, and he almost fancied that he could see the strange faces in the shadows of the garden and feel their hot breath upon his cheek.

His passage through the streets of Pendragon woke him from his dreams; its almost startling modernity and obtrusive up-to-dateness laughed at his fancies. It was very much changed since he had been there before—like the garden, it was the very apotheosis of order and modern methods. "The Pendragon Hotel" astonished him by its stone pillars, its glimpse of a wonderful, cool, softly carpeted hall, its official in gold buttons who stood solemnly magnificent on the steps, the admiration of several small boys who looked up into his face with wide-open eyes.

Harry remembered the old "Pendragon Hotel," a dirty, unmethodical place, with beds that were never clean. It had been something of a scandal, but its landlord had been an amusing fellow and a capital teller of stories.

The shops dazzled him by their brilliance. The hairdresser's displayed a wonderful assortment of wigs in the window; coloured bottles of every size and hue glittered in the chemist's; diamonds flashed in the jeweller's—the street seemed glorious to his colonial eyes.

The streets were not very crowded, and no one seemed to be in a hurry. Auckland had been rather a busy little town—no one had had very much time to spare—but here, under the mellow September sun, people lingered and talked, and the time and place seemed to stand still with the pleasant air of something restfully comfortable, and, above all, containing nothing that wasn't in the very best taste. It was this air of polite gentility that struck Harry so strongly. It had never been like that in the old days; a ragged unkempt place of uncertain manners and a very evident poverty. He rather resented its new polish, and he regretted once more that he had not sought a London tailor before coming down to Cornwall.

He suddenly recognised a face—a middle-aged, stout gentleman, with a white waistcoat and the air of one who had managed to lead a virtuous life and, nevertheless, accumulate money; he was evidently satisfied with both achievements. It was Barbour, Bunny Barbour. He had been rather a good chap at school, with some taste for adventure. He had had a wider horizon than most of them; Harry remembered how Bunny had envied him in New Zealand. He looked prosperous and sedate now, and the world must have treated him well. Harry spoke to him and was received with effusion. "Trojan, old man! Well, I never! I'm damned if I'd have recognised you. How you've changed! I heard you were coming back; your boy told me—fine chap that, Trojan, you've every reason to be proud. Well, to be sure! Come in and have a whisky and see the new club-rooms! Just been done up, and fairly knocks spots out of the old place."

He was extremely cordial, but Harry felt that he was under criticism. Barbour's eyes looked him up and down; there was almost a challenge in his glance, as though he said, "We are quite ready to receive you if you are one of us. But you must move with the times. It's no good for you to be the same as in the old days. We've all changed, and so must you!"

The club was magnificent. Harry stared in amazement at its luxury and comfort. Its wonderful armchairs and soft carpets, its decorations and splendid space astonished him. The old place had seemed rather fine to him as a boy, but he saw now how bad it had really been. He sank into one of the armchairs with that strange sense of angry resentment that he had felt before in the street gaining hotly upon him.

"It's good, isn't it?" said Barbour, smiling with an almost personal satisfaction, as though he had been largely responsible for the present improvements. "The membership's going up like anything, and we're thinking of raising subscriptions. Very decent set of fellows on it, too. Oh! we're getting along splendidly here. You must have noticed the change in the place!"

"I should think I have," said Harry—the tone of his voice was a little regretful; "but it's not only here—it's the whole town. It's smartened up beyond all knowing. But I must confess that, dirty and dingy as they were, I regret the old club-rooms. There was something extraordinarily homely and comfortable about them. Do you remember that old armchair with the hole in it? Gone long ago, of course, but I shall never sit in anything as nice again."

"Ah, sentiment," said Barbour, smiling; "you won't find much of it in Pendragon nowadays. It doesn't do. Sentimentalists are always Tories, you'll find; always wanting to keep the old things, and all against progress. We're all for progress now. We've got some capital men on the Town Council—Harding, Belfast, Rogers, Snaith—you won't remember them. There's some talk of pulling down the Cove and building new lodging-houses there. We're crowded out in the summer, and there are more people every year."

"Pull down the Cove?" said Harry, aghast; "but you can't. It's been there for hundreds of years; it's one of the most picturesque places in Cornwall."

"That's the only thing," said Barbour regretfully. "It acts rather well as a draw for painters and that sort of person, and it makes some pretty picture postcards that are certain to sell. Oh, I suppose they'll keep it for a bit, but it will have to go ultimately. Pendragon's changing."

There was no doubt that it was, and Harry left the club some quarter of an hour later with dismay in his heart. He had dreamed so long of the old times, the old beauties, the old quiet spirit of unprogressive content, that this new eagerness to be up-to-date and modern, this obvious determination to make Pendragon a watering-place of the most detestable kind, horrified him.

As he passed down the crooked, uneven stone steps that led to the Cove, he felt indignant, almost unhappy. It was as if a friend had been insulted in his presence and he had been unable to defend him. They said that the Cove must go, must make way for modern jerry-built lodging-houses, in order that middle-class families from London and Manchester might be sufficiently accommodated.

The Cove had meant a great deal to him when a boy—mystery, romance, pirates and smugglers, strange Cornish legends of saints and sinners, knights and men-at-arms. The little inn, "The Bended Thumb," with its irregular red-brick floor and its smoke-stained oaken rafters, had been the theatre of many a stirring drama—now it was to be pulled down. It was a wonderfully beautiful morning, and the little, twisting street of the Cove seemed to dance with its white shining cobbles in the light of the sun. It was mysterious as ever, but colours lingered in every corner. Purple mists seemed to hang about the dark alleys and twisting ways; golden shafts of light flashed through the open cottage doorways into rooms where motes of dust danced, like sprites, in the sun; smoke rose in little wreaths of pearl-grey blue into the cloudless sky; there was perfect stillness in the air, and from an overflowing pail that stood outside "The Bended Thumb," the clear drip, drip of the water could be heard falling slowly into the white cobbles, and close at hand was the gentle lap of the sea, as it ran up the little shingly beach and then dragged slowly back again with a soft, reluctant hiss.

It was the Cove in its gentlest mood. No one was about; the women were preparing the dinner and the men were away at work. No strange faces peered from inhospitable doorways; there was nothing to-day that could give the stranger a sense of outlawry, of almost savage avoidance of ordinary customs and manners. Harry's heart beat wildly as he walked down the street; there was no change here; it was as he had left it. He was at home here as he could never be in that new, strident Pendragon with its utter disregard of tradition and beauty.

He saw that it was late and hurried back. He had discovered a great deal during the morning.

At lunch he spoke of the changes that he had seen. Clare smiled. "Why, of course," she said. "Twenty years is a long time, and Pendragon has made great strides. For my part, I am very glad. It brings money to the shopkeepers, and the place will be quite fashionable in a few years' time. We're all on the side of progress up here," she added, laughing.

"But the Cove?" said Harry. "Barbour tells me that they are thinking of pulling it down to make way for lodging-houses or something."

"Well, why not?" said Clare. "It is really very much in the way where it is, and is, I am told, extremely insanitary. We must be practical nowadays or we are nothing; you have to pay heavily for being romantic."

Harry felt again that sensation of personal affront as though some close friend, bound to him by many ties, had been attacked violently in his presence. It was unreasonable, he knew, but it was very strong.

"And you, Robin," he said, "what do you think of it?"

"I agree with Aunt Clare," answered Robin lightly, as though it were a matter that interested him very little. "If the place is in the way, it ought to go. He's a sensible man, Barbour."

"The fact is, Harry," said Garrett, "you haven't changed quite as fast as the place has. You'll see the point of view in a few weeks' time."

He felt unreasonably, ridiculously angry. They were all treating him as a child, as some one who would grow up one day perhaps, but was, at present at any rate, immature in thought and word; even with Robin there was a half-implied superiority.

"But the Cove!" he cried vehemently. "Is it nothing to any of you? After all that it has been to us all our lives, to our people, to the whole place, are you going to root it out and destroy it simply because the town isn't quite big enough to put up all the trippers that burden it in the summer? Don't you see what you will lose if you do? I suppose you think that I am sentimental, romantic, but upon my word I can't see that you have improved Pendragon very much in all these twenty years. It was charming once—a place with individuality, independence; now it is like anywhere else—a miniature Brighton."

He knew that he was wasting his words. There was a pause, and he felt that they were all three laughing at him—yes, Robin as well. He had only made a fool of himself; they could not understand how much he had expected during those weary years of waiting—how much he had expected and how much he had missed.

Clare looked round the room and was relieved to find that only Beldam was present. If one of the family was bent on being absurd, it was as well that there should only be one of the servants to hear him.

"You know that you are to be on your trial this afternoon, Harry?" she said.

"My trial?" he repeated, bewildered.

"Yes—it's my at-home day, you know—first Thursdays—and, of course, they'll all come to see you. We shall have the whole town——" She looked at him a little anxiously; so much depended on how he behaved, and she wasn't completely reassured by his present manner.

If he astonished them all this afternoon by saying things about the Cove like that, it would be too terrible!

"How horrible!" he said, laughing. "I'm very much afraid that I shan't do you justice, Clare. I'm no good at small conversation."

His treating it so lightly made it worse, and she wondered how she could force him to realise the seriousness of it.

"All the nicest people in Pendragon," she said; "and they are rather ridiculously critical, and of course they talk."

He looked at her and laughed. "I wish they were Maories," he said, "I shouldn't be nearly so frightened!"

She leant over the table to emphasise her words. "But it really does make a difference, Harry. First impressions count a lot. You'll be nice to them, won't you?"

The laugh had left his eyes. It was serious, as he knew. He had had no idea that he would have, so to speak, "funked" it so. It was partly, of course, because of Robin. He did not want to make a fool of himself before the boy. He was already beginning to realise what were the things that counted with Robin.

The real pathos of the situation lay in his terrible anxiety to do the right thing. If he had taken it quietly, had trusted to his natural discretion and had left circumstances to develop of themselves, he would have, at any rate, been less self-conscious. But he could not let it alone. He had met Auckland society often enough and had, indeed, during his later years, been something of a society man, but there everything was straight-forward and simple. There was no tradition, no convention, no standard. Because other people did a thing was no reason why you should do it—originality was welcomed rather than otherwise.

But here there were so many things that you must do, and so very, very many that you mustn't; and if you were a Trojan, matters were still more complicated.

It was after half-past four when he entered the drawing-room, and Clare was pouring out tea. Five or six ladies were already there, and a clergyman of ample proportions and quite beautifully brushed hair. He was introduced—"Mrs. le Terry—Miss Ponsonby—Miss Lucy Ponsonby—Miss Werrel—Miss Thisbe Werrel—Mr. Carrell—our rector, Harry."

He shook hands and was terribly embarrassed. He was conscious at once of that same sense of challenge that he had felt with Barbour in the morning. They were not obviously staring, but he knew that they were rapidly summing him up. He coloured foolishly, and stood for a moment awkwardly in the middle of the room.

"Tea, Harry?" said Clare. "Scones down by the fire. Everybody else is all right—so look after yourself."

He found himself by Mrs. le Terry, a small, rather pretty woman with wide-open blue eyes, and a mass of dark brown hair hidden beneath a large black hat that drooped over one ear. She talked rapidly and with few pauses. She was, he discovered, one of those persons whose conversation was a series of exclamation marks. She was perpetually astonished, delighted, and disappointed with an amount of emotion that left her no breath and gave her hearers a small opinion of her sincerity. "It's too terribly funny," she said, opening her eyes very wide indeed, "that you should have been in that amazing place, New Zealand—all sheep and Maories, isn't it?—and if there's one thing that I should be likely to detest more than mutton I'm sure it would be Maories. Too dreadful and terrible! But you look splendidly well, Mr. Trojan. I never, really never, saw any one with such a magnificent colour! I suppose that it's that gorgeous sun, and it never rains, does it? Too delightful! If there's one thing that I *do* adore, it's the sun!"

"Well, I don't know about that," said Harry, laughing; "we had rain pretty often in Auckland, and——"

"Oh," she said, breaking in upon him, "that's too curious, because, do you know, I thought you never had rain at all, and I do detest rain so. It's too distressing when one has a new frock or must go to some stupid place to see some one. But I'm too awfully glad that you've come here, Mr. Trojan. We do want waking up a little, you know, and I'm sure you're the very person to do it. It would be too funny if you were to wake us all up, you know."

Harry was pleased. There were no difficulties here, at any rate. Hadn't Robin mentioned Mrs. le Terry as one of the leaders of Fallacy Street? He suddenly lost his shyness and wanted to become confidential. He would tell her how glad he was to be back in England again; how anxious he was to enter into all the fun and to take his part in all the work. He wondered what she felt about the Cove, and he hoped that she would be an enemy to its proposed destruction.

But she yielded him no opportunity of speaking, and he speedily discovered her opinion on the Cove. "And such changes since you went away! Quite another place, I'm glad to say. Pendragon is the sweetest little town, and even the dear, dirty trippers in the summer are the most delightful and amusing people you ever saw. And now that they talk of pulling down that horrid, dirty old Cove, it will be too splendid, with lodging-houses and a bandstand; and they do talk of an Esplanade—that would be too delightful!"

While she was speaking, he watched the room curiously. Robin had come in and was standing by the fireplace talking to the Miss Werrels, two girls of the athletic type, with short skirts and their hair brushed tightly back over their foreheads. He was leaning with one arm on the mantelpiece, and was looking down on the ladies with an air of languid interest: his eyes were restless, and every now and again glanced towards his father. The two Miss Ponsonbys were massive ladies of any age over fifty. Clad in voluminous black silk, with several little reticules and iron chains, their black hair bound in tight coils at the back of their heads, each holding stiffly her teacup with a tenacity that was worthy of a better cause, they were awe-inspiring and militant. In spite of their motionless gravity, there was something aggressive in their frowning brows and cold, expressionless eyes. Harry thought that he had never seen two more terrifying persons. Clare was talking to the prosperous clergyman; he smiled continually, and now and again laughed in reply to some remark, but it was always something restrained and carefully guarded. He was obviously a man who laid great store by exterior circumstances. That the sepulchre should be filled with dead men's bones might cause him pain, but that it should be unwhitened would be, to him, a thing far more terrible.

Clare turned round and addressed the room generally.

"Mr. Carrell has just been telling me of the shocking state of the Cove," she said. "Insanitary isn't the word, apparently. Things have gone too far, and the only wise measure seems to be to root the place up completely. It is sad, of course—it was a pretty old place, but it has had its day."

"I've just been telling your brother about it, Miss Trojan," said Mrs. le Terry. "It's quite too terrible, and I'm sure it's very bad for all of us to have anything quite so horrible so close to our houses. There's no knowing what dreadful things we may not all of us be catching at this very moment——"

She was interrupted by two new arrivals—Mrs. and Miss Bethel. They were a curious contrast. The mother was the strangest old lady that Harry had ever seen. She was tiny in stature, with snow-white hair and cheeks that were obviously rouged; she wore a dress of curious shot silk decorated with much lace, and her fingers were thick with jewels; a large hat with great purple feathers waved above her head. It was a fantastic and gaudy impression that she made, and there was something rather pitiful in the contrast between her own obvious satisfaction with her personal appearance and the bizarre, almost vulgar, effect of such strangely contrasted colours. She came mincing into the room with her head a little on one side, but in spite of, or perhaps because of, her rather anxious smiles, it was obvious that she was not altogether at her ease.

The girl who followed her was very different. Tall and very dark, she was clothed quite simply in grey; her hair was wonderful, although it was at present hidden to some extent by her hat, but its coal-black darkness had something intent, almost luminous, about it, so that, paradoxically, its very blackness held hidden lights and colours. But it was her manner that Harry especially noticed. She followed her mother with a strange upright carriage of the head and flash of the eyes that were almost defiant. She was evidently expecting no very civil reception, and she seemed to face the room with hostility and no very ready eagerness to please.

The effect on the room was marked. Mrs. le Terry stopped speaking for a moment and rustled her skirts with a movement of displeasure, the Miss Ponsonbys clutched their teacups even tighter than before and their brows became more clouded, the Miss Werrels smiled confidentially at each other as though they shared some secret, and even Robin made a slight instinctive movement of displeasure.

Harry felt at once an impulse of sympathy towards the girl. It was almost as if this sudden hostility had made them friends: he liked that independence of her carriage, the pride in her eyes. Mrs. le Terry's voice broke upon his ears.

"Which must be, Mr. Trojan, extraordinarily provoking. To go there, I mean, and find absolutely no one in—all that way, too, and a horribly wet night, and no train until nine o'clock."

In his endeavours to pick up the thread of the conversation he lost sight of their meeting with Clare.

She, indeed, had greeted them with all the Trojan coldness; nothing could have been more sternly formal than her "Ah! Mrs. Bethel, I'm so glad that you were able to come. So good of you to trouble to call. Won't you have some tea? Do find a seat somewhere, Miss Bethel. I hope you won't mind our all having finished."

Harry was introduced and took them their tea. It was obvious that, for some reason unknown to him, their presence there was undesired by all the company present, including Clare herself. He also knew instinctively that their coming there had been some act of daring bravery, undertaken perhaps with the hope that, after all, it might not be as they had feared.

The old lady's hand trembled as she took her teacup; the colour had fled from her face, and she sat there white and shaking. As Harry bent over her with the scones, he saw to his horror that a tear was trembling on her eyelid; her throat was moving convulsively.

At the same instant he knew that the girl's eyes were fixed upon his; he saw them imploring, beseeching him to help them. It was a difficult situation, but he smiled back at the girl and turned to the old lady.

"Do try these scones, Mrs. Bethel," he said; "they are still hot and I can recommend them strongly. I'm so glad to meet you; my sister told me only this morning that she hoped you would come this afternoon, as she wanted us to become acquainted."

It was a lie, but he spoke it without hesitation, knowing that it would reach Clare's ears. The little lady smiled nervously and looked up at him.

"Ah, Mr. Trojan," she said, "it's very good of you, I'm sure. We are only too delighted. It's not much gaiety that we can offer you here, but such as it is——"

She was actually making eyes at him, the preposterous old person. It was really a little pitiful, with her gorgeous colours, and her trembling assumption of a coquettish youth that had left her long ago. Her attempt to storm a difficult position by the worst of all possible tactics made him extremely sorry for the daughter, who was forced to look on in silence. His thoughts, indeed, were with the girl—her splendid hair, her eyes, something wild, almost rebellious, that found a kindred note in himself; curiously, almost absurdly, they were to a certain degree allies although they had not spoken. He talked to her a little and she mentioned the Cove.

"It is a test of your Cornish ancestry," she said—"if you care for it, I mean. So many people here look on it as a kind of rubbish-heap—picturesque but untidy—and it is the most beautiful place in the world."

"I am glad that you feel like that," he said quietly; "it meant a lot to me as a boy. I have been sorry to find how unpopular it is now; but I see that it still has its supporters."

"Ah, you must talk to father," she said. "He is always there. We are a little old-fashioned, I'm afraid."

There was in her voice, in her smile, something that stirred him strangely. He felt as though he had met her before—a long while ago. He recognised little characteristics, the way that she pushed back her hair when she was excited, the beautiful curve of her neck when she raised her eyes to his, the rise and fall of her bosom—it was all strangely, individually familiar, as though he had often watched her do the same things in the same way before, in some other place....

He had forgotten the others—Clare, Robin, the Miss Ponsonbys, Mrs. le Terry; and when they had all gone, he did not realise that he had in any way neglected them.

After Miss Bethel had left the room, followed by the preposterous old mother, he stood at the window watching the lights of the town shining mistily through the black network of trees in the drive. He must meet her again.

Clare spoke to him and he turned round. "I'm afraid you have made the Miss Ponsonbys enemies for life," she said; "you never spoke to them once. I warned you that they were the most important people in the place."

"Oh! the Miss Ponsonbys!" said Harry carelessly, and Robin stood amazed.

CHAPTER III

Robin's rooms, charming as they were, with their wide windows opening on to tossing sea and the sharp bend of the grey cliffs stretching to distant horizons, suffered from overcrowding.

His sitting-room, with its dark red wallpaper and several good prints framed in dark oak—Burne-Jones' "Study for Cupid's Masque," Hunt's "Hireling Shepherd," and Whistler's "Battersea Bridge" were the best—might have been delightful had he learned to select; but at the present stage in his development he hated rejecting anything as long as it reached a certain standard. His appreciations were wide and generous, and his knowledge was just now too superficial to permit of discerning criticism. The room, again, suffered from a rather effeminate prettiness. There were too many essentially trivial knick-knacks—some fans, silver ornaments, a charming little ebony clock, and a generous assortment of gay, elegantly worked cushions. The books, too, were all in handsome editions—Meredith in green leather with a gold-worked monogram, Pater in red half-morocco, Swinburne in light-blue with red and gold tooling—rich and to some extent unobtrusive, but reiterating unmistakably the first impression that the room had given, the mark of something superficial.

Robin was there now, dressing for dinner. He often dressed in his sitting-room, because his books were there. He liked to open a book for a moment before fitting his studs into his shirt, and how charming to read a verse of Swinburne before brushing his hair—not so much because of the Swinburne, but rather because one went down to dinner with a pleasant feeling of culture and education. To-night he was in a hurry. People had stayed so late for tea (it was still the day after his father's arrival), and he had to be at the other end of the town by half-past seven. What a nuisance going out to dinner was, and how he wished he wasn't going to-night.

The fact that the dinner promised, in all probability, to afford something of a situation did not, as was often the case, give him very much satisfaction. Indeed it was the reverse. The situation was going to be extremely unpleasant, and there was every likelihood that Robin would look a fool. Robin's education had been a continuous insistence on the importance of superficiality. It had been enforced while he was still in the cradle, when a desire to kick and fight had been always checked by the quiet reiteration that it was not a thing that a Trojan did. Temper was not a fault of itself, but an exhibition of it was; simply because self-control was a Trojan virtue. At his private school he was taught the great code of brushing one's hair and leaving the bottom button of one's waistcoat undone. Robbery, murder, rape—well, they had all played their part in the Trojan history; but the art of shaking hands and the correct method of snubbing a poor relation, if properly acquired, covered the crimes of the Decalogue.

It was not that Robin, either then or afterwards, was a snob. He thought no more of a duke or a viscount than of a plain commoner, but he learnt at once the lesson of "Us—and the Others." If you were one of the others—if there was a hesitation about your aspirates, if you wore a tail-coat and brown boots—then you were non-existent, you simply did not count.

When he left Eton for Cambridge, this Code of the Quite Correct Thing advanced beyond the art of Perfect Manners; it extended to literature and politics, and, in fact, everything of any importance. He soon discovered what were the things for "Us" to read, whom were the painters for "Us" to admire, and what were the politics for "Us" to applaud. He read Pater and Swinburne and Meredith, Bernard Shaw and Galsworthy and Joseph Conrad, and had quite definite ideas about all of them. He admired Rickett's stage effects, and thought Sholto Douglas's portraits awfully clever, and, of course, Max's Caricatures were masterly. I'm not saying that he did not really admire these things—in many things his appreciation was genuine enough—but if it should happen that he cared for "The Christian" or "God's Good Man," he speedily smothered his admiration and wondered how he could be such a fool. To do him justice, he never had any doubt that those whose judgment he followed were absolutely right; but he followed them blindly, often praising books or pictures that he had never read or seen because it was the thing to do. He read quite clever papers to "The Gracchi" at Cambridge, but the most successful of all, "The Philosophy of Nine-pins according to Bernard Shaw," was written before he had either seen or read any of that gentleman's plays. He was, in fact, in great danger of developing into a kind of walking *Rapid Review* of other people's judgments and opinions. He examined nothing for himself; his standard of the things to be attained in this world was fixed and unalterable; to have an unalterable standard at twenty-one is to condemn oneself to folly for life.

And now, as he was dressing for dinner, two things occupied his mind: firstly, his father; in the second place, the situation that he was to face in half-an-hour's time.

With regard to his father, Robin was terribly afraid that he was one of the Others. He had had his suspicions from the first—that violent entry, the loud voice and the hearty laugh, the bad-fitting clothes, and the perpetual chatter at dinner; it had all been noisy, unusual, even a little vulgar. But his behaviour at tea that afternoon had grieved Robin very much. How could he be so rude to the light and leading of Fallacy Street? It could only have been through ignorance; it could only have been because he really did not know how truly great the Miss Ponsonbys were. But then, to spend all his time with the Bethels, strange, odd people, with the queerest manners and an uncertain history, whom Fallacy Street had decided to cut!

No, Robin was very much afraid that his father must be ranked with the Others. He had not expected very much after all; New Zealand must be a strange place on all accounts; but his father seemed to show no desire to improve, he seemed quite happy and contented, and scarcely realised, apparently, the seriousness of his mistakes.

But, after all, the question of his father was a very minor affair as compared with the real problem that he must answer that evening. Robin had met Dahlia Feverel in the summer of the preceding year at Cambridge. He had thought her extremely beautiful and very fascinating. Most of his college friends had ladies whom they adored; it was considered quite a thing to do—and so Robin adored Dahlia.

No one knew anything about the Feverels. The mother was kept in the background and the father was dead—there was really only Dahlia; and when Robin was with her he never thought of questioning her as to antecedents of earlier history. For two months he loved her passionately, chiefly because he saw her very seldom. When he went down at the end of the summer term he felt that she was the only thing in the world worth living for. He became Byronic, scowled at Aunt Clare, and treated Garrett's cynicism with contempt. He wrote letters to her every day full of the deepest sentiments and a great deal of amazingly bad poetry. Clare wondered what was the matter, but asked no questions, and was indeed far too firmly convinced of the efficacy of the Trojan system to have any fears of mental or moral danger.

Then Miss Feverel made a mistake; she came with her mother to stay at Pendragon. For the first week Robin was blissfully happy—then he began to wonder. The best people in Pendragon would have nothing to do with the Feverels. Aunt Clare, unaware that they were friends of Robin's, pronounced them "commonly vulgar." The mother was more in evidence than she had been at Cambridge, and Robin passed from dislike to horror and from horror to hatred. Dahlia, too, seemed to have changed. Robin had loved her too passionately hitherto to think of the great Division. But soon he began to wonder. There were certain things—little unimportant trifles, of course—that made him rather uneasy; he began to have a horrible suspicion that she was one of the Others; and then, once the suspicion was admitted, proof after proof came forward to turn it into certainty.

How horrible, and what an escape! His visits to the little lodging-house overlooking the sea where Dahlia played the piano so enchantingly, and Mrs. Feverel, a solemn, rather menacing figure, played silently and mournfully continuous Patience, were less and less frequent. He was determined to break the matter off; it haunted his dreams, it troubled him all day; he was forced to keep his acquaintanceship with them secret, and was in perpetual terror lest Aunt Clare should discover it. He had that most depressing of unwished-for possessions, a skeleton; its cupboard-door swung creakingly in the wind, and its bones rattled in his ears.

No, the thing must come to an end at once, and completely. They had invited him to dinner and he had accepted, meaning to use the occasion for the contemplated separation. He had thought often enough of what he would say—words that had served others many times before in similar situations. He would refer to their youth, the affair should be a midsummer episode, pleasant to look back upon when they were both older and married to more worthy partners; he would be a brother to her and she should be a sister to him——but, thank God for his escape!

He believed that the Trojan traditions would carry him through. He was not quite sure what she would do—cry probably, and remonstrate; but it would soon be over and he would be at peace once more.

He dressed slowly and with his usual care. It would be easier to speak with authority if there was no doubt about his appearance. He decided to walk, and he passed through the garden into the town, his head a buzzing repetition of the words that he meant to say. It was a beautiful evening; a soft mist hid the moon's sharper outline, but she shone, a vague circlet of light through a little fleet of fleecy white cloud. Although it was early in September, some of the trees were beginning to change their dark green into faint gold, and the sharp outline of their leaves stood out against the grey pearl light of the sky. As he passed into the principal street of Pendragon, Robin drew his coat closer about him, like some ancient conspirator. He had no wish to be stopped by an inquisitive friend; his destination demanded secrecy. Soon the lights and asphalt of the High Street gave place to dark, twisting paths and cobbled stones. These obscure and narrow ways were rather pathetic survivals of the old Pendragon. At night they had an almost sinister appearance; the lamps were at very long intervals and the old houses leaned over the road with a certain crazy picturesqueness that was, at the same time, exceedingly dangerous. There were few lights in the windows and very few pedestrians on the cobbles; the muffled roar of the sea sounded close at hand. And, indeed, it sprang upon you quite magnificently at a turn of the road. To-night it scarcely moved; a ripple as the waves licked the sand, a gentle rustle as of trees in the wind when the pebbles were dragged back with the ebb—that was all. It seemed strangely mysterious under the misty, uncertain light of the moon.

The houses facing the sea loomed up darkly against the horizon—a black contrast with the grey of sea and sky. It was No. 4 where the Feverels lived. There was a light in the upper window and some one was playing the piano. Robin hesitated for some minutes before ringing the bell. When it had rung he heard the piano stop. For a few seconds there was no sound; then there were steps in the passage and the door was opened by the very dowdy little maid-of-all-work whose hands were always dirty and whose eyes were always red, as though with perpetual weeping.

With what different eyes he saw the house now! On his first visit, the sun had dazzled his eyes; there had been flowers in the drawing-room and she had come to meet him in some charming dress; he had stood enraptured at the foot of the stairs, deeming it Paradise. Now the lamp in the hall flared with the wind from the door, and he was acutely conscious of a large rent in the dirty, faded carpet. The house was perfectly still—it might have been a place of ghosts, with the moon shining mistily through the window on the stairs and the strange, insistent murmur of the sea beating mysteriously through the closed doors!

There was no one in the drawing-room, and its appalling bad taste struck him as it had never done before. How could he have been blind to it? The glaring yellow carpet, the bright purple lamp-shades, the gilt looking-glass over the fireplace, and, above all, dusty, drooping paper flowers in bright china vases ranged in a row by the window. Of course, it might be merely the lodgings. Lodgings always were like that—but to live with them for months! To attempt no change, to leave the flowers, and the terrible oil-painting "Lost in the Snow"—an obvious British Public appeal to a pathos that simply shrieked at you, with its hideous colours and very material snow-storm. No, Robin could only repeat once more, What an escape!

But had he, after all, escaped? He was not quite sure, as he stood by the window waiting. It might be difficult, and he was unmistakably nervous.

Dahlia closed the door, and stood there for a moment before coming forward.

"Robin—at last!" and she held out both hands to him. They were the same words that his aunt had used to his father last night, he remembered foolishly, and at once they seemed strained, false, ridiculous!

He took her hand and said something about being in time; then, as she seemed to expect it, he bent down and kissed her.

She was pretty in a rather obvious way. If there had been less artificiality there would have been more charm; of middle height, she was slim and dark, and her hair, parted in the middle, fell in waves over her temples. She affected a rather simple, aesthetic manner that suited her dark eyes and rather pale complexion. You said that she was intense until you knew her. To-night she wore a rather pretty dress of some dark-brown stuff, cut low at the neck, and with her long white arms bare. She had obviously taken a good deal of trouble this evening, and had undoubtedly succeeded.

"And so Sir Robert has deigned to come and see his humble dependants at last!" she said, laughing. "A whole fortnight, Robin, and you've not been near us."

"I'm dreadfully sorry," he said, "but I've really been too terribly busy. The Governor coming home and one thing and another——"

He felt gauche and awkward, the consciousness of what he must say after dinner weighed on him heavily. He could hardly believe that there had ever been a time when he had talked eagerly, passionately—he cursed himself for a fool.

"Yes, we've been very lonely and you're a naughty boy," said Dahlia. "But now you are here I won't scold you if you promise to tell me everything you've done since last time——"

"Oh! done?" said Robin vaguely; "I really don't know—the usual sort of thing, I suppose—not much to do in Pendragon at any time."

She had been looking at him curiously while he was speaking. Now she suddenly changed her voice. "I've been so lonely without you, dear," she said, speaking almost in a whisper; "I fancied—of course it was silly of me—that perhaps there was some one else—that you were getting a little tired of me. I was—very unhappy. I nearly wrote, but I was afraid that—some one might see it. Letters are always dangerous. But it's very lonely here all day—with only mother. If you could come a little oftener, dear—it means everything to me."

Her voice was a little husky as though tears were not far away, and she spoke in little short sentences—she seemed to find it hard to say the words.

Robin suddenly felt a brute. How could he ever tell her of what was in his mind? If it was really so much to her he could never leave her—not at once like that; he must do it gradually.

She was sitting by him on the sofa and looked rather delightful. She had the pathetic expression that always attracted him, and he felt very sorry indeed. How blank her days would be without him! Part of the romance had always been his rôle of King Cophetua, and tears sprang to his eyes as he thought of the poor beggar-maid, alone, forlornly weeping, when he had finally withdrawn his presence.

"I think it is partly the sea," she said, putting her hand gently on his sleeve. "When one is sitting quite alone here in the evening with nothing to do and no one to talk to, one hears it so plainly—it is almost frightening. You know, Robin, old boy, I don't care for Pendragon very much. I only came here because of you—and now—if you never come to see us——"

She stopped with a little catch in her voice. Her hand fastened on his sleeve; their heads were very close together and her hair almost brushed his cheek.

He really was an awful brute, but at the same time it was rather nice—that she should care so much. It would be terrible for her when he told her what was in his mind. She might even get very ill—he had read of broken hearts often enough; and she was extraordinarily nice just now—he didn't want to hurt her. But still a fellow must think of his career, his future, and that sort of thing.

Mrs. Feverel entered—ponderous, solemn, dressed in a black silk that trails behind her in funereal folds. Her hands were clammy to the touch and her voice was a deep bass. She said very little, but sat down silently by the window, forming, as she always did, a dark and extremely solid background. Robin hated and feared her. There was something sinister in her silence—something ominous in her perpetual black. He had never heard her laugh.

Dahlia was laughing now. "I'm a selfish brute, Bobby," she said, "to bother you with my silly little complaints when we want to be cheerful. We'll have a good time this evening, won't we? We'll sing some of those Rubinstein's duets after dinner, and I've got a new song that I've been learning especially for you. And then there's your father; I do want to hear all about him so much—he must be so interesting, coming from New Zealand. Mother and I saw a gentleman in the town this morning that we thought must be him. Tall and brown, with a light brown moustache and a dark blue suit. It must be splendid to have a father again after twenty years without him."

Her voice dropped a little, as though to refer gently to her own fatherless condition.

Mrs. Feverel, a dark shadow in the window, sighed heavily.

"Oh! the Governor!" said Robin, a little irritably. "No! It's rather difficult—he doesn't seem to know what to do and say. I suppose it's being in New Zealand so long! It makes it rather difficult for me."

He spoke as one suffering under an unjust accusation. It was bad luck, and he wondered vaguely why Dahlia had been so interested; why should she care, unless, and the idea struck him with horror, she already regarded him as a prospective father-in-law?

Dinner was announced by the grimy little maid. Robin took the dark figure of Mrs. Feverel on his arm and made some hesitating remark about the weather—but he had the curious and unpleasant sensation of her seeing through him most thoroughly and clearly. He felt ridiculously like a captive, and his doubts as to his immediate escape increased. The gaudy drawing-room, the dingy stairs, the gas hissing in the hall, had been, in all conscience, depressing enough, but now this heavy, mute, ominous woman, trailing her black robes so funereally behind her, seemed, to his excited fancy, some implacable Frankenstein created by his own thrice-cursed folly.

The dinner was not a success. The food was bad, but that Robin had expected. As he faced the depression of it, he was more than ever determined to end it, conclusively, that evening, but Mrs. Feverel's gloom and Dahlia's little attempts at coquettish gaiety frightened him. The conversation, supported mainly by Dahlia, fell into terrible lapses, and the attempts to start it again had the unhappy air of desperate remedies doomed to failure. Dahlia's pathetic glances failed of their intent. Robin was too deeply engaged in his own gloomy reflections to notice them, but her eyes filled with tears, and at last her efforts ceased and a horrible, gloomy silence fell like a choking fog upon them.

"Will you smoke, Robin?" she said, when at last the dessert, in the shape of some melancholy oranges and one very attenuated banana, was on the table. "Egyptian or Turkish—or will you have a pipe?"

He took a cigarette clumsily from the box and his fingers trembled as he lit first hers and then his own—he was so terribly afraid of cutting a ridiculous figure. He sat down again and beat a tattoo on the tablecloth. Mrs. Feverel, with some grimly muttered excuse, left the room. She watched him a moment from the other side of the table and then she came over to him. She bent over his chair, leaning her hands on his shoulders.

"Robin, what is it?" she said. "What's happened?"

"Nothing," he said gloomily. "It's all right——"

"Oh! do you suppose I haven't seen?" She bent closer to him and pressed her cheek against his. "Robin, old boy—you're not getting tired of me? You're tired or cross to-night—I don't know. I've been very patient all this time—waiting for you—hoping that you would come—longing for you—and you never came—all these many weeks. Then I thought that, perhaps, you were too busy or were afraid of people talking—but, at last, there was to be to-night; and I've looked forward to it—oh! so much!—and now you're like this!"

She was nearly crying, and there was that miserable little catch in her voice. He did feel an awful cad—he hadn't thought that she would really care so much as this; but still it had to be done some time, and this seemed a very good opportunity.

He cleared his throat, and, beating the carpet with his foot, tried to speak with dignity as well as feeling—but he only succeeded in being patronising.

"You know," he said quickly, and without daring to look at her, "one's had time to think. I don't mean that I'm sorry it's all been as it has—we've had a ripping time—but I'm not sure—one can't be certain—that it's best for it to go on—quite like this. You see, old girl, it's so damned serious. Of course my people have ideas about my marrying—of course the Trojans have always had to be careful. People expect it of them——"

He stopped for a moment.

"You mean that I'm not good enough?"

She had stepped back from his chair and was standing with her back to the wall. He got up from his chair and turned round and faced her, leaning with his hands on the table. But he could not face her for long; his eyes dropped before the fury in hers.

"No, no, Dahlia—how stupid of you!—of course it's not that. It's really rather unkind of you to make it harder for me. It's difficult enough to explain. You're good enough for any one, but I'm not quite sure, dear, whether we'd be quite the people to marry! We'd be splendid friends, of course—we'll always be that—but we're both very young, and, after all, it's rather hard for one to know. It was splendid at Cambridge, but I don't think we quite realised——"

"You mean you didn't," she broke in quickly. "I know well enough. Some one's been speaking to you, Robin."

"No—nobody." He looked at her fiercely. She had hurt his pride. "As if I'd be weak enough to let that make any difference. No one has said a word—only——"

"Only—you've been thinking that we're not quite good enough for you—that we'd soil your Trojan carpets and chairs—that we'd stain your Trojan relations. I—I know—I——"

And then she broke down altogether. She was kneeling by the table with her head in her arms, sobbing as though her heart would break.

"Oh, I say, Dahlia, don't! I can't bear to see you cry—it will be all right, old girl, to-morrow—it will really—and then you will see that it was wiser. You will thank me for speaking about it. Of course we'll always be good friends. I——"

"Robin, you don't mean it. You can't!" She had risen from her knees and now stood by him, timidly, with one hand on his arm. "You have forgotten all those splendid times at Cambridge. Don't you remember that evening on the Backs? Just you and I alone when there was that man singing on the other side of the water, when you said that we would be like that always—together. Oh, Robin dear, it can't have been all nothing to you."

She looked very charming with her eyes a little wet and her hair a little dishevelled. But his resolution must not weaken—now that he had progressed so far, he must not go back. But he put his arm round her.

"Really, old girl, it is better—for both of us. We can wait. Perhaps in a few years' time it will seem different again. We can think about it then. I don't want to seem selfish, but you must think about me a little. You must see how hard it has been for me to say this, and that it has only been with the greatest difficulty that I've been strong enough. Believe me, dear, it is harder for me than it is for you—much harder."

He was really getting on very well. He had had no idea that he would do it so nicely. Poor girl! it was hard luck—perhaps he had led her to expect rather too much—those letters of his had been rather too warm, a little indiscreet. But no doubt she would marry some excellent man of her own class—in a few years she would look back and wonder how she had ever had the fortune to know so intimately a man of Robin's rank! Meanwhile, the scene had better end as soon as possible.

She had let him keep his arm round her waist, and now she suddenly leant back and looked up in his face.

"Robin, darling," she whispered, "you can't mean it—not that we should part like this. Why, think of the times that we have had—the splendid, glorious times—and all that we're going to have. Think of all that you've said to me, over and over again———"

She crept closer to him. "You love me really, dear, all the same. It's only that some one's been talking to you and telling you that it's foolish. But that mustn't make any difference. We're strong enough to face all the world. You know that you said you were in the summer, and I'm sure that you are now. Wait till to-morrow, dear, and you'll see it all differently."

"I tell you nobody's been talking," he said, drawing his arm away. "Besides, if they did, it wouldn't make any difference. No, Dahlia, it's got to stop. We're too young to know, and besides, it would be absurd anyway. I know it's bad luck on you. Perhaps I said rather too much in the summer. But of course we'll always be good friends. I know you'll see it as I do in a little time. We've both been indiscreet, and it's better to draw back now than later—really it is."

"Do you mean it, Robin?"

She stood facing him with her hands clenched; her face was white and her eyes were blazing with fury.

"Yes, of course," he said. "I think it's time this ended———"

"Not before I've told you what I think of you," she cried. "You're a thief and a coward—you've stolen a girl's love and then you're afraid to face the world—you're afraid of what people will say. If you don't love me, you're tied to me, over and over again. You've made me promises—you made me love you—and now when your summer amusement is over you fling me aside—you and your fine relations! Oh! you gentlemen! It would be a good thing for the world if we were rid of the whole lot of you! You coward! You coward!"

He was taken aback by her fury.

"I say—Dahlia—" he stammered, "it's unfair——"

"Oh! yes!" she broke in, "unfair, of course, to you! but nothing to me—nothing to me that you stole my love—robbed me of it like a common thief—pretended to love me, promised to marry me, and now—now—Oh! unfair! yes, always for the man, never for the girl—she doesn't count! She doesn't matter at all. Break her heart and fling it away and nobody minds—it's as good as a play!"

She burst into tears, and stood with her head in her hands, sobbing as though her heart would break. It was a most distressing scene!

"Really, really, Dahlia," said Robin, feeling extremely uncomfortable (it was such a very good thing, he thought, that none of his friends could see him), "it's no use your taking it like this. I had better go—we can't do any good by talking about it now. To-morrow, when we can look at it calmly, it will seem different."

He moved to the door, but she made another attempt and put her hand timidly on his arm to stop him.

"No, no, Robin, I didn't mean what I said—not like that. I didn't know what I was saying. Oh, I love you, dear, I love you! I can't let you go like that. You don't know what it means to me. You are taking everything from me—when you rob a girl of her love, of her heart, you leave her nothing. If you go now, I don't care what happens to me—death—or worse, That's how you make a bad woman, Robin. Taking her love from her and then letting her go. You are taking her soul!"

But he placed her gently aside. "Nonsense, Dahlia," he said. "You are excited to-night. You exaggerate. You will meet a man much worthier than myself, and then you will see that I was right."

He opened the door and was gone.

She sat down at the table. She heard him open and shut the hall door, and then his steps echoed down the street, and at last there was silence. She sat at the table with her head bent, her eyes gazing at the oranges and the bananas. The house was perfectly silent, and her very heart seemed to have ceased to beat. Of course she did not realise it; it seemed to her still as though he would come back in a moment and put his arms round her and tell her that it was all a game—just to see if she had really cared. But the silence of the street and the house was terrible. It choked her, and she pulled at her frock to loosen the tightness about her throat. It was cruel of him to have gone away like that—but of course he would come back. Only why was that cold misery at her heart? Why did she feel as if some one had placed a hand on her and drawn all her life away, and left her with no emotion or feeling—only a dull, blank, despair, like a cold fog through which no sun shone?

For she was beginning to realise it slowly. He had gone away, after telling her, brutally, frankly, that he was tired of her—that he had, indeed, never really cared for her. That was it—he had never cared for her—all those things that he had promised in the summer had been false, words without any meaning. All that idyll had been hollow, a sham, and she had made it the centre of her world.

She got up from the table and swayed a little as she stood. She pressed her hands against her forehead as though she would drive into her brain the fact that there would be no one now—no one at all—it was all a lie, a lie, a lie!

The door opened softly and Mrs. Feverel stole in. "Dahlia—what has he done?"

She looked at her as though she could not see her.

"Oh, nothing," she said slowly. "He did nothing. Only it's all over—there is not going to be any more."

And then, as though the full realisation of it had only just been borne in upon her, she sat down at the table again and burst into passionate crying.

Mrs. Feverel watched her. "I knew it was coming, my dear—weeks ago. You know I told you, only you wouldn't listen. Lord! it was plain enough. He'd only been playing the same game as all the rest of them."

Dahlia dried her eyes fiercely. "I'm a fool to make so much of it," she said. "I wasn't good enough—he said—not good enough. His people wouldn't like it and the rest—Oh! I've been a fool, a fool!"

Her mood changed to anger again. Even now she did not grasp it fully, but he had insulted her. He had flung back in her face all that she had given him. Injured pride was at work now, and for a moment she hated him so that she could have killed him gladly had he been there. But it was no good—she could not think about it clearly; she was tired, terribly tired.

"I'm tired to death, mother," she said. "I can't think to-night."

She stumbled a little as she turned to the door.

"At least," said Mrs. Feverel, "there are the letters."

But Dahlia had scarcely heard.

"The letters?" she said.

"That he wrote in the summer. You have them safe enough?"

But the girl did not reply. She only climbed heavily up the dark stairs.

CHAPTER IV

Clare Trojan was having her breakfast in her own room. It was ten o'clock, and a glorious September morning, and the sparrows were twittering on the terrace outside as though they considered it highly improper for any one to have breakfast between four walls when Nature had provided such a splendid feast on the lawn.

Clare was reading a violent article in the *National Review* concerning the inadequacy of our present solution of the housing problem; but it did not interest her.

If the world had only been one large Trojan family there would have been no problem. The trouble was that there were Greeks. She did dimly realise their existence, but the very thought of them terrified her. Troy must be defended, and there were moments when Clare was afraid that its defenders were few; but she blinded herself to the dangers of attack. "There are no Greeks, there *are* no Greeks." Clare stood alone on the Trojan walls and defied that world of superstition and pagan creeds. With the armour of tradition and an implicit belief in the watchword of all true Trojan leaders, "Qui dort garde," she warded the sacred hearths; but there were moments when her eyes were opened and signs were revealed to her of another world—something in which Troy could have no place; and then she was afraid.

She was considering Harry, his coming, and his probable bearing on present conditions, and she knew that once again the Trojan walls were in danger. It seemed to her, as she sat there, cruelly unfair that the son of the House, the man who in a little while would stand before the world as the head of the Trojan tradition, should be the chief instrument in the attempted destruction of the same. She had not liked Harry in the old days. She had always, even as a girl, a very stern idea of the dignity of the House. Harry had never fulfilled this idea, had never even attempted to. He had been wild, careless, undisciplined, accompanying strange uncouth persons on strange uncouth adventures; he had been almost a byword in the place. No, she had not liked him; she had almost hated him at one time. And then after he had gone away she had deliberately forgotten him; she had erased his name from the fair sheet of the Trojan record, and had hoped that the House would never more be burdened by his undisciplined history. Then she had heard that there was a son and heir, and her one thought had been of capture, deliverance of the new son of the House from his father's influence. She was not deliberately cruel in her determination; she saw that the separation must hurt the father, but she herself was ready to make sacrifice for the good of the House and she expected the same self-denial in others. Harry made no difficulties. New Zealand was no place for a lonely widower to bring up his boy, and Robin was sent home. From that moment he was the centre of Clare's world; much self-denial can make a woman good, only maternity can make her divine. To bring the boy up for the House, to tutor him in all the little and big things that a Trojan must know and do, to fit him to take his place at the head of the family on a later day; all these things she laboured for, day and night without ceasing, and without divided interests. She loved the boy, too, passionately, with more than a mother's love, and now she looked back over what had been her life-work with pride and satisfaction. She had tried to forget Harry. She hoped, although she never dared to face the thought in her heart, that he would die there, away in that foreign country, without coming back to them again. Robin was hers now; she had educated him, loved him, scolded him—he was all hers, she would brook no division. Then, when she had heard that Harry was to come home, it had been at first more than she could bear. She had burst into wild incoherent protests;

she had prayed that an accident might happen to him and that he might never reach home. And then the Trojan pride and restraint had come to her aid. She was ashamed, bewildered, that she could have sunk to such depths; she prepared to meet him calmly and quietly; she even hoped that, perhaps, he might be so changed that she would welcome him. And, after all, he would in a little time be head of the House. Robin, too, was strongly under her influence, and it was unlikely that he would leave her for a man whom he had never known, for whom he could not possibly care.

It was this older claim of hers with regard to Robin that did, she felt, so obviously strengthen her position, and now that Harry had really returned, she thought that her fears need not trouble her much longer—he did all the things that Robin disliked most. His boisterousness, heartiness, and good-fellowship, dislike of everyday conventionality, would all, she knew, count against him with Robin. She had seen him shrink on several occasions, and each time she had been triumphantly glad. For she was frightened, terribly frightened. Harry was threatening to take from her the one great thing around which her life was centred; if he robbed her of Robin he robbed her of everything, and she must fight to keep him. That it would come to a duel between them she had long foreseen, she had governed for so long that she would not easily yield her place now; but she had not known that she would feel as she did about Robin, she had not known that she would be jealous—jealous of every look and word and motion. She had never known what jealousy was before, but now in the silence of the golden, sunlit room, with only the twittering of the birds on the lawn to disturb her thoughts, she faced the facts honestly without shrinking, and she knew that she hated her brother. Oh! why couldn't he go back again to his sheep-shearing! Why had he come to disturb them! It was not his environment, it was not his life at all! She felt that they could never lead again that same quiet, ordered existence; like a gale of wind he had burst their doors and broken their windows, and now the house was open, desolate, to the world.

She went up to her father's room, as was her custom every morning after breakfast. He was lying at his open window, watching, with those strange, restless eyes of his, the great expanse of sea and sky stretching before him. His room was full of light and air. Its white walls and ceiling, great bowls of some of the last of the summer's roses, made it seem young and vigorous and alive. It was almost a shock to see that huddled, dying old man with his bent head and trembling hands—but his eyes were young, and his heart.

As she looked at him, she wondered why she had never really cared for him. At first she had been afraid; then, as she grew older and a passionate love for and pride in the family as a conservative and ancient institution developed in her, that fear became respect, and she looked up to her father from a distance, admiring his reserve and pride but never loving him; and now that respect had become pity, and above all a great longing that he might live for many, many years, securing the household gods from shame and tending the fire on the Trojan hearth. For at the moment of his death would come the crisis—the question of the new rule. At one time it had seemed certain that Robin would be king, with herself a very vigilant queen-regent. But now that was all changed. Harry had come home, and it was into his hands that the power would fall.

She had often wondered that she knew her father so little. He had always been difficult to understand; a man of two moods strongly opposed—strangely taciturn for days together, and then brilliantly conversational, amusing, and a splendid companion. She had never known which of these attitudes was the real one, and now that he was old she had abandoned all hope of ever answering the question. His moods were more strongly contrasted than ever. He often passed quickly from one to the other. If she had only known which was the real one; she felt at times that his garrulity was a blind—that he watched her almost satirically whilst he talked. She feared his silences terribly, and she used often to feel that a moment was approaching when he would reveal to her definitely and finally some plot that he had during those many watchful years been forming. She knew that he had never let her see his heart—he had never taken her into his confidence. She had tried to establish some more intimate relationship, but she had failed; and now, for many years, she had left it at that.

But she wanted to know what he thought of Harry. She had waited for a sign, but he had given none; and although she had watched him carefully she had discovered nothing. He had not mentioned his son—a stranger might have thought that he had not noticed him. But Clare knew him too well to doubt that he had come to some definite conclusion in the matter.

She bustled cheerfully about the room, humming a little tune and talking to him, lightly and with no apparent purpose. He watched the gulls fly past the open window, his eyes rested on a golden flash of sun that struck some shining roof in the Cove, but his mind was back in the early days when he had played his game with the best and had seen the bright side of the world.

"He was a rake, Jack Crayle"—he seemed scarcely conscious that Clare was in the room—"a rake but a good heart, and an amusing fellow too. I remember meeting old Rendle and Hawdon Sallust—Hawdon of the eighties, you know—not the old man—he kept at home—all three of them at White's, Rendle and Sallust and Crayle; Jack bet Rendle he wouldn't stop the next man he met in the street and claim him as an old friend and bring him in—and, by Jove, he took it and brought him in, too—sort of tramp chap he was, too—dirty, untidy fellow—but Rendle was game serious—by Gad, he was. Said he was an old friend that had fallen on evil times—gave him a drink and won the bet—'63 that was—the year Bailey won that polo match against old Tom Radley—all the town was talking of it. By Gad, he could ride, Bailey could. Why——"

"It's time for your medicine, father," said Clare, breaking ruthlessly in upon the reminiscences.

"Eh, dear, yes," he said, looking at her curiously. "You're never late, Clare, always up to time. Yes, yes, well, well; in '63 that was. I remember it like yesterday—old Tom—particular friend he was of mine then, although we broke afterwards—my fault too, probably, about a horse it was. I———"

But Clare gave him his medicine, first tying a napkin round his neck lest she should spill the drops. He looked at her, smiling, over the napkin.

"You were always a girl for method," he said again; "not like Harry."

She looked at him quickly, but could guess nothing; she was suddenly frightened, as she so often was when he laughed like that. She always expected that some announcement would follow. It was almost as if he had threatened her.

"Harry?" she said. "No. But he is very like he used to be in some ways. It is nice to have him back again—but—well, he will find Pendragon rather different from Auckland, I'm afraid."

Sir Jeremy said nothing. He lay there without moving; Clare untied the napkin, and put back the medicine, and wheeled the chair into a sunnier part of the room and away from the window.

"You must get on with Harry, Clare," he said suddenly, sharply.

"Why, yes," she answered, laughing a little uneasily. "Of course we get on. Only his way of looking at things was always a little different—even, perhaps, a little difficult to understand"; and then, after a little pause, "I am stupid, I know. It was always hard for me to see like other people."

But he was not listening to her. He was smiling at the sun, and the birds on the lawn, and the flashing gold of the distant sand.

"No, you never saw like Harry," he said at last. "You want to be old to understand," and he would say no more.

He talked to her no more that morning, and she was vaguely uneasy. What was he thinking about Harry, and how did his opinion influence the situation?

She fancied that she saw signs of rebellion. For many years he had allowed her to do what she would, and although she had sometimes wondered whether he was quite as passive as she had fancied, she had had no fear of any disturbance. Now there was something vaguely menacing in his very silences. And, in some undefined way, the pleasure that he took in the cries of birds, the plunge and chatter of the sea as it rose and fell on the southern shore, the glint of the sun on the gold and green distances of rock and moor was alarming. She herself did not understand those things; indeed, she scarcely saw them, and was inclined to despise any one who loved any unpractical beauty, anything that was not at least traditional. And now this was a bond between her father and Harry. They had both loved wild, uncivilised things, and it was this very trait in their character that had made division between them before. But now what had been in those early years the cause of trouble was their common ground of sympathy.

They shared some secret of which she knew nothing, and she was afraid lest Robin should learn it too.

She went about her housekeeping duties that morning with an uneasy mind. The discipline below stairs was excellent because she was feared. It was not that she was hasty-tempered or unjust; indeed the cook, who had been there for many years, said that she had never seen Miss Clare angry, and her justice was a thing to marvel at. She always gave people their due, and exactly their due; she never over-praised or blamed, and that was why people said that she was cold; it was also, incidentally, responsible for her excellent discipline.

She was, as Sir Jeremy had said, a woman of amazing method. But the attitude of her actual household helped her; they were all, by education and environment, Trojans. Whatever they had been before they entered service at "The Flutes"—Radicals, Socialists, Dissenters, or Tones—at the moment of passing the threshold they were transformed into Trojans. Other things fell from them like a mantle, and in their serious devotion to traditional Conservatism they were examples of the true spirit of Feudalism. Beldam, the butler, had long ago graduated as Professor in the system. Coming as page-boy in earlier years, he had acquired the by no means easy art of Trojan diplomacy. It was now his duty to overhaul, as it were, every servant that passed the gates; an overhauling, moreover, done seriously and with much searching of the heart. Were you a Trojan? That is, do you consider that you are exceptionally fortunate in being chosen to perform menial but necessary duties in the Trojan household? Will you spend the rest of your days, not only in performing your duties worthily, but also in preaching to a blind and misguided world the doctrine of Trojan perfection and superiority? If the answer were honestly affirmative, you were accepted; otherwise, you were expelled with a fortnight's wages and eternal contempt.

Even the scullerymaid was not spared, but had to pass an examination in rites and rituals so severe that one unfortunate, Annie Grace Marks, after Beldam had spoken to her severely for half-an-hour, burst out with an impetuous, "Thank Gawd, she was a Marks, which was as good as the High and Mighty any day of the week, and better, for there wasn't no pride in the Marks and never 'ad been."

She received her dismissal that same evening.

But the case of Annie Marks was an isolated one. Rebellion was very occasional, and, for the most, the servants stayed at "The Flutes"—partly because the pay was good, and partly because the very reiteration of Trojan supremacy gave them a feeling of elevation very pleasant to their pride. In accordance with all true feudal law, you lost your own sense of birth and ancestry and became in a moment a Trojan; for Smith, Jones, and Robinson this was very comforting.

So Clare had very little trouble, and this morning she was able to finish her duties speedily, and devote her whole attention to the crisis that threatened the family.

She decided to see Garrett, and made her way to his room. He was writing, and seemed disturbed by her entry. He had been working for some years on a book to be entitled, "Our Aristocracy: its Threatened Supremacy." He was still engaged on the preliminary chapter, "Some aspects of historical aristocracy," and it had developed into a somewhat minute account of Trojan past history. He had no expectations of ever concluding the work, but it gave him a pleasant sense of importance and seemed in some vague way to be of value to the Trojan family.

He was always happy when at work, although he effected very little; but, after all, the great stylists always worked slowly. His style was, it is true, somewhat commonplace; but his rather minute output allowed him to rank, in his own estimation, with Pater and Omar Khayyám, and disdain the voluminous facility of Thackeray and Dickens. He was, he felt, one of the "precious" writers, and so long as no one saw his work he was able both to comfort himself and to impress others with the illusion.

It was said vaguely in Pendragon that "Garrett Trojan was a clever fellow—was writing a book—said to be brilliant, of great promise—no, he hadn't seen it, but——" etc.

So Garrett looked at his sister a little resentfully.

"I hope it's important, Clare," he said, "because—well, you know, the morning's one's time for work, and once one gets off the track it's difficult to get back; not that I've done much, you know, only half a page—but this kind of thing can't move quickly."

"I'm sorry, Garrie," she answered, "but you've got to talk to me. There are things about which I want your advice."

She did not really want it; she had decided on her line of conduct, and nothing that he could say would alter her decision—but it flattered him, and she needed his help.

"Well, of course," he said, pushing his chair back and coming to the fire, "if it's anything I can do— What is it, Clare? Household or something in the town?"

"Oh, nothing," she laughed at him. "Don't be worried, Garrie; I know it's horrid to disturb you, and there's really nothing—only—well, after all, there is only us, isn't there? for acting together I mean—and I want to know what line you're going on."

"Oh! about Harry?" He looked at her sharply for a moment. "You know that I object to lines, Clare. They are dangerous things." He implied that he was above them. "Of course there are times when it is necessary to—well, to be decisive; but at present it seems to me that we must wait for the situation to develop—it will, of course."

"I knew that you would say that," she said impatiently. "But it won't do; the situation *has* developed. You always preferred to look on—it is, as you say, less dangerous; but here I must have your help. Harry has been back a week; he is, for you and me, unchanged. The situation, as far as we go, is the same as it was twenty years ago. He is not one of us, he never was, and, to do him justice, never pretended to be. We, or at any rate I, imagined that he would be different now, after all that time. He is exactly the same." She paused.

"Well?" he said. "All that for granted, it's true enough. What's the trouble?"

"Things aren't the same though, now. There is father, and Robin. Father has taken to Harry strongly. He told me so just now. And for Robin——"

"Scarcely captivated," said Garrett drily. "Have you seen them together? Hardly domestic——"

Then he looked at her again and laughed. "And that pleases you, Clare."

"Of course," she answered him firmly. "There is no good in hedging. He is no brother of ours, Garrett. He is, what is more important still, no Trojan, and after all family counts for something. We don't like him, Garrett. Why be sentimental about it? He will follow father—and it will be soon—*après, le déluge*. For ourselves, it does not matter. It is hard, of course, but we have had our time, and there are other things and places. It is about Robin. I cannot bear to think what it would mean if he were alone here with Harry, after all these years."

"He would not stay."

"You think that?" Clare said eagerly. "It is so hard to know. He is still only a boy. Of course Harry shocks him now, shocks everything—his sense of decency, his culture, his pride—but that will wear off; he will get used to it—and then——"

It had been inevitable that the discussion should come, and Garrett had been waiting. He had no intention of going to find her, he would wait until she came to him, but he had been anxious to know her opinion. For himself the possibility of Harry's return had never presented itself. After all those years he would surely remain where he was. In yielding his son he had seemed to abandon all claim to any rights of inheritance, and Garrett had thought of him as one comfortably dead. He had contemplated his own ultimate succession with the pleasurable certainty that it was absolutely the right thing. In his love for a rather superficial tradition he was a perfect Trojan, and might be relied on to continue existing conditions without any attempt at radical changes. Clare, too, would be of great use.

But in a moment what had been, in his mind, certainty was changed into impossibility; instead of a certain successor he had become some one whose very existence was imperilled—his existence, that is, on the only terms that were in the least comfortable. Everything that made life worth living was threatened. Not that his brother would turn him out; he granted Harry the very un-Trojan virtues of generosity and affection for humanity in general—a rather foolish, gregarious open-handedness opposed obviously to all decent economy. But Harry would keep him—and the very thought stirred Garrett to a degree of anger that his sluggish nature seldom permitted him. Kept! and by Harry! Harry the outlaw! Harry the rebel! Harry the Greek! Garrett scarcely loved his brother when he thought of it.

But it was necessary that some line of action should be adopted, and he was glad that Clare had taken the first step.

"You don't think," he said doubtfully, "that he could be induced to go back?"

"What!" cried Clare, "after these years and the way he has waited! Why, remember that first evening! He will never leave this again. He has been dreaming about it too long!"

"I don't know," said Garrett. "He'll be at loggerheads with the town very soon. He has been saying curious things to a good many people. He objects to all improvement and says so. The place will soon be too hot for him."

But Clare shook her head. "No," she said. "He will soon find out about things—and then, in a little, when he takes father's place, what people think odd and unpleasant now will be original and strong. Besides, he would never go, whatever might happen, because of Robin."

"Ah, yes, there is Robin. It will be curious to watch developments there. Randal comes to-day, doesn't he?"

"Yes, this afternoon. A most delightful boy. I'm afraid that he may find Harry tiresome."

"We must wait," Garrett said finally; "in a week's time we shall see better. But, Clare, don't be rash. There is father—and, besides, it will scarcely help Robin."

"Oh! no melodrama," she said, laughing and moving towards the door. "Only, we understand each other, Garrie. Things won't do as they are—or, as they promise to be."

Garrett returned, with a sigh of relief, to his papers.

For Harry the week had been a series of bitter disappointments. He woke gradually from his dreams and saw that everything was changed. He was in a new world and he was out of place. Those dreams had been coloured, fantastically, beautifully. In the white pebbles, the golden sand, the curling grey smoke of the Cove, he had formed pictures that had lightened many dreary and lonely hours in Auckland. He was to come back; away from that huge unwieldy life in which comfort had no place and rest was impossible, back to all the old things, the wonderful glorious things that meant home and tradition and, above all, love. He was a sentimentalist, he knew that now. It had not been so in those old days; the life had been too adventurous and exciting, and he had despised the quiet comforts of a stay-at-home existence. But now he knew its value; he would come home and take his place as head of the family, as father, as citizen—he had learnt his lesson, and at last it was time for the reward.

But now that he had come home he found that the lesson was not learnt, or, perhaps, that the learning had been wasted; he must begin all over again. Garrett and Clare had not changed; they had made no advances and had shown him quite plainly, in the courteous Trojan fashion, that they considered his presence an intrusion, that they had no place in their ranks that he could fill. He was, he saw it plainly, no more in line with them than he had been twenty years before. Indeed, matters were worse. There was no possibility of agreement—they were poles apart.

With the town, too, he was an "outsider." The men at the Club thought him a bore—a person of strange enthusiasms and alarming heresies. By the ladies he was considered rough: as Mrs. le Terry had put it to Miss Ponsonby, he was a kind of too terrible bushranger without the romance! He was gauche, he knew, and he hated the tea-parties. They talked about things of which he knew nothing; he was too sincere to cover his convictions with the fatuous chatter that passed, in Fallacy Street society, for brilliant wit. That it was fatuous he was convinced, but his conviction made matters no easier for him.

But his attitude to the town had been, it must be confessed, from the very first a challenge. He had expected things that were not there; he had thought that his dreams were realities, and when he had demanded golden colours and had been shown stuff of sombre grey, there had been wild rebellion and impatient discontent with the world. He had thought Pendragon amazing in its utter disregard of the things that were to him necessities, but he had forgotten that he himself despised so completely things that were to Pendragon essentials. He had asked for beauty and they had given him an Esplanade; he had searched for romance and had discovered the new hotel; he dreamed of the sand and blue water of the Cove and had awaked to find the place despised and contemned—a site for future boarding-houses.

The town had thought him at first entertaining; they had made allowances for a certain rather picturesque absurdity consequent on backwoods and the friendship of Maories—men had laughed at the Club and detailed Harry Trojan's latest with added circumstances and incident, and for a while this was amusing. But his vehemence knew no pause, and he stated his disgust at the practical spirit of the new Pendragon with what seemed to the choice spirits at the Club effrontery. They smiled and then they sneered, and at last they left him alone.

So Harry found himself, at the end of the first week after his return, alone in Pendragon.

He had not, perhaps, cared for their rejection. He had come, like Gottwalt in *Flegejahre*, "loving every dog, and wishing that every dog should love him"—but he had seen, at once, that his way must be apart from theirs, and in that knowledge he had tried to find the comfort of a minority certain of its own strength and disdainful of common opinion. He had marvelled at their narrow vision and was unaware that his own point of view was equally narrow.

And, after all, there was Robin. Robin and he would defy Pendragon and laugh at its stupid little theories and short-sighted plans. And then, slowly, irresistibly, he had seen that he was alone—that Robin was on the side of Pendragon. He refused to admit it even now, and told himself again and again that the boy was naturally a little awkward at first—careless perhaps—certainly constrained. But gradually a wall had been built up between them; they were greater strangers now than they had been on that first evening of the return. Ah! how he had tried! He had thought that, perhaps, the boy hated sentiment and he had held himself back, watching eagerly for any sign of affection, ready humbly to take part in anything, to help in any difficulty, to laugh, to sympathise, to take his place as he had been waiting to do for so many years.

But Robin had made no advances, showed no sign. He had almost repulsed him—had at least been absolutely indifferent. They had had a walk together, and Harry had tried his best—but the attempt had been obvious, and at last there had come a terrible silence; they had walked back through the streets of Pendragon without a word.

Everything that Harry had said had been unfortunate. He had praised the Cove enthusiastically, and Robin had been contemptuous. He had never heard of Pater and had confounded Ibsen with Jerome K. Jerome. He had praised cricket and met with no reply. Twice he had seen Robin's mouth curl contemptuously, and it had cut him to the heart.

Poor Harry! he was very lonely. During the last two days he had been down in the Cove; he had found his way into the little inn and got in touch with some of the fishermen. But they scarcely solaced his loneliness. He had met Mary Bethel on the downs, and for a moment they had talked. There was no stiffness there; she had looked at him simply as a friend, with no hostility, and he had been grateful.

At last he had begun to look forward to the coming of Robin's friend, Randal. He was, evidently, a person to whom Robin looked up with great admiration. Perhaps he would form in some way a link, would understand the difficulties of both, and would help them. Harry waited, eagerly, and formed a picture of Randal in his mind that gave him much encouragement.

He was in his room now; it was half-past four, and the carriage had just passed up the drive. He looked anxiously at his ties and hesitated between light green, brown, and black. He had learnt the importance of these things in his son's eyes. He was going next week to London to buy clothes; meanwhile he must not offend their sense of decency, and he hesitated in front of his tie-box like a girl before her first dance. The green was terribly light. It was a good tie, but perhaps not quite the thing. Nothing seemed to go properly with his blue suit—the brown was dull and uninteresting—it lacked character; any one might have worn it, and he flung it back almost scornfully into the box. The black was really best, but how dismal! He seemed to see all his miserable loneliness and disappointment in its dark, sombre colour. No, that would never do! He must be bright, amusing, cheerful—anything but dull and dismal. So he put on the green again, and went down to the drawing-room. Randal was a young man of twenty-four—dark, tall, and slight, with a rather weary look in the eyes, as of one who had discovered the hollow mockery of the world and wondered at the pleasures of simple people. He was perfectly dressed, and had arrived, after much thought and a University education, at that excellent result when everything is right, as it were, by accident—as though no thought had been taken at all. As soon as a man appears to have laboured for effect, then he is badly dressed. Randal was good-looking. He had very dark eyes and thin, rather curling lips, and hair brushed straight back from his forehead.

The room was in twilight. It was Clare's morning-room, chosen because it was cosy and favoured intimacy. She was fond of Randal and liked to mother him; she also respected his opinions. The windows looked over the sea and the blinds were not drawn. The twilight, like a floating veil, hovered over sea and land; the last faint colours of the sunset, gold and rose and grey, trembled over the town.

Harry was introduced. Randal smiled, but his hand was limp; Harry felt a little ashamed of his own hearty grasp and wished that he had been less effusive. Randal's suit was dark blue and he wore a black tie; Harry became suddenly conscious of his daring green and, taking his tea, went and sat in the window and watched the town. The first white colours of the young moon, slipping from the rosy-grey cloud, touched faintly the towers of the ruined church on the moor; he fancied that he could just see the four stones shining darkly grey against the horizon, but it was difficult to tell in that mysterious half-light. Robin was sitting under the lamp by the door. The light caught his hair, but his face was in shadow. Harry watched him eagerly, hungrily. Oh! how he loved him, his son!

Randal was discussing some people with whom he had been staying—a little languidly and without any very active interest. "Rather a nice girl, though," he said. "Only such a dreadful mother. Young Page-Rellison would have had a shot, I do believe, if it hadn't been for the mother—wore a wig and talked Cockney, and fairly grabbed the shekels in bridge."

"And what about the book?" Clare asked.

"Oh! going on," said Randal. "I showed Cressel a chapter the other day—you know the New Argus man; and he was very nice about it. Of course, some of the older men won't like it, you know. It fairly goes for their methods, and I flatter myself hits them pretty hard once or twice. You know, Miss Trojan, it's the young school you've got to look to nowadays; it's no use going back to those mid-Victorians—all very well for the schoolroom—cause and effect and all that kind of thing—but we must look ahead—be modern and you will be progressive, Miss Trojan."

"That's just what I'm always saying, Mr. Randal," said Clare, smiling. "We're fighting a regular battle over it down here, but I think we will win the day."

Randal turned to Harry. "And you, sir," he said, "are with us, too?"

Harry laughed. He knew that Robin was looking at him. "I have been away," he said, "and perhaps I have been a little surprised at the strides that things have made. Twenty years is a long time, and I was romantic and perhaps foolish enough to expect that Pendragon would be very much the same when I came back. It has changed greatly, and I am a little disappointed."

Clare looked up. "My brother has lost touch a little, Mr. Randal," she said, "and I don't think quite sees what is good for the place—indeed, necessary. At any rate, he scarcely thinks with us."

"With *us*." There was emphasis on the word. That meant Robin too. Randal glanced at him for a moment and then he turned to Robin—father and son! A swift drawing of contrasts, perhaps with an inevitable conclusion in favour of his own kind. It was suddenly as though the elder man was shut out of the conversation; they had, in a moment, forgotten his very presence. He sat in the dusk by the window, his head in his hands, and terrible loneliness at his heart; it hurt as he had never known before that anything could hurt. He had never known that he was sensitive; in Auckland it had not been so. He had never felt things then, and had a little despised people that had minded. But there had been ever, in the back of his mind, the thought of those days that were coming when, with his son at his side, he could face all things. Well, now he had his son—there, with him in the room. The irony of it made him clench his hands, there in the dark, whilst they talked in the lighted room behind him.

"Oh! King's is going to pot," Randal was saying. "I was down in the Mays and they were actually running with the boats—they seemed quite keen on going up. The decent men seem to have all gone."

Robin was paying very little attention. He was looking worried, and Clare watched him a little anxiously. "I hope you will be able to stay with us some days, Mr. Randal," she said. "There are several new people in Pendragon whom I should like you to meet."

Randal was charmed. He would love to stop, but he must get back to London almost immediately. He was going over to Germany next week and there were many arrangements to be made.

"Germany!" It was Robin who spoke, but the voice was not his usual one. It was alive, vibrating, startling. "Germany! By Jove! Randal—are you really going?"

"Why, of course," a little wearily; "I have been before, you know. Rather a bore, but the Rainers—you remember them, Miss Trojan—are going over to the Beethoven Festival at Bonn and are keen on my going with them. I wasn't especially anxious, but one must do these things, you know."

"Robin was there a year ago—Germany, I mean—and loved it. Didn't you, Robin?"

"Germany? It was Paradise, Heaven—what you will. Rügen, the Harz, Heidelberg, Worms——" He stopped and his voice broke. "I'm a little absurd about it still," he said, as though in apology for such unnecessary enthusiasm.

"Oh! you're young, Robin," said Randal, laughing. "When you've seen as much as I have you'll be blasé. Not that one ought to be, but Germany—well, it hardly lasts, I think. Rügen—why, it rained and there were mists round the Studenkammer, and how those people eat at the Jagdschloss! Heidelberg! picture postcards and shocking hotels—Oh! No, Robin, you'll see all that later. I wish you were going instead of me, though."

Harry had looked up at the sound of Robin's voice. It had been a new note. There had been an eagerness, an enthusiasm, that meant life and something genuine.

Hope that had been slowly dying revived again. If Robin really cared for Germany like that, then they had something in common. With that spark a fire might be kindled. A red-gold haze as of fire burnt in the night sky, over the town. Stars danced overhead, a little wind, beating fitfully at the window, seemed to carry the light of the moon in its tempestuous track, blowing it lightly in silver mists and clouds over the moor. The Wise Men were there, strong and dark and sombre, watching over the lighted town and listening patiently to the ripple and murmur and life of the sea at their feet. In the little inn at the Cove men were sitting over the roaring fire, telling tales—strange, weird stories of a life that these others did not know. Harry had heard them when he was a boy—those stories—and he had felt the spell and the magic. There had been life in them and romance.

Perhaps they were there again to-night, just as they had been twenty years before. The stars called to him, the lighted town, the dusky, softly breathing sea, the loneliness of the moor. He must get out and away. He must have sympathy and warmth and friendship; he had come back to his own people with open arms and they had no place for him. His own son had repulsed him. But Cornwall, the country of his dreams, the mother of his faith, the guardian of his honour, was there—the same yesterday, to-day, and for ever. He would search for her and would find her—even though it were on the red-brick floor of the tavern in the Cove.

He turned round and found that the room was empty. They had forgotten him and left him—without a word. The light of the lamp caught the silver of the tea-things, and flashed and sparkled like a flame.

Harry Trojan softly opened the door, passed into the dim twilight of the hall, picked up his hat, and stepped into the garden.

CHAPTER V

As he felt the crunch of the gravel beneath his feet he was possessed with the spirit of adventure. The dark house behind him had been holding him captive. It had held him against his will, imprisoning him, tormenting him, and the tortures that he had endured were many and severe. He had not known that he could have felt it so much—that absolute rejection of him by everything in which he had trusted; but he would mind these things no longer—he would even try not to mind Robin! That would be hard, and as he thought of it even now for a moment tears had filled his eyes. That, however, was cowardice. He must fling away the hopes of twenty years and start afresh, with the knowledge won of his experience and the strength that he had snatched from his wounds.

And after all a man was a fool to mope and whine when that wind from the sea was beating in his ears and the sea scents of clover and poppies and salt stinging foam were brought to his nostrils, and the trees rustled like the beating of birds' wings in the velvety star-lighted sky.

A garden was wonderful at night—a place of strange silences and yet stranger sound: trees darkly guarding mysterious paths that ran into caverns of darkness; the scents of flowers rising from damp earth heavy with dew; flowers that were weary with the dust and noise of the day and slept gently, gratefully, with their heads drooping to the soil, their petals closed by the tender hands of the spirits of the garden. The night-sounds were strangely musical. Cries that were discordant in the day mingled now with the running of distant water, the last notes of some bird before it slept, the measured harmony of a far-away bell, the gentle rustle of some arrival in the thickets; the voice that could not be heard in the noisy chatter of the day rose softly now in a little song of the night and the dark trees and the silver firelight of the stars.

And it was all very romantic, of course. Harry Trojan had flung his cares behind him and stepped over the soft turf of the lawns, a free adventurer. It was not really very late, and there was an hour before dinner; but he was not sure that he minded about that—they would be glad to dine without him. There crossed his mind the memory of a night in New Zealand. He had been walking down to the harbour in Auckland, and the moon had shone in the crooked water-side streets, its white, cold light crossed with dark black shadows of roofs and gables. Suddenly a woman's voice called for help across the silence, and he had turned and listened. It had called again, and, thinking that he might help some one in distress, he had burst a dark, silent door, stumbled up crooked wooden stairs, and entered an empty room. As he passed the door there was a sound of skirts, and a door at the other end of the room had closed. There was no one there, only a candle guttering on the table, the remains of a meal, a woman's hat on the back of a chair; he had waited for some time in silence, he had called and asked if there was any one there, he had tried the farther door and found it shut—and so, cursing himself for a fool, he had passed down into the street again and the episode had ended. There was really nothing in it—nothing at all; but it was the atmosphere, the atmosphere of romantic adventure shot suddenly across a rather drab and colourless existence, and he had liked to dwell on the possibilities of the affair and ask himself about it. Who was the woman, and why had she cried out? Why was there no one in the room? And why had no one answered him?

He did not know and really he did not care, and, indeed, it was better that the affair should be left in vague and incomplete outline. It was probably commonplace enough, had one only known, and sordid too, perhaps. But to-night was just such a night as that other. He would go to the Cove and find his romance where he had left it twenty years ago. It was the hour in Pendragon when shops are closing and young men and maidens walk out. There were a great many people in the street; girls with white, tired faces, young men with bright ties and a self-assertive air—a type of person new to Pendragon since Harry's day. The young man who served you respectfully, almost timidly, behind the counter was now self-assertive, taking the middle of the street with a flourish of his cane. Fragments of conversation came to Harry's ears—

"Mother being out I thought as 'ow I might venture—not but what she'd kick up a rare old fuss———"

"So I told 'er it weren't no business of 'ers and the sooner she caught on to the idea the better for all parties, seein' as 'ow————"

"Well, I never did! and you told 'im that, did yer? I always said you'd some pluck if you really wanted to————"

A gramophone from an open window up the street shrieked the alluring refrain of "She's a different girl again," and a man who had established himself at the corner under the protecting glare of two hissing gas-jets urged on the company present an immediate acceptance of his stupendous offer. "Gold watches for 'alf a crown—positively for one evening in order to clear—all above board. Solid gold and cheap at a sovereign."

The plunge into the cool depths of the winding little path that led down to the Cove was delicious. Oh! the contrast of it! The noise and ugly self-assertion of the town, flinging its gas-jets against the moon and covering the roll of the sea with the shriek of the gramophone. He crossed through the turnstile at the bend of the road and passed up the hill that led to the Cove. At a bend the view of the sea came to him, the white moonlight lying, a path of dancing shining silver, on the grey sweep of the sea. A wind was blowing, turning the grey into sudden points of white—like ghostly hands rising for a moment suddenly from immensity and then sinking silently again, their prayers unanswered.

As he passed up the hill he was aware of something pattering beside him; at first it was a little uncanny in that dim, uncertain light, and he stopped and bent down to the road. It was a dog, a fox-terrier of a kind, dirty, and even in that light most obviously a mongrel. But it jumped up at him and put its paws on his knee.

"Well, company's company," he said with a laugh. "I don't know where you've sprung from, but we'll travel together for a bit." The dog ran up the hill, and for a moment stood out against the moon—a shaggy, disreputable dog with a humorous stump of a tail. He stood there with one ear flapping back and the other cocked up—a most ridiculous figure.

Harry laughed again and the dog barked; they walked down the hill together.

The Cove was dark, but from behind shuttered windows lamps twinkled mysteriously, and the red glow from the inn flung a circle of light down the little cobbled street. The beat of the sea came solemnly like the tramp of invisible armies from the distance. There was no other sound save the tremble of the wind in the trees.

Harry pushed open the door of the inn and entered, followed by the dog. The place was the same; nothing had been changed. There was the old wooden gallery where the fiddle had played such merry tunes. The rough uneven floor had the same holes, the same hills and dales. The great settle by the fire was marked, as in former years, with mysterious crosses and initials cut by jack-knives in olden days. The two lamps shone in their accustomed places—one over the fire, another by the window. The door leading to the bar was half open, and in the distance voices could be heard, but the room itself seemed to be empty.

A great fire leapt in the fireplace and the gold light of it danced on the red-brick floor. The peculiar scent as of tobacco and ale and the salt of the sea, and, faintly, the breath of mignonette and geraniums, struck out the long intervals since Harry had been there before. Twenty years ago he had breathed the same air; and now he was back there again and nothing was changed. The dog had run to the fire and sat in front of it now, wagging his stump of a tail, his ear cocked. Harry laughed and sat down in the settle; the burden of the last week was flung off and he was a free man.

A long, lean man with a straggling beard stood in the doorway and watched him; then he came forward. "Mr. Harry," he said, and held out his hand.

Harry started up. "I'm sorry," he said, stammering, "I don't remember."

"We were wonderin'," said the long, thin man slowly, "when you was comin' down. Not that you'd remember faces—that's not to be expected—especially in foreign parts which is confusing and difficult for a man—but I'm Bill Tregarvis what have had you out fishin' many's the time—not that you'd remember faces," he said again, looking a little timidly at him.

But he did! Harry remembered him perfectly! Bill Tregarvis! Why, of course—many was the time they had seen life together—he had had a wife and two boys.

Harry wrung his hand and laughed.

"Remember, Bill! Why, of course! It was only for a moment. I had got the face all right but not the name. Yes, I have, as a matter of fact, come before, but there were things that have made it difficult at first, and of course there was a lot to do up there. But it's good to be down here! The other place is changed; I had been a bit disappointed, but here it is just the same—the same old lights and smells and sea, and the same old friends———"

"Yer think that?" Tregarvis looked at him. "Because we'd been fearing that all your travelling and sight-seeing might have harmed you—that you'd be thinking a bit like the folk up-along with their cars and gas and filth. Aye, it's a changed world up there, Mr. Harry; but down-along there's no difference. It's the sea keeps us steady."

And then they talked about the old adventurous days when Harry had been eighteen and the world had been a very wonderful place: the herring fishing, the bathing, the adventures on the moor, the tales at night by candlelight, the fun of it all. The room began to fill, and one after another men came forward and claimed friendship on the score of old days and perils shared. They received him quite simply—he was "Mr. Harry," but still one of themselves, taking his place with them, telling tales and hearing them in return.

There were nine or ten of them, and a wild company they made, crowding round the fire, with the flames leaping and flinging gigantic shadows on the walls. The landlord, a short, ruddy-faced man with white hair and a merry twinkle of the eye, was one of the best men that Harry had ever known.

He was a man whose modesty was only equalled by his charity; a man of great humour, wide knowledge of the most varied subjects, and above all a passionate faith in the country of his birth, Cornwall. He was, like most Cornishmen, superstitious, but his belief in Nature as a wise and beneficent mother, stern but never unjust, controlled his will and justified his actions. In those early days Harry had worshipped him with that whole-hearted adoration bestowed at times by young hero-worshippers on those that have travelled a little way along the path and have learnt their lesson wisely. Tony Newsome's influence had done more for Harry in those early years than he had realised, but he knew now what he owed to him as he sat by his side and recalled those other days. They had written once or twice, but Tony was no correspondent and hated to have a pen between his fingers.

"Drive a horse, pull a boat, shoot a gun, mind a net—but God help me if I write," he had said. Not that he objected to books; he had read a good deal and cared for it—but "God's air in the day and a merry fire at night leaves little room for pen and ink" was his justification.

He treated Harry now as his boy of twenty years ago, and laughed at him and scolded him as of old. He did not question him very closely on the incidents of those twenty years, and indeed, with them all, Harry noticed that there was very little curiosity as to those other countries. They welcomed him quietly, simply. They were glad that he was there again, sitting with them, taking his place naturally and easily—and again the twenty years seemed as nothing.

He sat with the dog at his feet. Newsome's hand was on his knee, and every once and again he gave a smothered chuckle. "I knew you'd come back, Mr. Harry," he said. "I just waited. Once the sea has got hold of you it doesn't loosen its grip so quick. I knew you'd come back."

They told wild stories as they had been telling them for many years at the same hour in the same place—strange things seen at sea, the lights and mists of the moor, survivals of smuggling days and fights on the beach under the moon; and it always was the sea. They might leave it for a moment perhaps, but they came back to it—the terror of it, the joy of it, the cruelty of it; the mistress that held them chained, that called their children and would not be denied, the god that they served.

They spoke of her softly with lowered voices and a strange reverence. They had learnt her moods and her dangers; they knew that she could caress them, and then, of a sudden, strike them down—but they loved her.

And she had claimed Harry again. Everything for which he had been longing during that past week had come to him at last; their friendship, their faith in an old god, and above all that sense of a great adventure, for the spirit of which he had so diligently been searching. "Up-along" life was an affair of measured rules and things foreseen. "Down-along" it was a game of unending surprises and a gossamer web shot with the golden light of romance.

High-falutin perhaps, but to Harry, as he sat before the fire with the strange dog and those ten wild men, words and pictures came too speedily to admit of a sense of the absurd.

An old man, with a long white beard and a shaking hand, knew strange tales of the moor. When the mists creep up and blot out the land, then the four grey stones take life and are the giants of old, and strange sacrifices are grimly performed. Talse Carlyon had seen things late on a moonlit night with the mists swimming white and silvery-grey over the moor. He had lost his way and had met a man of mighty size who had led him by the hand. There had been spirits about, and at the foot of the grey stone a pool of blood—he had never been the same man since.

"There are spirits and spirits," said the old man solemnly, "and there 'm some good and some bad, for the proper edification of us mortals, and, for my part, it's not for the like of us to meddle."

He stroked his beard—a very gloomy old man with a blind eye. Harry remembered that he had had a wife twenty years before, so he inquired about her.

"Dead," said the old man fiercely, "dead—and, thank God, she went out like a candle."

He muttered this so fiercely that Harry said no more, and the white beard shone in the light of the fire, and his blind eye opened and shut like a box, and his wrinkled hand shook on his knee. The fishing had been bad of late, and here again they spoke as if some personal power had been at work. There were few there who had not lost some one during the years that they had served her, and the memory of what this had been and the foreshadowing of the dangerous future hung over them in the room. Songs were sung, jokes were made, but they were the songs and laughter of men on guard, with the enemy to be encountered, perhaps, in the morning.

Harry sat in his corner of the great seat, watching the leaping of the flames, his hand on Newsome's shoulder, listening to the murmuring voices at his side. He scarcely knew whether he were awake or sleeping; their laughter came to him dimly, and it seemed that he was alone there with only Newsome by his side and the dog sleeping at his feet. The tobacco smoke hung in grey-blue wreaths above his head and the gold light of the two lamps shone mistily, without shape or form. Perhaps it was really a dream. The old man with the white beard and the blind eye was sleeping, his head on his breast. A man with a vacant expression was telling a tale, heavily, slowly, gazing at the fire. The others were not listening—or at any rate not obviously so. They, too, gazed at the fire—it had, as it were, become personal and mesmerised the room. Perhaps it was a dream. He would wake and find himself at "The Flutes." There would be Clare and Garrett and—Robin! He would put all that away now; he would forget it for a moment, at least. He had failed them; they had not wanted him and had told him so,—but here they had known him and loved him; they had welcomed him back as though there had been no intervening space of years.

They at least had known what life was. They had not played with it, like those others. They had not surrounded themselves with barricades of artificiality, and glanced through distorting mirrors at their own exaggerated reflection; they had seen life simply, fearlessly, accepting their peril like men and enjoying their fate with the greatness of soul that simplicity had given them. They were not like those others; those on the hill had invaded the sea with noisy clamour, had greeted her familiarly and offered her bathing-machines and boarding-houses; these others had reverenced her and learnt to know her, alone on the downs in the first grey of the dawn, or secretly, when the breakers had rolled in over the sand, carrying with them the red and gold of some gorgeous sunset.

He contrasted them in his mind—the Trojans and the Greeks. He turned round a little in his seat and listened to the story: "It were a man—a strange man with horns and hoofs, so he said—and a merry, deceiving eye; but he couldn't see him clear because of the mist that hung there, with the moon pushing through like a candle, he said. The man was laughing to himself and playing with leaves that danced at his feet under the wind. It can't have been far from the town, because Joe heard St. Elmo's bell ringin' and he could hear the sea quite plain. He ..."

The voice seemed to trail off again into the distance; Harry's thoughts were with his future. What was he to do? It seemed to him that his crisis had come and was now facing him. Should he stay or should he flee? Why should he not escape—away into the country, where he could live his life without fear, where there would be no contempt, no hampering family traditions? Should he stay and wait while Robin learnt to hate him? At the thought his face grew white and he clenched his hands. Robin ... Robin ... Robin ... it always came back to that—and there seemed no answer. That dream of love between father and son, the dream that he had cherished for twenty years, was shattered, and the bubble had burst....

"So Joe said he didn't know but he thought it was to the left and down through the Cove—to the old church he meant; and the man laughed and danced with the leaves through the mist; and once Joe thought he was gone, and there he was back again, laughin'."

No, he would face it. He would take his place as he had intended—he would show them of what stuff he was made—and Robin would see, at last. The boy was young, it would of course take time——

The door of the inn opened and some one came in. The lamps flared in the wind, and there was a cry from the fireplace. "Mr. Bethel! Well, I'm right glad!"

Harry started. Bethel—that had been the name of his friend—the girl who had come to tea. The new-comer was a large man, over six feet in height, and correspondingly broad. His head was bare, and his hair was a little long and curly. His eyes were blue and twinkled, and his face was pleasantly humorous and, in the mouth and chin, strong and determined. He wore a grey flannel suit with a flannel collar, and he was smoking a pipe of great size. Newsome, starting to his feet, went forward to meet him. Bethel came to the fire and talked to them all; there was obviously a free companionship between them that told of long acquaintance. He was introduced to Harry.

"I've heard of you, Mr. Trojan," he said, "and have been expecting to meet you. I think that we have interests in common—at least an affection for Cornwall."

Harry liked him. He looked at him frankly between the eyes—there was no hesitation or disguise; there had been no barrier or division; and Harry was grateful.

Bethel sat down by the fire, and a discussion followed about matters of which Harry knew nothing. There was talk of the fishing prospects, which were bad; a gloom fell upon them all, and they cursed the new Pendragon—the race had grown too fast for them and competition was too keen. But Harry noticed that they did not yet seem to have heard of the proposed destruction of the Cove. Then he got up to go. They asked him to come again, and he promised that he would. Bethel rose too.

"If you don't object, Mr. Trojan," he said, "I'll make one with you. I had only looked in for a moment and had never intended to stay. I was on my way back to the town."

They went out into the street together, and Harry shivered for a moment as the wind from the sea met them.

"Ah, that's good," Bethel said; "your fires are well enough, but that wind is worth a bag of gold."

They walked for a little in silence, and then Harry said: "Those are a fine lot of men. They know what life really is."

Bethel laughed. "I know what you feel about them. You are glad that there's no change. Twenty years has made little difference there. It is twenty years, isn't it?"

"Yes," said Harry. "One thinks that it is nothing until one comes back, and then one thinks that it's more than it really is."

"Yes, you're disappointed," Bethel said. "I know. Pendragon has become popular, and to your mind that has destroyed its beauty—or, at any rate, some of it."

"Well, I hate it," Harry said fiercely, "all this noise and show. Why couldn't they have left Pendragon alone? I don't hate it for big places that are, as it were, in the line of march. I suppose that they must move with the day. That is inevitable. But Pendragon! Why—when I was a boy, it was simply a little town by the sea. No one thought about it or worried about it: it was a place wonderfully quiet and simple. It was too quiet for me then; I should worship it now. But I have come back and it has no room for me."

"I haven't known it as long as you," Bethel answered, "but I confess that the very charm of it lies in its contrast. It is invasion, if you like, but for that very reason exciting—two forces at work and a battle in progress."

"With no doubt as to the ultimate victory," said Harry gloomily. "Yes, I see what you mean by the contrast. But I cannot stand there and see them dispassionately—you see I am bound up with so much of it. Those men to-night were my friends when I was a boy. Newsome is the best man that I have ever known, and there is the place; I love every stone of it, and they would pull it down."

They had left the Cove and were pressing up a steep path to the moor. The moon was struggling through a bank of clouds; the wind was whistling over their heads.

Bethel suddenly stopped and turned towards Harry. "Mr. Trojan," he said, "I'm going to be impulsive and perhaps imprudent. There's nothing an Englishman fears so much as impulse, and he is terribly ashamed of imprudence. But, after all, there is no time to waste, and if you think me impertinent you have only to say so, and the matter ends."

Harry laughed. "I am delighted," he began, but the other stopped him.

"No, wait a moment. You don't know. I'm afraid you'll think that I'm absurd—most people will tell you that I am worse. I want you to try to be a friend of mine, at any rate to give me a chance. I scarcely know you—you don't know me at all—but; one goes on first impressions, and I believe that you would understand a little better than most of these people here—for one thing you have gone farther and seen more————"

There was a little pause. Harry was surprised. Here was what he had been wanting—friendship; a week ago he would have seized it with both hands; now he was a little distrustful; a week ago it would have been natural, delightful; now it was unusual, even a little absurd.

"I should be very glad," he said gravely. "I—scarcely————"

"Oh," Bethel broke in, "we shall come together naturally—there's no fear of that. I could see at once that you know the mysteries of this place just as I do. Those others here are blind. I've been waiting for some one who would understand. But I don't want you to listen to those other people about me; they will tell you a good deal—and most of it's true. I don't blame 'em, but I'm curiously anxious for you not to think with them. It's ridiculous, I know, when I had never seen you before. If you only knew how long I'd been waiting—to talk to some one—about—all this."

He waved his hand and they stopped. They were standing on the moor. Above their head mighty grey clouds were driving like fleets before the wind, and the moon, a cold, lifeless thing, a moon of chiselled marble, appeared, and then, as though frightened at the wild flight of the clouds, vanished. The sea, pearl grey, lay like mist on the horizon, and its voice was gentle and tired, as though it were slowly dying into sleep. They were near the Four Stones—gaunt, grey, and old. The dog had followed Harry from the inn and now ran, a white shadow, in front of him.

"Let me tell you," Bethel said, "about myself. You know I was born in London—the son of a doctor with a very considerable practice. I received an excellent education, Rugby and Cambridge, and was trained for the law. I was, I believe, a rather ordinary person with a rather more than ordinary power of concentration, and I got on. I built up a business and was extremely and very conventionally happy. I married and we had a little girl. And then, one summer, we came down to Cornwall for our holiday. It was St. Ives. I remember that first morning as though it were yesterday. It was grey with the sea flinging great breakers. There was a smell of clover and cornflowers in the air, and great sheets of flaming poppies in the cornfields. But there was more than that. It was Cornwall, something magical, and that strange sense of old history and customs that you get nowhere else in quite the same way. Ah! but why analyse it?—you know as well as I do what I mean. A new man was born in me that day. I had been sociable and fond of little quite ordinary pleasures that came my way, now I wanted to be alone. Their conversation worried me; it seemed to be pointless and concerned with things that did not matter at all. I had done things like other men—now it was all to no purpose. I used to lie for hours on the cliffs watching the sea. I was often out all day, and I met all sorts of people, tramps, wasters, vagabonds, and they seemed the only people worth talking to. I met some strange fellows but excellent company—and they knew, all of them, the things that I knew; they had been out all night and seen the moon and the stars change and the first light of the dawn, and the little breeze that comes in those early hours from the sea, bringing the winds of other countries with it. And they were merry, they had a philosophy—they knew Cornwall and believed in her.

"Well—the holiday came to an end, and I had to go back! London. My God! After that I struggled—I went to my work every day with the sound of that sea in my ears and the vision of those moors always there with me. And the freedom! If you have tasted that once, if you have ever got really close so that you can hear strange voices and see beauties of which you had never dreamt, well, you will never get back to your old routine again. I don't care how strong you are—you can't do it, man. Once she's got hold of you, nothing counts. That was eighteen years ago. I kept my work for a year, but it was killing me. I got ill—I nearly died; once I ran away at night and tried to get to the sea. But I came back—there were my wife and girl. We had a little money, and I gave it all up and we came to live down here. I have done nothing since; rather shameful, isn't it, for a strong man? They have thought that here; they think that I am a waster—by their lights I am. But the things I have learnt! I didn't know what living was until I came here! I knew nothing, I did nothing, I was a dead man. What do I care for their thoughts of me! They are in the dark!"

He had spoken eagerly, almost breathlessly. He was defending his position, and Harry knew that he had been waiting for years to say these things to some one of his own kind who would understand. And he understood only too well! Had he not himself that very evening been tempted to escape, to flee his duty? He had resisted, but the temptation had been very strong—that very voice of Cornwall of which Bethel had spoken—and if it were to return he did not know what answer he might give. But he was not thinking of Bethel; his thoughts were with the wife and daughter. That poor pathetic little woman—and the girl——

"And your wife and daughter?" he said. "What of them?"

"They are happy," Bethel said eagerly. "They are indeed. I don't see them very often, but they have their own interests—and friends. My wife and I never had very much in common—Ah! you're going to scold," he said, laughing, "and say just what all these other horrid people say. But I know. I grant it you all. I'm a waster—through and through; it's damnably selfish—worst of all, in this energetic and pushing age, it's idle. Oh! I know and I'm sorry—but, do you know, I'm not ashamed. I can't see it seriously. I wouldn't harm a fly. Why can't they let me alone? At least I am happy."

They had reached the outskirts of the town by this time and Bethel stopped before a little dark house with red shutters and a tiny strip of garden.

"Here we are!" said he. "This is my place. Come in and smoke! It must be past your dinner hour up at 'The Flutes.' Come and have something with me."

Harry laughed. "They have already ceased wondering at my erratic habits," he said. "New Zealand is a bad place for method."

He followed Bethel in. It was a tiny hall, and on entering he stumbled over an umbrella-stand that lounged forward in a rickety position. Bethel apologised. "We're in a bit of a mess," he said. "In fact, to tell the truth, we always are!" He hung his coat in the hall and led the way into the dining-room. Mrs. Bethel and her daughter came forward. The little woman was amazing in a dress of bright red silk and an absurd little yellow lace cap. Only half the table was laid; for the rest a shabby green cloth, spotted with ink, formed a background for an incoherent litter of papers and needlework. The walls were lined with books and there were some piled on the floor.

A cold shoulder of mutton, baked potatoes in their skins, a melancholy glass dish containing celery, and a salad bowl startlingly empty, lay waiting on the table.

"Anne," said Bethel, "I've brought a guest—up with the family port and let's be festive."

His great body seemed to fill the room, and he brought with him the breath of the sea and the wind. He began to carve the mutton like Siegfried making battle with Fafner, and indeed again and again during the evening he reminded Harry of Siegfried's impetuous humour and rejoicing animal spirits.

Mrs. Bethel was delighted. Her little eyes twinkled with excitement, her yellow cap was pushed awry, and her hands trembled with pleasure. It was obvious that a visitor was an unusual event. Miss Bethel had said very little, but she had given Harry that same smile that he had seen before. She busied herself now with the salad, and he watched her white fingers shine under the lamplight and the white curve of her neck as she bent over the bowl. She was dressed in some dark stuff—quite simple and unassuming, but he thought that he had never seen anything so beautiful.

He said very little, but he was quietly happy. Bethel did not talk very much; he was eating furiously—not greedily, but with great pleasure and satisfaction. Mrs. Bethel talked continuously. Her eyes shone and her cap bobbed on her head like a live thing.

"I said, Mr. Trojan, after our meeting the other day, that you would be a friend. I said so to Mary coming back. I felt sure that first day. It is so nice to have some one new in Pendragon—one gets used, you know, to the same faces and tired of them. In my old home, Penlicott in Surrey, near Marlwood Beeches—you change at Grayling Junction—or you used to; I think you go straight through now. But *there* you know we knew everybody. You really couldn't help it. There was really only the Vicar and the Doctor, and he was so old. Of course there were the Draytons; you must have heard of Mr. Herbert Drayton—he paints things—I forget quite what, but I know he's good. They all lived there—such a lot of them and most peculiar in their habits; but one gets used to anything. They all lived together for some time, about fifteen there were. Mother and I dined there once or twice, and they had the funniest dining-room with pictures of Job all round the room that were most queer and rather disagreeable; and they all liked different things to drink, so they each had a bottle—of something—separately. It looked quite funny to see the fifteen bottles, and then 'Job' on the wall, you know."

But he really hadn't paid very much attention to her. He had been thinking and wondering. How was it that a man like Bethel had married such a wife? He supposed that things had been different twenty years ago, with them as with him. It was strange to think of the difference that twenty years could make. She had been, perhaps, a little pretty, dainty thing then—the style of girl that a strong man like Bethel would fall in love with. Then he thought of Miss Bethel—what was her life with a mother like that and a father who never thought about her at all? She must, he thought, be lonely. He almost hoped that she was. It gave them kinship, because he was lonely too. The conversation was not very animated; Mrs. Bethel was suddenly silent—she seemed to have collapsed with the effort, and sat huddled up in her chair, with her hands in her lap.

He realised that he had said nothing to Miss Bethel, and he turned to her. "You know London?" he said. He wondered whether she longed for it sometimes—its excitement and life.

"Oh yes," she said quickly; "we were there, you know, a long while ago, and I've been up once or twice since. But it makes one feel so dreadfully small, as if one simply didn't count, and no woman likes that."

"Pendragon makes one feel smaller," Harry said. "When one is of no account even in a small place, then one is small indeed."

He had not intended to speak bitterly, but she had caught the sound of it in his voice and she was suddenly sorry for him. She had been a little afraid of him before—even on that terrible afternoon at "The Flutes"; but now she saw that he was disappointed—he had expected something and it had failed him.

She said nothing then, and the meal came to an end. Bethel dragged Harry into his study to see the books. There was the same untidiness here. The table was littered with papers and pens, tobacco jars, numerous pipes, some photographs. From the floor to the ceiling were books—rows on rows—flung apparently into the shelves with no order or method.

"I'm no good as far as books go," said Harry, laughing. "There never was such a heathen. There have always been other things to do, and I must confess it is a mystery to me how men get time to read at all. If I do get time I'm generally done up, and a novel's the only thing I'm fit for."

"Ah, then, you don't know the book craze," Bethel Said. "It's worse than drink. I've seen it absolutely ruin a man. You can't stop—if you see a book you must get it, whether you really want it or no. You go on buying and buying and buying. You get far more than you can ever read. But you're a miser and you hate even lending them. You sit in your room and count the covers, and you're no fit company for man or beast."

Harry looked at him—"You've known it?"

"Oh yes! I've known it. I'm a bit better now—I'm out such a lot. But even now there's a great deal here that I've never read, and I add to it continually. The worst of it is," he said, laughing, "that we can't afford it. It's very hard on Mary and the wife, but I'm a rotten loafer, and that's the end of it."

He said it so gaily and with so little sense of responsibility that you couldn't possibly think that it weighed on him. But he looked such a boy, standing there with his hands in his pockets and that half-penitent, half-humorous look in his eyes, that you couldn't be angry. Harry laughed.

"Upon my word, you're amazing!"

"Oh! you'll get sick of me. It's all so selfish and slack, I know. But I struggled once—I'm in the grip now." He talked about Borrow and displayed a little grey-bound "Walden" with pride. He spoke of Richard Jefferies with an intimate affection as though he had known the man.

He gave Harry some of his enthusiasm, and he lent him "Lavengro." He described it and Harry compared mentally Isobel Berners with Mary Bethel.

Then they went up to the little drawing-room—an ugly room, but redeemed by a great window overlooking the sea, and a large photograph of Mary on the mantelpiece. Under the light of the lamp the silver frame glittered and sparkled.

He sat by the window and talked to her, and again he had that same curious sense of having known her before: he spoke of it.

"I expect it's in another existence then," she said; "as I've never been into New Zealand and you've never been out of it—at least, since I've been born. But, of course, I've talked about you to Robin. We speculated, you know. We hadn't any photographs much to help us, and it was quite a good game."

"Ah! Robin!"

"I want to speak to you about him," she said, turning round to him. "You won't think me interfering, will you? but I've meant to speak ever since the other day. I was afraid that, perhaps—don't think it dreadfully rude of me—you hadn't quite understood Robin. He's at a difficult age, you know, and there are a lot of things about him that are quite absurd. And I have been afraid that you might take those absurdities for the real things and fancy that that was all that was there. Cambridge—and other things—have made him think that a certain sort of attitude is essential if you're to get on. I don't think he even sincerely believes in it. But they have taught him that he must, at least, seem to believe. The other things are there all right, but he hides them—he is almost ashamed of any one suspecting their existence."

"Thank you!" Harry said quietly. "It is very kind of you and I'm deeply grateful. It's quite true that Robin and I haven't seemed to hit it off properly. I expect that it is my fault. I have tried to see his point of view and have the same interests, but every effort that I've made has seemed to make things worse. He distrusts me, I think, and—well—of course, that hurts. All the things in which I had hoped we would share have no interest for him."

"Don't you think, perhaps," she said, "that you've been a little too anxious—perhaps, a little too affectionate? I am speaking like this because I care for Robin so much. We have been such good friends for years now, and I think he has let me see a side of him that he has hidden from most people. He is curiously sensitive, and really, I think, very shy; and most of all, he has a perfect horror of being absurd. That is what I meant about your being affectionate. He would think, perhaps, that the rest were laughing at him. It's as if you were dragging something that was very sacred and precious out into the light before all those others. Boys are like that; they are terrified lest any one should know what good there is in them—it isn't quite good form."

They were silent for some time. Harry was throwing her words like a searchlight on the events of the past week, and they revealed much that had been very dark and confused. But he was thinking of her. Their acquaintance seemed to have grown into intimacy already.

"I can't thank you enough," he said again.

"It is so nice of you," she said laughing, "not to have thought it presumptuous of me. But Robin is a very good friend of mine. Of course you will find out what a sterling fellow he is—under all that superficiality. He is one of my best friends here!"

He got up to go. As he held out his hand, he said: "I will tell you frankly, Miss Bethel, that Pendragon hasn't received me with open arms. I don't know why it should—and twenty years in New Zealand knocks the polish off. But it has been delightful this evening—more than you know."

"It has been nice for us too," Mary answered. "I don't know that Pendragon is exactly thronging our door night and day—and a new friend is worth having. You see I've claimed you as a friend because you listened so patiently to my sermon—that's a sure test."

She had spoken lightly but he had felt the bitterness in her voice. Life was hard for her too, then? He knew that he was glad.

"I shall come back," he said.

"Please," she answered.

He said good-bye to Mrs. Bethel and she pressed his hand very warmly. "You are very kind to take pity on us," she said, ogling him under the gas in the hall; "I hope you will come often."

Bethel said very little. He walked with him to the gate and laughed. "We're absurd, aren't we, Trojan?" he said. "But don't neglect us altogether. Even absurdity is refreshing sometimes."

But Harry went up the hill with a happier heart than he had had since he entered Pendragon.

That promise of adventure had been fulfilled.

CHAPTER VI

Randal was only at "The Flutes" two days, but he effected a good deal in that time. He did nothing very active—called on Mrs. le Terry and rode over the Downs once with Robin—but he managed to leave a flock of very active impressions behind him. That, as he knew well, was his strong point. He could not be with you a day without vaguely, almost indistinctly, but nevertheless quite certainly, influencing your opinions. He never said anything very definite, and, on looking back, you could never assert that he had positively taken any one point of view; but he had left, as it were, atmosphere—an assurance that this was the really right thing to do, this the proper attitude for correct breeding to adopt. It was always, with him, a case of correct breeding, and that was why the Trojans liked him so very much. "Randal," as Clare said, "knew so precisely who were sheep and who were goats, and he showed you the difference so clearly."

Whenever he came to stay some former acquaintances were dropped as being, perhaps, not quite the right people. He never said that any one was not the right person, that would be bad breeding, but you realised, of your own accord, that they were not quite right. That was why the impression was so strong—it seemed to come from yourself; your eyes were suddenly opened and you wondered that you hadn't seen it before.

He said very little of Trojan people this time; the main result of his visit was its effect on Harry's position.

Had you been a stranger you would have noticed nothing; the motto of the gentleman of good breeding is, "The end and aim of all true opinions is the concealing of them from the wrong person."

Randal was exceedingly polite to Harry, so polite that Robin and Clare knew immediately that he disapproved, but Harry was pleased. Randal spoke warmly to Robin. "You are lucky to have such a father, Bob; it's what we all want, you and I especially, a little fresh air let into our Cambridge dust and confusion; it's most refreshing to find some one who cares nothing about all those things that have seemed to us, quite erroneously probably, so valuable. You should copy him, Robin."

But Robin made no reply. He understood perfectly. There had been some qualities in his father that he had, deep down in his nature, admired. He had seemed to be without doubt a man on whom one could rely in a tight corner, and in spite of himself he had liked his father's frankness. It was unusual. There was always another meaning in everything that Robin's friends said, but there was never any doubt about Harry. He missed the fine shades, of course, and was lamentably lacking in discrimination, but you did know where you were. Robin had, almost reluctantly, admired this before the coming of Randal. But now there could be no question. When Randal was there you had displayed before you the complete art of successful allusion. Nothing was ever directly stated, but everything was hinted, and you were compelled to believe that this really was the perfection of good breeding. Robin admired Randal exceedingly. He took his dicta very seriously and accepted his criticism. The judgment of his father completed the impression that he had begun to receive. He was impossible. Randal was going by the 10.45, and he would walk to the station.

"A whiff of fresh air, Robin, is absolutely essential. You must walk down with me. I hate to go, Miss Trojan."

"Very soon to return, I hope, Mr. Randal," answered Clare. She liked him, and thought him an excellent influence for Robin.

"Thank you—it's very kind—but one's busy, you know. It's been hard enough to snatch these few days. Besides, Robin isn't alone in the same way now. He has his father."

Clare made no reply, but her silence was eloquent.

"I'm sorry for him, Miss Trojan," he said. "He is, I'm afraid, a little out of it. Twenty years, you know, is a long time."

Clare smiled. "He is unchanged," she said. "What he was as a boy, he is now."

"He is fortunate," Randal said gravely. "For most of us experience has a jostling series of shocks ready. Life hurts."

He said good-bye with that air of courtly melancholy that Clare admired so much. He shook Harry warmly by the hand and expressed a hope of another meeting.

"I should be delighted," Harry said. "What sort of time am I likely to catch you in town?"

But Randal, alarmed at this serious acceptance of an entirely ironical proposal, was immediately vague and gave no definite promise. Harry watched them pass down the drive, then he turned back slowly into the house.

It was one of those blue and gold days that are only to be realised perfectly in Cornwall—blue of the sky and the sea, gold on the roofs and the rich background of red and brown in the autumn-tinted trees, whilst the deep green of the lawns in front of the house seemed to hold both blues and golds in its lights and shadows. The air was perfectly still and the smoke from a distant bonfire hung in strange wreaths of grey-blue in the light against the trees, as though carved delicately in marble.

Randal discussed his prospects. He spoke, as he invariably did with regard to his past and future, airily and yet impressively: "I don't like to make myself too cheap," he said. "There are things any sort of fellow can do, and I must say that I shrink from taking bread out of the mouths of some of them. But of course there are things that one *must* do—where special knowledge is wanted—not that I'm any good, you know, but I've had chances. Besides, one must work slowly. Style's the thing—Flaubert and Pater for ever—the doctrine of the one word."

Robin looked at him with admiration.

"By Jove, Randal, I wish I could write; I sometimes feel quite—well, it sounds silly—but inspired, you know—as if one saw things quite differently. It was very like that in Germany once or twice."

"Ah, we're all like that at times," Randal spoke encouragingly. "But don't you trust it—an *ignis fatuus* if ever there was one. That is why we have bank clerks at Peckham and governesses in Bloomsbury writing their reminiscences. It's those moments of inspiration that are responsible for all our over-crowded literature."

They had chosen the path over the fields to the station, and suddenly at the bend of the hill the sea sprang before them, a curving mirror that reflected the blue of the sky and was clouded mistily with the gold of the sun. That sudden springing forward of the sea was always very wonderful, even when it had been seen again and again, and Robin stopped and shaded his eyes with his hand.

"It's fine, isn't it, Randal?" he said. "One gets fond of the place."

He was a little ashamed to have betrayed such feeling and spoke apologetically. He went on hurriedly. "There was an old chap in Germany—at Worms—who was most awfully interesting. He kept a little bookshop, and I used to go down and talk to him, and he said once that the sea was the most beautiful dream that the world contained, but you must never get too near or the dream broke, and from that moment you had no peace."

Randal looked at Robin anxiously. "I say, old chap, this place is getting on your nerves; always being here is bad for you. Why don't you come up to town or go abroad? You're seedy."

"Oh, I'm all right," Robin said, rather irritably. "Only one wonders sometimes if—" he broke off suddenly. "I'm a bit worried about something," he said.

He was immediately aware that he had said nothing to Randal about the Feverel affair and he wondered why. Randal would have been the natural person to talk to about it; his advice would have been worth having. But Robin felt vaguely that it would be better not. For some strange reason, as yet unanalysed, he scarcely trusted him as he had done in the old days. He was still wondering why, when they arrived at the station.

They said good-bye affectionately—rather more affectionately than usual. There was a little sense of strain, and Robin felt relieved when the train had gone. As he hurried from the platform he puzzled over it. He could hold no clue, but he knew that their friendship had changed a little. He was sorry.

As he turned down the station road he decided that life was becoming very complicated. There was first his father; that oughtn't in the nature of things to have complicated matters at all—but it was complicated, because there was no knowing what a man like that would do. He might let the family down so badly; it was almost like having gunpowder in your cellar. Randal had thought him absurd. Robin saw that clearly, and Randal's opinion was that of all truly sensible people. But, after all, the real complication was the Feverel affair. It was now nearly ten days since that terrible evening and nothing had happened. Robin wasn't sure what *could* have happened, but he had expected something. He had waited for a note; she would most assuredly write and her letter would serve as a hint, he would know how to act; but there had been no sign. On the day following the interview he had felt, for the most part, relief. He was suddenly aware of the burden that the affair had been, he was a free man; but with this there had been compunction. He had acted like a brute; he was surprised that he could have been so hard, and he was a little ashamed of meeting the public gaze. If people only realised, he thought, what a cad he was, they would assuredly have nothing to do with him. As the days passed, this feeling increased and he was extremely uncomfortable. He had never before doubted that he was a very decent fellow—nothing, perhaps, exceptional in any way, but, judged by every standard, he passed muster. Now he wasn't so sure, he had done something that he would have entirely condemned in another man, and this showed him plainly and most painfully the importance that he placed on the other man's opinion. He was beginning to grow his crop of ideas and he was already afraid of the probable harvest.

That his affection for Dahlia was dead there could be no question, but that it was buried, either for himself or the public, was, most unfortunately, not the case. He was afraid of discovery for the first time in his life, and it was unpleasant. Dahlia herself would be quiet; at least, he was almost sure, although her outbreak the other evening had surprised him. But he was afraid of Mrs. Feverel. He felt now that she had never liked him; he saw her as some grim dragon waiting for his inevitable surrender. He did not know what she would do; he was beginning to realise his inexperience, but he knew that she would never allow the affair to pass quietly away. To do him justice, it was not so much the fear of personal exposure that frightened him; that, of course, would be unpleasant—he would have to face the derision of his enemies and the contempt of those people whom formerly he had himself despised. But it was not personal contempt, it was the disgrace to the family; the house was suddenly threatened on two sides—his father, the Feverels—and he was frightened. He saw his name in the papers; the Trojan name dragged through the mud because of his own folly—Oh! it must be stopped at all costs. But the uncertainty of it was worrying him. Ten days had passed and nothing was done. Ten days, and he had been able to speak of it to no one; it had haunted him all day and had spoiled his sleep; first, because he had done something of which he was ashamed, and secondly, because he was afraid that people might know.

There were the letters. He remembered some of the sentences now and bit his lip. How could he have been such a fool? She must give them back—of course she would; but there was Mrs. Feverel.

The uncertainty was torturing him—he must find out how matters were, and suddenly, on the inspiration of the moment, he decided to go and see Dahlia at once. Things could not be worse, and at least the uncertainty would be ended. The golden day irritated him, and he found the dark gloom of the Feverels' street a relief. A man was playing an organ at the corner, and three dirty, tattered children were dancing noisily in the middle of the road. He watched them for a moment before ringing the bell, and wondered how they could seem so unconcerned, and he thought them abandoned.

He found Dahlia alone in the gaudy drawing-room. She gave a little cry when she saw who it was, and her cheeks flushed red, and then the colour faded. He noticed that she was looking ill and rather untidy. There were dark lines under her eyes and her mouth was drawn. There was an awkward pause; he had sat down with his hat in his hand and he was painfully ill at ease.

"I knew you would come back, Robin," she began at last. "Only you have been a long time—ten days. I have never gone out, because I was afraid that I would miss you. But I knew that you would be sorry after the other night, because you know, dear, you hurt me terribly, and for a time I really thought you meant it."

"But I do mean it," Robin broke in. "I did and I do. I'm sorry, Dahlia, for having hurt you, but I thought that you would see it as I do—that it must, I mean, stop. I had hoped that you would understand."

But she came over and stood by him, smiling rather timidly. "I don't want to start it all over again," she said. "It was silly of me to have made such a fuss the other night. I have been thinking all these ten days, and it has been my fault all along. I have bothered you by coming here and interfering when I wasn't really wanted. Mother and I will go away again and then you shall come and stay, and we shall be all alone—like we were at Cambridge. I have learnt a good deal during these last few days, and if you will only be patient with me I will try very hard to improve."

She stood by his chair and laid her hand on his arm. He would have thrilled at her touch six months before—now he was merely impatient. It was so annoying that the affair should have to be reopened when they had decided it finally the other night. He felt again the blind, unreasoning fear of exposure. He had never before doubted his bravery, but there had never been any question of attack—the House had been, it seemed, founded on a rock, he had never doubted its stability before. Now, with all the cruelty of a man who was afraid for the first time, he had no mercy.

"It is over, Dahlia—there is no other possibility. We had both made a mistake; I am sorry and regret extremely if I had led you to think that it could ever have been otherwise. I see it more clearly than I saw it ten days ago—quite plainly now—and there's no purpose served in keeping the matter open; here's an end. We will both forget. Heroics are no good; after all, we are man and woman—it's better to leave it at that and accept the future quietly."

He spoke coldly and calmly, indeed he was surprised that he could face it like that, but his one thought was for peace, to put this spectre that had haunted him these ten days behind him and watch the world again with a straight gaze—he must have no secrets.

She had moved away and stood by the fireplace, looking straight before her. She was holding herself together with a terrible effort; she must quiet her brain and beat back her thoughts. If she thought for a moment she would break down, and during these ten days she had been schooling herself to face whatever might come—shame, exposure, anything—she would not cry and beg for pity as she had done before. But it was the end, the end, the end! The end of so much that had given her a new soul during the last few months. She must go back to those dreary years that had had no meaning in them, all those purposeless grey days that had stretched in endless succession on to a dismal future in which there shone no sun. Oh! he couldn't know what it had all meant to her—it could be flung aside by him without regret. For him it was a foolish memory, for her it was death.

The tears were coming, her lips were quivering, but she clenched her hands until the nails dug into the flesh. The sun poured in a great flood of colour through the window, and meanwhile her heart was broken. She had read of it often enough and had laughed—she had not known that it meant that terrible dull throbbing pain and no joy or hope or light anywhere. But she spoke to him quietly.

"I had thought that you were braver, Robin. That you had cared enough not to mind what they said. You are right: it has all been a mistake."

"Yes," he said doggedly, without looking at her. "We've been foolish. I hadn't thought enough about others. You see after all one owes something to one's people. It would never do, Dahlia, it wouldn't really. You'd never like it either—you see we're different. At Cambridge one couldn't see it so clearly, but here—well, there are things one owes to one's people, tradition, and, oh! lots of things! You have got your customs, we have ours—it doesn't do to mix."

He hadn't meant to put it so clearly. He scarcely realised what he had said because he was not thinking of her at all; it was only that one thing that he saw in front of him, how to get out, away, clear of the whole entanglement, where there was no question of suspicion and possible revelation of secrets. He was not thinking of her.

But the cruelty of it, the naked, unhesitating truth of it, stung her as nothing had ever hurt her before—it was as though he had struck her in the face. She was not good enough, she was not fit. He had said it before, but then he had been angry. She had not believed it; but now he was speaking calmly, coldly—she was not good enough!

And in a moment her idol had tumbled to the ground—her god was lying pitifully in the dust, and all the Creed that she had learnt so patiently and faithfully had crumbled into nothing. Her despair seemed, for the moment, to have gone; she only felt burning contempt—contempt for him, that he could seem so small—contempt for herself, that she could have worshipped at such altars.

She turned round and looked at him.

"That is rather unfair. You say that I am not your equal socially. Well, we will leave it at that—you are quite right—it is over."

He lowered his eyes before her steady gaze. At last he was ashamed; he had not meant to put it brutally. He had behaved like a cad and he knew it. Her white face, her hands clenched tightly at her side, the brave lift of her head as she faced him, moved him as her tears and emotions had never done.

He sprang up and stood by her.

"Dahlia, I've been a brute, a cad—I didn't know what I had said—I didn't mean it like that, as you thought. Only I've been so worried, I've not known where to turn and—oh, don't you see, I'm so young. I get driven, I can't stand up against them all."

Why, he was nearly crying. The position was suddenly reversed, and she could almost have laughed at the change. He was looking at her piteously, like a boy convicted of orchard-robbing—and she had loved him, worshipped him! Five minutes ago his helplessness would have stirred her, she would have wanted to take him and protect him and comfort him; but now all that was past—she felt only contempt and outraged pride: her eyes were hard and her hands unclenched.

"It is no good, Robin. You were quite right. There is an end of everything. It was a mistake for both of us, and perhaps it is as well that we should know it now. It will spare us later."

So that was the end. He felt little triumph or satisfaction; he was only ashamed.

He turned to go without a word. Then he remembered—"There are the letters?"

"Ah! you must let me keep them—for a memory." She was not looking at him, but out of the window on to the street. A cab was slowly crawling in the distance—she could see the end of the driver's whip as he flicked at his horses.

"You can't—you don't mean——?" Robin turned back to her.

"I mean nothing—only I am—tired. You had better go. We will write if there is anything more."

"Look here!" Robin was trembling from head to foot. "You must let me have them back. It's serious—more than you know. People might see them and—my God! you would ruin me!"

He was speaking melodramatically, and he looked melodramatic and very ridiculous. He was crushing his bowler in his hands.

"No. I will keep them!" She spoke slowly and quite calmly, as though she had thought it all out before. "They are valuable. Now you must go. This has been silly enough—Good-bye."

She turned to the window and he was dismissed. His pride came to the rescue; he would not let her see that he cared, so he went—without another word.

She stood in the same position, and watched him go down the street. He was walking quickly and at the same time a little furtively, as though he was afraid of meeting acquaintances. She turned away from the window, and then, suddenly, knelt on the floor with her head in her hands. She sobbed miserably, hopelessly, with her hands pressed against her face.

And Mrs. Feverel found her kneeling there in the sunlight an hour later.

"Dahlia," she said softly, "Dahlia!"

The girl looked up. "He has gone, mother," she said. "And he is never coming back. I sent him away."

And Mrs. Feverel said nothing.

CHAPTER VII

There were times when Harry felt curiously, impressively, the age of the house. It was not all of it old, it had been added to from time to time by successive Trojans; but there had, from the earliest days, been a stronghold on the hill overlooking the sea and keeping guard.

He had had a wonderful pride in it on his return, but now he began to feel as though he had no right in it. Surely if any one had a right to such a heritage it was he, but they had isolated him and told him that he had no place there. The gardens, the corners and battlements of the house, the great cliff falling sheer to the sea, had had no welcome for him, and when he had claimed his succession they had refused him. He was beginning to give the stocks and stones of the House a personal existence. Sometimes at night, when the moon gave the place grey shadows and white lights, or in the early morning when the first birds were crying in the trees and the sea was slowly taking colour from the rising sun, in the perfect stillness and beauty of those hours the house had seemed to speak to him with a new voice. He imagined, fantastically at times, that the white statues in the garden watched him with grave eyes, wondering what place he would take in the chronicles of the House.

It was Sunday afternoon, and he was alone in the library. That was a room that had always appealed to him, with its dark red walls covered from floor to ceiling with books, its wide stone fireplace, its soft, heavy carpets, its wonderfully comfortable armchairs. It seemed to him the very perfection of that spirit of orderly comfort and luxurious simplicity for which he had so earnestly longed in New Zealand. He sat in that room for hours, alone, thinking, wondering, puzzling, devising new plans for Robin's surrender and rejecting them as soon as they were formed.

He was sitting by the fire now, hearing the coals click as they fell into the golden furnace that awaited them. He was comparing the incidents of the morning with those of the preceding Sunday, and he knew that things were approaching a crisis. Clare had scarcely spoken to him for three days. Garrett and Robin had not said a word beyond a casual good-morning. They were ignoring him, continuing their daily life as though he did not exist at all. He remembered that he had felt his welcome a fortnight before a little cold—it seemed rapturous compared with the present state of things.

They had driven to church that morning in state. No one had exchanged a word during the whole drive. Clare had sat quietly, in solemn magnificence, without moving an eyelid. They had moved from the carriage to the church in majestic procession, watched by an admiring cluster of townspeople. He had liked Clare's fine bearing and Robin's carriage; there was no doubt that they supported family traditions worthily, but he felt that, in the eyes of the world, he scarcely counted at all. It was a cold and over-decorated church, with an air of wealth and lack of all warm emotions that was exactly characteristic of its congregation. Harry thought that he had never seen a gathering of more unresponsive people. An excellent choir sang Stainer in B flat with perfect precision and fitting respect, and the hymns and psalms were murmured with proper decorum. The clergyman who had come to tea on the day after Harry's arrival preached a carefully calculated and excellently worded sermon. Although his text was the publican's "Lord, be merciful to me, a sinner," it was evident that his address was tinged with the Pharisee's self-congratulations.

A little gathering was formed in the porch after the service, and Mrs. le Terry, magnificent in green silk and an enormous hat, was the only person who took any interest in Harry, and she was looking over his head during the conversation in order, apparently, to fix the attention of some gentleman moving in the opposite direction.

At lunch Harry had made a determined effort towards cheerfulness. He had learnt that heartiness was bad manners and effusion a crime, so he was quiet and restrained. But his efforts failed miserably; Robin seemed worried and his thoughts were evidently far away, Clare was occupied with the impertinence of some stranger who had thrust himself into the Trojan pew at the last moment, and Garrett was repeating complacently a story that he had heard at the Club tending to prove the unsanitary condition of the lower classes in general and the inhabitants of the Cove in particular. After lunch they had left him alone; he had not dared to petition Robin for a walk, so, sick at heart and miserably lonely, he had wandered disconsolately into the library. He had taken from one of the shelves the volume T-U of *The Dictionary of National Biography*, and had amused himself by searching for the names of heroes in Trojan annals.

There was only one who really mattered—a certain Humphrey Trojan, 1718-1771; a man apparently of poor circumstances and quite a distant cousin of the main branch, one who had been in all probability despised by the Sir Henry Trojan of that time. Nevertheless he had been a person of some account in history and had, from the towers of the House, watched the sea and the stars to some purpose. He had been admitted, Harry imagined, into the sacred precincts after his researches had made him a person of national importance, and it was amusing to picture Sir Henry's pride transformed into a rather obsequious familiarity when "My cousin, Humphrey, had been honoured by an interview with his Majesty and had received an Order at the royal hand"—amusing, yes, but not greatly to the glory of Sir Henry. Harry liked to picture Humphrey in his days of difficulty—sturdy, persevering, confident in his own ability, oblivious of the cuts dealt him by his cousin. Time would show.

He let the book fall and gazed at the fire, thinking. After all, he was a poor creature. He had none of that perseverance and belief in his own ultimate success, and it was better, perhaps, to get right out of it, to throw up the sponge, to turn tail, and again there floated before him that wonderful dream of liberty and the road—of a relationship with the world at large, and no constraint of family dignity and absurd grades of respectability. Off with the harness; he had worn it for a fortnight and he could bear it no longer. Bethel was right; he would follow the same path and find his soul by losing it in the eyes of the world. But after all, there was Robin. He had not given it a fair trial, and it was only cowardice that had spoken to him.

The clock struck half-past three and he went upstairs to see his father. The old man seldom left his bed now. He grew weaker every day and the end could not be far away. He had no longer any desire to live, and awaited with serene confidence the instant of departure, being firmly convinced that Death was too good a gentleman to treat a Trojan scurvily, and that, whatever the next world might contain, he would at least be assured of the respect and deference that the present world had shown him. His mind dwelt continually on his early days, and, even when there was no one present to listen, he repeated anecdotes and reminiscences for the benefit of the world at large. His face seemed to have dwindled considerably, but his eyes were always alive—twinkling over the bedclothes like lights in a dark room. His mouth never moved, only his hand, claw-like and yellow as parchment, clutched the bedclothes and sometimes waved feebly in the air to emphasise his meaning. He had grown strangely intolerant of Clare, and although he submitted to her offices as usual, did so reluctantly and with no good grace; she had served him faithfully and diligently for twenty years and this was her reward. She said nothing, but she laid it to Harry's charge.

Sir Jeremy's eyes twinkled when he saw his son. "Hey, Harry, my boy—all of 'em out, aren't they? Devilish good thing—no one to worry us. Just give the pillows a punch and pull that table nearer—that's right. Just pull that blind up—I can't see the sea."

The room had changed its character within the last week. It was a place of silences and noiseless tread, and the scent of flowers mingled with the intangible odour of medicine. A great fire burnt in the open fireplace, and heavy curtains had been hung over the door to prevent draughts.

Harry moved silently about the room, flung up the blind to let in the sun, propped up the pillows, and then sat down by the bed.

"You're looking better, father," he said; "you'll soon be up again."

"The devil I will," said Sir Jeremy. "No, it's not for me. I'm here for a month or two, and then I'm off. I've had my day, and a damned good one too. What do you think o' that girl now, Harry—she's fine—what?"

He produced from under the pillow a photograph, yellow with age, of a dancer—jet-black hair and black eyes, her body balanced on one leg, her hands on her hips. "Anonita Sendella—a devilish fine woman, by gad—sixty years ago that was—and Tom Buckley and I were in the running. He had the money and I had the looks, although you wouldn't think it now. She liked me until she got tired of me and she died o' drink—not many like that nowadays." He gazed at the photograph whilst his eyes twinkled. "Legs—by Heaven! what legs!" He chuckled. "Wouldn't do for Clare to see that; she was shaking my pillows this mornin' and I was in a deuce of a fright—thought the thing would tumble out."

He lay back on his pillows thinking, and Harry stared out of the window. The end would come in a month or two—perhaps sooner; and then, what would happen? He would take his place as head of the family. He laughed to himself—head of the family! when Clare and Garrett and Robin all hated him? Head of the family!

The sky was grey and the sea flecked with white horses. It was shifting colours to-day like a mother-of-pearl shell—a great band of dark grey on the horizon, and then a soft carpet of green turning to grey again by the shore. The grey hoofs [Transcriber's note: roofs?] of the Cove crowded down to the edge of the land, seeming to lean a little forward, as though listening to what the sea had to say; the sun, breaking mistily through the clouds, was a round ball of dull gold—a line of breakwater, far in the distance, seemed ever about to advance down the stretch of sea to the shore, as though it would hurl itself on the cluster of brown sails in the little bay, huddling there for protection. Head of the House! What was the use, when the House didn't want him?

His father was watching him and seemed to have read his thoughts. "You'll take my place, Harry?" he said. "They won't like it, you know. It was partly my fault. I sent you away and you grew up away, and they've always been here. I've been wanting you to come back all this time, and it wasn't because I was angry that I didn't ask you—but it was better for you. You don't see it yet; you came back thinking they'd welcome you and be glad to see you, and you're a bit hurt that they haven't. They've been hard to you, all of 'em—your boy as well. I've known, right enough. But it cuts both ways, you see. They can't see your point of view, and they're afraid of the open air you're letting in on to them. You're too soft, Harry; you've shown them that it hurts, and they've wanted it to hurt. Give 'em a stiff back, Harry, give 'em a stiff back. Then you'll have 'em. That's like us Trojans. We're devilish cruel because we're devilish proud; if you're kind we hurt, but if you do a bit of hurting on your own account we like it."

"I've made a mess of it," Harry said, "a hopeless mess of it. I've tried everything, and it's all failed. I'd better back out of it——" Then, after a pause, "Robin hates me——"

Sir Jeremy chuckled.

"Oh no, he doesn't. He's like the rest of us. You wanted him to give himself away at once, and of course he wouldn't. They're trying you and waiting to see what you'll do, and Robin's just following on. You'll be all right, only give 'em a stiff back, the whole crowd of 'em."

Suddenly his wrinkled yellow hand shot out from under the bedclothes and he grasped his son's. "You're a damned fine chap," he said, "and I'm proud of you—only you're a bit of a fool—sentimental, you know. But you'll make more of the place than I've ever done, God bless you——" after which he lay back on his pillows again, and was soon asleep.

Harry waited for a little, and then he stole out of the room. He told the nurse to take his place, and went downstairs.

It was four o'clock, and he was going to tea at the Bethels'. He had been there pretty frequently during the past week—that and the Cove were his only courts of welcome. He knew that his going there had only aggravated his offences in the eyes of his sister, but that he could not help. Why should they dictate his friends to him?

The little drawing-room was neat and clean. There were some flowers, and the chairs and sofa were not littered with books and needlework and strange fragments of feminine garments. Mrs. Bethel was gorgeous in a green silk dress and the paint was more obtrusive than ever. Her eyes were red as though she had been crying, and her hair as usual had escaped bounds.

Mary was making tea and smiled up at him. "Shout at father," she said. "He's downstairs in the study, browsing. He'll come up when he knows you are here."

Harry went to the head of the stairs and called, and Bethel came rushing up. Sunday made no difference to his clothes, and he wore the grey suit and flannel collar of their first meeting.

His greeting was, as ever, boisterous. "Hullo! Trojan! that's splendid! I was afraid they'd carry you off to that church of yours or you'd have a tea-party or something. I'm glad they've spared you."

"No, I went this morning," Harry answered, "all of us solemnly in the family coach. I thought that was enough for one day."

"We used to have a carriage when papa was alive," said Mrs. Bethel, "and we drove to church every Sunday. We were the only people beside the Porsons, and theirs was only a pony-cart."

"Well, for my part, I hate driving," said Mary. "It puts you in a bad temper for the sermon."

"Let's have tea," said Bethel. "I'm as hungry as though I'd listened to fifty parsons."

And, indeed, he always was. He ate as though he had had no meal for a month at least, and he had utterly demolished the tea-cake before he realised that no one else had had any.

"Oh, I say, I'm so sorry," he said ruefully. "Mary, why didn't you tell me? I'll never forgive myself——" and proceeded to finish the saffron buns.

"All the same," said Mary, "we're going to church to-night, all of us, and if you're very good, Mr. Trojan, you shall come too."

Harry paused for a moment. "I shall be delighted," he said; "but where do you go?"

"There's a little church called St. Sennan's. You haven't heard of it, probably. It's past the Cove—on a hill looking over the sea. It's the most tumble-down old place you ever saw, and nobody goes there except a few fishermen, but we know the clergyman and like him. I like the place too—you can listen to the sea if you're bored with the sermon."

"The parson is like one of the prophets," said Bethel. "Too strong for the Pendragon point of view. It's a place of ruins, Trojan, and the congregation are like a crowd of ancient Britons—but you'll like it."

Mrs. Bethel was unwontedly quiet—it was obvious that she was in distress; Mary, too, seemed to speak at random, and there was an air of constraint in the room.

When they set off for church the grey sky had changed to blue; the sun had just set, and little pink clouds like fairy cushions hung round the moon. As they passed out of the town, through the crooked path down to the Cove, Harry had again that strong sense of Cornwall that came to him sometimes so suddenly, so strangely, that it was almost mysterious, for it seemed to have no immediate cause, no absolute relation to surrounding sights or sounds. Perhaps to-night it was in the misty half-light of the shining moon and the dying sun, the curious stillness of the air so that the sounds and cries of the town came distinctly on the wind, the scent of some wild flowers, the faint smell of the chrysanthemums that Mary was wearing at her breast.

"By Jove, it's Cornwall," he said, drawing a great breath. He was walking a little ahead with Mary, and he turned to her as she spoke. She was walking with her head bent, and did not seem to hear him. "What's up?" he said.

"Nothing," she answered, trying to smile.

"But there is," he insisted. "I'm not blind. I've bored you with my worries. You might honour me with yours."

"There isn't anything really. One's foolish to mind, and, indeed, it's not for myself that I care—but it's mother."

"What have they done?"

"They don't like us—none of them do. I don't know why they should; we aren't, perhaps, very likeable. But it is cruel of them to show it. Mother, you see, likes meeting people—we had it in London, friends I mean, lots of them, and then when we came here we had none. We have never had any from the beginning. We tried, perhaps a little too hard, to have some. We gave little parties and they failed, and then people began to think us peculiar, and if they once do that here you're done for. Perhaps we didn't see it quite soon enough and we went on trying, and then they began to snub us."

"Snub you?"

"Yes, you know the kind of thing. You saw that first day we met you——"

"And it hurts?"

"Yes—for mother. She still tries; she doesn't see that it's no good, and each time that she goes and calls, something happens and she comes back like she did to-day. I don't suppose they mean to be unkind—it is only that we are, you see, peculiar, and that doesn't do here. Father wears funny clothes and never sees any one, and so they think there must be something wrong——"

"It's a shame," he said indignantly.

"No," she answered, "it isn't really. It's one's own fault—only sometimes I hate it all. Why couldn't we have stayed in London? We had friends there, and father's clothes didn't matter. Here such little things make such a big difference"—which was, Harry reflected, a complete epitome of the life of Pendragon.

"I'm not whining," she went on. "We all have things that we don't like, but when you're without a friend——"

"Not quite," he said; "you must count me." He stopped for a moment. "You *will* count me, won't you?"

"You realise what you are doing," she said. "You are entering into alliance with outcasts."

"You forget," he answered, "that I, also, am an outcast. We can at least be outcasts together."

"It is good of you," she said gravely; "I am selfish enough to accept it. If I was really worth anything, I would never let you see us again. It means ostracism."

"We will fight them," he answered gaily. "We will storm the camp"; but in his heart he knew that their stronghold, with "The Flutes" as the heart of the defence, would be hard to overcome.

They climbed up the hill to the little church with the sea roaring at their feet. A strong wind was blowing, and, for a moment, at a steep turn of the hill, she laid her hand on his arm; at the touch his heart beat furiously—in that moment he knew that he loved her, that he had loved her from the first moment that he had seen her, and he passed on into the church.

It was, as Bethel had said, almost in ruins—the little nave was complete, but ivy clambered in the aisles and birds had built their nests in the pillars. Three misty candles flickered on the altar, and some lights burnt over the pulpit, but there were strange half-lights and shadows so that it seemed a place of ghosts. Through the open door the night air blew, bringing with it the beating of the sea, and the breath of grass and flowers. The congregation was scanty; some fishermen and their wives, two or three old women, and a baby that made no sound but listened wonderingly with its finger in its mouth. The clergyman was a tall man with a long white beard and he did everything, even playing the little wheezy harmonium. His sermon was short and simple, but was listened to with rapt attention. There was something strangely intense about it all, and the hymns were sung with an eagerness that Harry had never heard elsewhere. This was a contrast with the church of the morning, just as the Cove was a contrast with Pendragon; the parting of the ways seemed to face Harry at every moment of his day—his choice was being urgently demanded and he had no longer any hesitation.

Newsome was there, and he spoke to him for a moment on coming out. "You'll be lonely 'up-along,'" he said; "you belong to us."

They all four walked back together.

"How do you like our ancient Britons?" said Bethel.

"It was wonderful," said Harry. "Thank you for taking me."

They were all very silent, but when they parted at the turning of the road Bethel laughed. "Now you are one of us, Trojan. We have claimed you."

As he shook Mary's hand he whispered, "This has been a great evening for me."

"I was wrong to grumble to you," she answered. "You have worries enough of your own. I release you from your pledge."

"I will not be released," he said.

That night Clare Trojan, before going to bed, went into Garrett's room. He was working at his book, and, as usual, hinted that to take such advantage of his good-nature by her interruption was unfair.

"I suppose to-morrow morning wouldn't do instead, Clare—it's a bit late."

"No, it wouldn't—I want you to listen to me. It's important."

"Well?" He seated himself in the most comfortable chair and sighed. "Don't be too long."

She was excited and stood over him as though she would force him to be interested.

"It's too much, Garrett. It's got to stop."

"What?"

"Harry. Some one must speak to him."

Garrett smiled. "That, of course, will be you, Clare—you always do; but if it's my permission that you want you may have it and welcome. But we've discussed all this before. What's the new turn of affairs?"

"No. I want more than your permission; we must take some measures together. It's no good unless we act at once. Miss Ponsonby told me this afternoon—it has become common talk—the things he does, I mean. She did not want to say anything, but I made her. He goes down continually to some low public-house in the Cove; he is with those Bethels all day, and will see nothing of any of the decent people in the place—he is becoming a common byword."

"It is a pity," Garrett said, "that he cannot choose his friends better."

"He must—something must be done. It is not for ourselves only, though of course that counts. But it is the House—our name. They laugh at him, and so at all of us. Besides, there is Robin."

Garrett looked at his sister curiously—he had never seen her so excited before. But she found it no laughing matter. Miss Ponsonby would not have spoken unless matters had gone pretty far. The Cove! The Bethels! Robin's father!

For, after all, it was for Robin that she cared. She felt that she was fighting his battles, and so subtly concealed from herself that she was, in reality, fighting her own. She was in a state of miserable uncertainty. She was not sure of her father, she was not sure of Robin, scarcely sure of Garrett—everything threatened disaster.

"What will you do?" Garrett had no desire that the responsibility should be shifted in his direction; he feared responsibility as the rock on which the ship of his carefully preserved proprieties might come to wreck.

"Do? Why, speak—it must be done. Think of him during the whole time that he has been here—not only to Pendragon, but to us. He has made no attempt whatever to fit in with our ways or thoughts; he has shown no desire to understand any of us; and now he must be pulled up, for his own sake as well as ours."

But Garrett offered her little assistance. He had no proposals to offer, and was barren of all definite efforts; he hated definite lines of any kind, but he promised to fall in with her plans.

"I will come down to breakfast," she said, "and will speak to him afterwards."

Garrett nodded wearily and went back to his work. On the next morning the crisis came.

Breakfast was a silent meal at all times. Harry had learnt to avoid the cheerful familiarity of his first morning—it would not do. But the heavy solemnity of the massive silver teapot, the ham and cold game on the sideboard, the racks of toast that were so needlessly numerous, drove him into himself, and, like his brother and son, he disappeared behind folds of newspaper until the meal was over.

Clare frequently came down to breakfast, and therefore he saw nothing unusual in her appearance. The meal was quite silent; Clare had her letters—and he was about to rise and leave the room, when she spoke.

"Wait a minute, Harry. I want to say something. No, Robin, don't go—what I'm going to say concerns us all."

Garrett remained behind his newspaper, which showed that he had received previous warning. Robin looked up in surprise, and then quickly at his father, who had moved to the fireplace.

"About me, Clare?" He tried to speak calmly, but his voice shook a little. He saw that it was a premeditated attack, but he wished that Robin hadn't been there. He was, on the whole, glad that the moment had come; the last week had been almost unbearable, and the situation was bound to arrive at a crisis—well, here it was, but he wished that Robin were not there. As he looked at the boy for a moment his face was white and his breath came sharply. He had never loved him quite so passionately as at that moment when he seemed about to lose him.

Clare had chosen her time and her audience well, and suddenly he felt that he hated her; he was immediately calm and awaited her attack almost nonchalantly, his hand resting on the mantelpiece, his legs crossed.

Clare was still sitting at the table, her face half turned to Harry, her glance resting on Robin. She tapped the table with her letters, but otherwise gave no sign of agitation.

"Yes—about you, Harry. It is only that I think we have reason—almost a right—to expect that you should yield a little more thoroughly to our wishes. Both *Garrett*"—this with emphasis—"and myself are sure that your failing to do so is only due to a misconception on your part, and it is because we are sure that you have only to realise them to give way a little to them, that I—we—are speaking."

"I certainly had not realised that I had failed in deference to your wishes, Clare."

"No, not failed—and it is absurd to talk of deference. It is only that I feel—we all feel"—this with another glance at Robin—"that it is naturally impossible for you to realise exactly what are the things required of us here. Things that would in New Zealand have been of no importance at all."

"Such as——?"

"Well, you must remember that we have, as it were, the eyes of all the town upon us. We occupy a position of some importance, and we are definitely expected to maintain that position without lack of dignity."

"Won't you come to the point, Clare? It is a little hard to see——"

"Oh, things are obvious enough—surely, Harry, you must see for yourself. People were ready to give you a warm welcome when you returned. I—we—all of us, were only too glad. But you repulsed us all. Why, on the very day after your arrival you were extremely—I am sorry, but there is no other word—discourteous to the Miss Ponsonbys. You have made your friends almost entirely amongst the fisher class, a strange thing, surely, for a Trojan to do, and you now, I believe, spend your evenings frequently in a low public-house resorted to by such persons—at any rate you have spent them neither here nor at the Club, the two obvious places. I am only mentioning these things because I think that you may not have seen that such matters—trivial as they may seem to you—reflect discredit, not only on yourself, but also, indirectly, on all of us."

"You forget, Clare, that I have many old friends down at the Cove. They were there when I was a boy. The people in Pendragon have changed very largely, almost entirely. There is scarcely any one whom I knew twenty years ago; it is, I should have thought, quite natural that I should go to see my old friends again after so long an absence."

He was trying to speak quietly and calmly. His heart was beating furiously, but he knew that if he once lost control, he would lose, too, his position. But, as he watched them, and saw their cold, unmoved attitude his anger rose; he had to keep it down with both hands clenched—it was only by remembering Robin that the effort was successful.

"Natural to go and see them on your return—of course. But to return, to go continually, no. I cannot help feeling, Harry, that you have been a little selfish. That you have scarcely seen our side of the question. Things have changed in the last twenty years—changed enormously. We have seen them, studied them, and, I think, understood them. You come back and face them without any preparation; surely you cannot expect to understand them quite as we do."

"This seems to me, I must confess, Clare, a great deal of concern about a very little matter. Surely I am not a person of such importance that a few visits to the Cove can ruin us socially?"

"Ah! that is what you don't understand! Little things matter here. People watch, and are, I am afraid, only too ready to fasten on matters that do not concern them. Besides, it is not only the Cove—there are other things—there are, for instance, the Bethels."

At the name Robin started. He liked Mary Bethel, had liked her very much indeed, but he had known that his aunt disapproved of them and had been careful to disguise his meetings. But the instant thought in his mind concerned the Feverels. If the Bethels were impossible socially, what about Dahlia and her mother? What would his aunt say if she knew of that little affair? And the question which had attacked him acutely during the last week in various forms hurt him now like a knife.

He watched his father curiously. He did not look as if he cared very greatly. Of course Aunt Clare was perfectly right. He had been selfishly indifferent, had cared nothing for their feelings. Randal had shown plainly enough how impossible he was. Indeed the shadow of Randal lurked in the room in a manner that would have pleased that young gentleman intensely had he known it. Clare had it continually before her, urging her, advising her, commanding her.

At the mention of the Bethels, Harry looked up sharply.

"I think we had better leave them out of the discussion." His voice trembled a little.

"Why? Are they so much to you? They have, however, a good deal to do with my argument. Do you think it was wise to neglect the whole of Pendragon for the society of the Bethels—people of whom one is an idler and loafer and the other a lunatic?" Clare was becoming excited.

"You forget, Clare, that I first met them in your drawing-room."

"They were there entirely against my will. I showed them that quite distinctly at the time. They will not come again."

"That may be. But they are, as you have said, my friends. I cannot, therefore, hear them insulted. They must be left out of the discussion."

On any other matter he could have heard her quietly, but the Bethels she must leave alone. He could see Mary, as he spoke, turning on the hill and laying her hand on his arm; her hair blew in the wind and the light in her eyes shone under the moon. He had for a moment forgotten Robin.

"At any rate, I have made my meaning clear. We wish you—out of regard for us, if for no other reason—to be a little more careful both of your company and of your statements. It is hard for you to see the position quite as we do, I know, but I cannot say that you have made any attempt whatsoever to see it with our eyes. It seems useless to appeal to you on behalf of the House, but that, too, is worth some consideration. We have been here for many hundreds of years; we should continue in the paths that our ancestors have marked out. I am only saying what you yourself feel, Garrett?"

"Absolutely." Garrett looked up from his paper. "I think you must see, Harry, that we are quite justified in our demands—Clare has put it quite plainly."

"Quite," said Harry. "And you, Robin?"

"I think that Aunt Clare is perfectly right," answered Robin coldly.

Harry's face was very white. He spoke rapidly and his hand gripped the marble of the mantelpiece; he did not want them to see that his legs were trembling.

"Yes. I am glad to know exactly where we stand. It is better for all of us. I might have taken it submissively, Clare, had you left out your last count against me. That was unworthy of you. But haven't you, perhaps, seen just a little too completely your own point of view and omitted mine? I came back a stranger. I was ready to do anything to win your regard. I was perhaps a little foolishly sentimental about it, but I am a very easy person to understand—it could not have been very difficult. I imagined, foolishly, that things would be quite easy—that there would be no complications. I soon found that I had made a mistake; you have taught me more during the last fortnight than I had ever learnt in all my twenty years abroad. I have learnt that to expect affection from your own relations, even from your son, is absurd—affection is bad form; that, of course, was rather a shock.

"You have had, all of you, your innings during the last fortnight. You have decided, with your friends, that I am impossible, and from that moment you have deliberately cut me. You have driven me to find friends of my own and then you have complained of the friends that I have chosen. That is completed—in a fortnight you have shown me, quite plainly, your position. Now I will show you mine. You have refused to have anything to do with me—for the future the position shall be reversed. I shall alter in no respect whatever, either my friendships or my habits. I shall go where I please, do what I please, see whom I please. We shall, of course, disguise our position from the world. I have learnt that disguise is a very important part of one's education. Our former relations from this moment cease entirely."

He was speaking apparently calmly, but his anger was at white-heat. All the veiled insults and disappointments of the last fortnight rose before him, but, above all, he saw Mary as though he were defending her, there, in the room. He would never forgive them.

Clare was surprised, but she did not show it. She got up from the table and walked to the door. "Very well, Harry," she said, "I think you will regret it."

Garrett rose too, his hand trembling a little as he folded his newspaper.

"That is, I suppose, an ultimatum," he said. "It is a piece of insolence that I shall not forget."

Robin was turning to leave the room. Harry suddenly saw him. He had forgotten him; he had thought only of Mary.

"Robin," he whispered, stepping towards him. "Robin—you don't think as they do?"

"I agree with my aunt," he said, and he left the room, closing the door quietly behind him.

Harry's defiance had left him. For a moment the only thing that he saw clearly in a world that had suddenly grown dark and cold was his son. He had forgotten the rest—his sister, Mary, Pendragon—it all seemed to matter nothing.

He had come from New Zealand to love his son—for nothing else.

He had an impulse to run after him, to seize him, and hold him, and force him to come back.

Then he remembered—his pride stung him. He would fight it out to the end; he would, as his father said, "show them a stiff back."

He was very white, and for a moment he had to steady himself by the table. The silver teapot, the ham, the racks of toast were all there—how strange, when the rest of the world had changed; he was quite alone now—he must remember that—he had no son. And he, too, went out, closing the door quietly behind him.

CHAPTER VIII

Some letters during this week:—

23 SOUTHWICK CRESCENT, W.,
October 10, 1906.

My dear Robin—I should have written before, I am ashamed of my omission, but my approaching departure abroad has thrown a great many things on my hands; I have a paper to finish for Clarkson and an essay for the *New Review*, and letter-writing has been at a standstill. It was delightful—that little peep of you that I got—and it only made me regret the more that it is impossible to see much of you nowadays. I cannot help feeling that there is a danger of vegetation if one limits oneself too completely to a provincial life, and, charming though Cornwall is, its very fascination causes one to forget the importance of the outer world. I fancied that I discerned signs that you yourself felt this confinement and wished for something broader. Well, why not have it? I confess that I see no reason. Come up to London for a time—go abroad—your beloved Germany is waiting for you, and a year at one of the Universities would be both amusing and instructive. These are only suggestions; I should hesitate to offer them at all were it not that there has always been such sympathy between us that I know you will not resent them. Of course, the arrival of your father has made considerable difference. I must say, honestly, that I regretted to see that you had not more in common. The fault, I expect, has been on both sides; as I said to you before, it has been hard for him to realise exactly what it is that we consider important. We—quite mistakenly possibly—have come to feel that certain things, art, literature, music, are absolutely essential to us, morally and physically. They are nothing at all to him, and I can quite understand that you have found it difficult—almost impossible—to grasp his standpoint. I must confess that he did not seem to me to attempt to consider yours; but it is easy, and indeed impertinent, to criticise, and I hope that, on the next occasion of your writing, I shall hear that things are going smoothly and that the first inevitable awkwardnesses have worn off.

I must stop. I have let my pen wander away with me. But do consider what I said about coming up to town; I am sure that it is bad for you in every way—this burial. Think of your friends, old chap, and let them see something of you.—Yours ever,

LANCELOT RANDAL.

"THE FLUTES," PENDRAGON,
October 12, 1906.

My dear Lance—Thanks very much for your letter. This mustn't pretend to be anything of a letter. I have a thousand things to do, and no time to do them. It was very delightful seeing you, and I, too, was extremely sorry we could not see more of you. My aunt enjoyed your visit enormously, and told me to remind you that you are expected here, for a long stay, on your return from Germany.

Yes, I was worried and am still. There are various things—"it never rains but it pours"—but I cannot feel that they are in the least due to my vegetating. I haven't the least intention of sticking here, but my grandfather is, as you know, very ill, and it is impossible for me to get away at present.

Resent what you said! Why, no, of course not. We are too good friends for resentment, and I am only too grateful for your advice. The situation here at this moment is peculiarly Meredithian—and, although one ought perhaps to be silent concerning it, I know that I can trust you absolutely and I need your advice badly. Besides, I must speak to some one about it; I have been thinking it over all day and am quite at a loss. There was battle royal this morning after breakfast, and my father was extremely rude to my aunt, acting apparently from quite selfish motives. I want to look at it fairly, but I can, honestly, see it in no other light. My aunt accused him of indifference with regard to the family good name. She, quite rightly, I think, pointed out that his behaviour from first to last had been the reverse of courteous to herself and her friends, and she suggested that he had, perhaps, scarcely realised the importance of maintaining the family dignity in the eyes of Pendragon. You remember his continual absences and the queer friendships that he formed. She suggested that he should modify these, and take a little more interest in the circle to which we, ourselves, belong. Surely there is nothing objectionable in all this; indeed, I should have thought that he would have been grateful for her advice. But no—he fired up in the most absurd manner, accused us of unfairness and prejudice, declared his intention of going his own way, and gave us all his congé. In fact, he was extremely rude to my aunt, and I cannot forgive him for some of the things that he said. His attitude has been absurd from the first, and I cannot see that we could have acted otherwise, but the situation is now peculiar, and what will come of it I don't know. I must dress for dinner—I am curious to see whether he will appear—he was out for lunch. Let me have a line if you have a spare moment. I scarcely know how to act.—Yours,

ROBERT TROJAN.

23 SOUTHWICK CRESCENT, W.,

October 14, 1906.

Dear Robin—In furious haste, am just off and have really no time for anything. I am more sorry than I can say to hear your news. I must confess that I had feared something of the kind; matters seemed working to a climax when I was with you. As to advice, it is almost impossible; I really don't know what to say, it is so hard for me to judge of all the circumstances. But it seems to me that your father can have had no warrant for the course that he took. One is naturally chary of delivering judgment in such a case, but it was, obviously, his duty to adapt himself to his environment. He cannot blame you for reminding him of that fact. Out of loyalty to your aunt, I do not see that you can do anything until he has apologised. But I will think of the matter further, and will write to you from abroad.—In great haste, your friend, LANCELOT RANDAL.

"THE FLUTES," PENDRAGON, CORNWALL,
October 13, 1906.
Dear Miss Feverel—I must apologise for forcing you to realise once more my existence. Any reminder must necessarily be painful after our last meeting, but I am writing this to request the return of all other reminders of our acquaintance that you may happen to possess; I enclose the locket, the ring, your letters, and the tie that you worked. We discussed this matter the other day, but I cannot believe that you will still hold to a determination that can serve no purpose, except perhaps to embitter feelings on both sides. From what I have known of you I cannot believe that you are indulging motives of revenge—but, otherwise, I must confess that I am at a loss.—Expecting to receive the letters by return, I am, yours truly,
ROBERT TROJAN.

9 SEA VIEW TERRACE, PENDRAGON, CORNWALL,
October 14, 1906.
Dear Mr. Trojan—Thank you for the locket, the ring, and the letters which I have received. I regret that I must decline to part with the letters; surely it is not strange that I should wish to keep them.—Yours truly, DAHLIA FEVEREL.

"THE FLUTES,"
October 15, 1906.
What do you mean? You have no right to them. They are mine. I wrote them. You serve no purpose by keeping them. Please return them at once—by return. I have done nothing to deserve this. Unless you return them, I shall know that you are merely an intriguing—; no, I don't mean that. Please send them back. Suppose they should be seen?—In haste, R. T.

9 SEA VIEW TERRACE, PENDRAGON, CORNWALL,
October 15, 1906.
My decision is unalterable.
D. F.

But Dahlia sat in the dreary little drawing-room watching the grey sea with a white face and hard, staring eyes.

She had sat there all day. She thought that soon she would go mad. She had not slept since her last meeting with Robin; she had scarcely eaten—she was too tired to think.

The days had been interminable. At first she had waited, expecting that he would come back. A hundred impulses had been at work. At first she had thought that she would go and tell him that she had not meant what she said; she would persuade him to come back, She would offer him the letters and tell him that she had meant nothing—they had been idle words. But then she remembered some of the things that he had said, some of the stones that he had flung. She was not good enough for him or his family; she had no right to expect that an alliance was ever possible. His family despised her. And then her thoughts turned from Robin to his family. She had seen Clare often enough and had always disliked her. But now she hated her so that she could have gladly killed her. It was at her door that she laid all the change in Robin and her own misery. She felt that she would do anything in the world to cause her pain. She brooded over it in the shabby little room with her face turned to the sea. How could she hurt her? There were the others, too—the rest of the family—all except Robin's father, who was, she felt instinctively, different. She thought that he would not have acted in that way. And then her thoughts turned back to Robin, and for a moment she fancied that she hated him, and then she knew that she still loved him—and she stared at the grey sea with misery in her heart and a dull, sombre confusion in her brain. No, she did not hate Robin, she did not really want to hurt him. How could she, when they had had those wonderful months together? Those months that seemed such centuries and centuries away. But, nevertheless, she kept the letters. Her mother had talked about them, had advised her to keep them. She did not mean to do anything very definite with them—she could not look ahead very far—but she would keep them for a little.

When she had seen Robin's handwriting again it had been almost more than she could bear. For some time she had been unable to tear open the envelope and speculated, confusedly, on the contents. Perhaps he had repented. She judged him by her own days and nights of utter misery and knew that, had it been herself, they would have driven her back crying to his feet. Perhaps it was to ask for another interview. That she would refuse. She felt that she could not endure another such meeting as their last; if he were to come to her without warning, to surprise her suddenly—her heart beat furiously at the thought; but the deliberate meeting merely for the purpose of his own advantage—no!

She opened the letter, read the cold lines, and knew that it was utterly the end. She had fancied, at their last meeting, that her love, like a bird shot through the heart, had fallen at his feet, dead; then, after those days of his absence, his figure had grown in her sight, glorified, resplendent, and love had revived again—now, with this letter she knew that it was over. She did not cry, she scarcely moved. She watched the sea, with the letter on her lap, and felt that a new Dahlia Feverel, a woman who would traffic no longer with sentiment, who knew the world for what it was—a hard, merciless prison with fiends for its gaolers—had sprung to birth.

She replied to him and showed her mother her answer. She scarcely listened to Mrs. Feverel's comments and went about her daily affairs, quietly, without confusion. She saw herself and Robin like figures in a play—she applauded the comedy and the tragedy left her unmoved. Robin Trojan had much to answer for.

He read her second letter with dismay. He had spent the day in solitary confinement in his room, turning the situation round and round in his mind, lost in a perfect labyrinth of suggested remedies, none of which afforded him any outlet. The thought of exposure was horrible; anything must be done to avoid that—disgrace to himself was bad enough; to be held up for laughter before his Cambridge friends, Randal, his London acquaintances—but disgrace to the family! That was the awful thing!

From his cradle this creed of the family had been taught him; he had learnt it so thoroughly that he had grown to test everything by that standard; it was his father's disloyalty to that creed that had roused the son's anger—and now, behold, the son was sinning more than the father! It was truly ironic that, three days after his attacking a member of the family for betraying the family, he himself should be guilty of far greater betrayal! How topsy-turvy the world seemed, and what was to be done?

The brevity and conciseness of Dahlia's last letter left him in no doubt as to her intentions. Breach of Promise! The letters would be read in court, would be printed in the newspapers for all the world to see. With youth's easy grasping of eternity, it seemed to him that his disgrace would be for ever. Beddoes' "Death's Jest-book" was lying open on his knee. Wolfram's song—

> Old Adam, the carrion crow,
> The old crow of Cairo;
> He sat in the shower, and let it flow
> Under his tail and over his crest;
> And through every feather
> Leaked the wet weather;
> And the bough swung under his nest;
> For his beak it was heavy with marrow.
> Is that the wind dying? Oh no;
> It's only two devils, that blow
> Through a murderer's bones, to and fro,
> In the ghost's moonshine—

had always seemed to him the most madly sinister verse in English literature. It had been read to him by Randal at Cambridge and had had a curious fascination for him from the first. He had found that the little bookseller at Worms had known it and had indeed claimed Beddoes for a German—now it seemed to warn him vaguely of impending disaster.

He did not see that he himself could act any further in the matter; she would not see him and writing was useless. And yet to leave the matter uncertain, waiting for the blow to fall, with no knowledge of the movements in the other camp, was not to be thought of. He must do something.

The moment had arrived when advice must be taken—but from whom? His father was out of the question. It was three days since the explosion, and there was an armed truce. He had, in spite of himself, admired his father's conduct during the last three days, and he was surprised to find that it was his aunt and uncle rather than his father who had failed to carry off the situation. He refused as yet to admit it to himself, but the three of them, his aunt, his uncle, and himself, had seemed almost frightened. His father was another person; stern, cold, unfailingly polite, suddenly apparently possessed of those little courtesies in which he had seemed before so singularly lacking. There had been conversation of a kind at meals, and it had always been his father who had filled awkward pauses and avoided difficult moments. The knowledge, too, that his father would, in a few months' time, be head of the house, was borne in upon him with new force; it might be unpleasant, but it would not, as he had formerly fancied, be ludicrous. A sign of his changed attitude was the fact that he rather resented Randal's letter and wished a little that he had not taken him into his confidence.

Nevertheless, to ask advice of his father was impossible. He must speak to his uncle and aunt. How hard this would be only he himself knew. He had never in their eyes failed, in any degree, towards the family honour. From whatever side the House might be attacked, it would not be through him. There was nothing in his past life, they thought, at which they would not care to look.

He realised, too, Clare's love for him. He had known from very early days that he counted for everything in her life; that her faith in the family centred in his own honour and that her hopes for the family were founded completely in his own progress—and now he must tell her this.

He could not, he knew, have chosen a more unfortunate time. The House had already been threatened by the conduct of the father; it was now to totter under blows dealt by the son. The first crisis had been severe, this would be infinitely more so. He hated himself for the first time in his life, and, in doing so, began for the first time to realise himself a little.

Well, he must speak to them and ask them what was to be done, and the sooner it was over the better. He put the Beddoes back into the shelf, and went to the windows. It was already dark; light twinkled in the bay, and a line of white breakers flashed and vanished, keeping time, it seemed, with the changing gleam of the lighthouse far out to sea. His own room was dark, save for the glow of the fire. They would be at tea; probably his father would not be there—the present would be a good time to choose. He pulled his courage together and went downstairs.

As he had expected, Garrett was having tea with Clare in her own room—the Castle of Intimacy, as Randal had once called it. Garrett was reading; Clare was sitting by the fire, thinking.

"She will soon have more to think about," thought Robin wretchedly.

She looked up as he came in. "Ah, Robin, that's splendid! I was just going to send up for you. Come and sit here and talk to me. I've hardly seen you to-day."

She had been very affectionate during the last three days—rather too affectionate, Robin thought. He liked her better when she was less demonstrative.

"Where have you been all the afternoon?"

"In my room. I've been busy."

"Tea? You don't mind it strong, do you, because it's been here a good long time? Gingerbread cake especially for you."

But gingerbread cake wasn't in the least attractive. Beddoes suited him much better:—

Is that the wind dying? Oh no;
It's only two devils, that blow
Through a murderer's bones, to and fro,
In the ghost's moonshine.

"Do you know Beddoes, aunt?"

"No, dear. What kind of thing is it? Poetry?"

"Yes. You wouldn't like it, though——only I've been reading him this afternoon. He suited my mood."

"Boys of your age shouldn't have moods." This from Garrett. "I never had."

Robin took his tea without answering, and sat down on the opposite side of the fire to his aunt. How was he to begin? What was he to say? There followed an awful pause—life seemed to have been full of pauses lately.

Clare was watching him anxiously. How had his father's outbreak affected him? She was afraid, from little things that she had seen, that he had been influenced. Harry had been so different those last three days—she could not understand it. She watched him eagerly, hungrily. Why was he not still the baby that she could take on her knees and kiss and sentimentalise over? He, too, she fancied, had been different during these last days.

"More tea, Robin? You'd better—it's a long while before dinner."

"No, thanks, aunt. I—that is—well, I've something I wanted to say."

He turned round in his chair and faced the fire. He would rather not look at her whilst he was speaking. Garrett put down his book and looked up. Was there going to be more worry? What had happened lately to the world? It seemed to have lost all proper respect for the Trojan position. He could not understand it. Clare drew her breath sharply. Her fears thronged about her, like shadows in the firelight—what was it? ... Was it Harry?

"What about, Robin? Is anything the matter?"

"Why, no—nothing really—it's only—that is—Oh, dash it all—it's awfully difficult."

There was another silence. The ticking of the clock drove Robin into further speech.

"Well—I've made a bit of a mess. I've been rather a fool and I want your advice."

Another pause, but no assistance save a cold "Well?" from Garrett.

"You see it was at Cambridge, last summer. I was an awful fool, I know, but I really didn't know how far it was going until—well, until afterwards———"

"Until—after what?" said Garrett. "Would you mind being a little clearer, Robin?"

"Well, it was a girl." Robin stopped. It sounded so horrible, spoken like that in cold blood. He did not dare to look at his aunt, but he wondered what her face was like. He pulled desperately at his tie, and hurried on. "Nothing very bad, you know. I meant, at first, anyhow—I met her at another man's—Grant of Clare—quite a good chap—and he gave a picnic—canaders and things up the river. We had a jolly afternoon and she seemed awfully nice and—her mother wasn't there. Then—after that—I saw a lot of her. Every one does at Cambridge—I mean see girls and all that kind of thing—and I didn't think anything of it—and she really *seemed* awfully nice then. There isn't much to do at Cambridge, except that sort of thing—really. Then, after term, I came down here, and I began to write. I'm afraid I was a bit silly, but I didn't know it then, and I used to write her letters pretty often, and she answered them. And—well, you know the sort of thing, Uncle Garrett—I thought I loved her———"

At this climax, Robin came to a pause, and hoped that they would help him, but they said no word until, at last, Garrett said impatiently, "Go on."

"Well," continued Robin desperately, "that's really all—" knowing, however, that he had not yet arrived at the point of the story. "She—and her mother—came down to live here—and then, somehow, I didn't like her quite so much. It seemed different down here, and her mother was horrid. I began to see it differently, and at last, one night, I told her so. Of course, I thought, naturally, that she would understand. But she didn't—her mother was horrid—and she made a scene—it was all very unpleasant." Robin was dragging his handkerchief between his fingers, and looking imploringly at the fire. "Then I went and saw her again and asked her for—my letters—she said she'd keep them—and I'm afraid she may use them—and—well, that's all," he finished lamely.

He thought that hours of terrible silence followed his speech. He sat motionless in his chair waiting for their words. He was rather glad now that he had spoken. It had been a relief to unburden himself; for so many days he had only had his own thoughts and suggestions to apply to the situation. But he was afraid to look at his aunt.

"You young fool," at last from Garrett. "Who is the girl?"

"A Miss Feverel—she lives with her mother at Sea view Terrace—there is no father."

"Miss Feverel? What! That girl! You wrote to her! You———"

At last his aunt had spoken. He had never heard her speak like that before—the "You!" was a cry of horror. She suddenly got up and went over to him. She bent over him where he sat, with head lowered, and shook him by the shoulder.

"Robin! It can't be true—you haven't written to that girl! Not love-letters! It is incredible!"

"It is true—" he said, looking up. "Don't look at me like that, Aunt Clare. It isn't so bad—other fellows——" but then he was ashamed and stopped. He would leave his defence alone.

"Is that all?" said Garrett. "All you have done, I mean? You haven't injured the girl?"

"I swear that's all," Robin said eagerly. "I meant no harm by it. I wrote the letters without thinking I——"

Clare stood leaning on the mantelpiece, her head between her hands.

"I can't understand it. I can't understand it," she said. "It isn't like you—not a bit. That girl and you—why, it's incredible!"

"That's only because you had your fancy idea of him, Clare," said Garrett. "We'd better pass the lamentation stage and decide what's to be done."

For once Garrett seemed practical; he was pleased with himself for being so. It had suddenly occurred to him that he was the only person who could really deal with the situation. Clare was a woman, Harry was out of the question, Robin was a boy.

"Have you spoken to your father?" he asked.

"No. Of course not!" Robin answered, rather fiercely. "How could I?"

Clare went back to her chair. "That girl! But, Robin, she's plain—quite—and her manners, her mother—everything impossible!"

It was still incredible that Robin, the work of her hands as it were, into whom she had poured all things that were lovely and of good report, could have made love to an ordinary girl of the middle classes—a vulgar girl with a still more vulgar mother.

But in spite of her vulgarity she was jealous of her. "You don't care for her any longer, Robin?"

"Now?—oh no—not for a long time—I don't think I ever did really. I can't think how I was ever such a fool."

"She still threatens Breach of Promise," said Garrett, whose mind was slowly working as to the best means of proving his practical utility. "That's the point, of course. That the letters are there and that we have got to get them back. What kind of letters were they? Did you actually give her hopes?"

Robin blushed. "Yes, I'm afraid I did—as well as I can remember, and judging by her answers. I said the usual sort of things——" He paused. It was best, he felt, to leave it vague.

But Clare had scarcely arrived at the danger of it yet—the danger to the House. Her present thought was of Robin; that she must alter her feelings about him, take him from his pedestal—a Trojan who could make love to any kind of girl!

"I can't think of it now," she said; "it's confusing. We must see what's to be done. We'll talk about it some other time. It's hard to see just at present."

Garrett looked puzzled. "It's a bit of a mess," he said. "But we'll see——"
and left the room with an air of importance.

Robin turned to go, and then walked over to his aunt, and put his hand on
her sleeve.

"Don't think me such a rotter," he said. "I am awfully sorry—it's about
you that I care most—but I've learnt a lesson; I'll never do anything like that
again."

She smiled up at him, and took his hand in hers.

"Why, old boy, no. Of course I was a little surprised. But I don't mind very
much if you care for me in the same way. That's all I have, Robin—your caring;
and I don't think it matters very much what you do, if I still have that."

"Of course you have," he said, and bent down and kissed her. Then he left
the room.

CHAPTER IX

"I'm worse to-day," said Sir Jeremy, looking at Harry, "and I'll be off under
a month."

He seemed rather pathetic—the brave look had gone from his eyes, and
his face and hands were more shrivelled than ever. He gave the impression of
cowering in bed as though wishing to avoid a blow. Harry was with him
continually now, and the old man was never happy if his son was not there. He
rambled at times and fancied himself back in his youth again. Harry had found
his father's room a refuge from the family, and he sat, hour after hour, watching
the old man asleep, thinking of his own succession and puzzling over the
hopeless tangle that seemed to surround him. How to get out of it! He had no
longer any thought of turning his back; he had gone too far for that, and they
would think it cowardice, but things couldn't remain as they were. What would
come out of it?

He had, as Robin had said, changed. The effect of the explosion had been
to reveal in him qualities whose very existence he had formerly never expected.
He even found, strangely enough, a kind of joy in the affair. It was like playing a
game. He had made, he felt, the right move and was in the stronger position. In
earlier days he had never been able to quarrel with any one. Whenever such a
thing had happened, he had been the first to make overtures; he hated the idea
of an enemy, his happiness depended on his friends, and sometimes now, when
he saw his own people's hostility, he was near surrender. But the memory of his
sister's words had held him firm, and now he was beginning to feel in tune with
the situation.

He watched Robin furtively at times and wondered how he was taking it
all. Sometimes he fancied that he caught glances that pointed to Robin's own
desire to see how *he* was taking it. Once they had passed on the stairs, and for a

moment they had both paused as though they would speak. It had been all Harry could do to restrain himself from flinging his arms on to his son's shoulders and shaking him for a fool and then forcing him into surrender, but he had held himself back, and they had passed on without a word.

After all, what children they all were! That's what it came to—children playing a game that they did not understand!

"I wish it would end," said Sir Jeremy; "I'm getting damned sick of it. Why can't he take you out straight away, and be done with it? Do you know, Harry, my boy, I think I'm frightened. It's lying here thinking of it. I never had much imagination—it isn't a Trojan habit, but it grows on one. I fancy—well, what's the use o' talking?" and he sank back into his pillows again.

The room was dark save for the leaping light of the fire. It was almost time to dress for dinner, but Harry sat there, forgetting time and place in the unchanging question, How would it all work out?

"By Gad, it's Tom! Hullo, old man, I was just thinking of you. Comin' round to Horrocks' to-night for a game? Supper at Galiani's—but it's damned cold. I don't know where that sun's got to. I've been wandering up and down the street all day and I can't find the place. I've forgotten the number—I can't remember whether it was 23 or 33, and I keep getting into that passage. There I am again! Bring a light, old man—it's so dark. What's that? Who's there? Can't you answer? Darn you, come out, you——" He sat up in bed, quivering all over. Harry put his hand on his arm.

"It's all right, father," he said. "No one's here—only myself."

"Ugh! I was dreaming—" he answered, lying down again. "Let's have some light—not that electric glare. Candles!"

Harry was sitting in the corner by the bed away from the fire. He was about to rise and move the candles into a clump on the mantelpiece when there was a tap on the door and some one came in. It was Robin.

"Grandfather, are you awake? Aunt Clare told me to look in on my way up to dress and see if you wanted anything?"

The firelight was on his face. He looked very young as he stood there by the bed. His face was flushed in the light of the fire. Harry's heart beat furiously, but he made no movement and said no word.

Robin bent over the bed to catch his grandfather's answer, and he saw his father.

"I beg your pardon." he stammered. "I didn't know——" He waited for a moment as though he were going to say something, or expected his father to speak. Then he turned and left the room.

"Let's have the candles," said Sir Jeremy, as though he had not noticed the interruption, and Harry lit them.

The old man sank off to sleep again, and Harry fell back into his own gloomy thoughts once more. They were always meeting like that, and on each occasion there was need for the same severe self-control. He had to remind himself continually of their treatment of him, of Robin's coldness and reserve.

At times he cursed himself for a fool, and then again it seemed the only way out of the labyrinth.

His love for his son had changed its character. He had no longer that desire for equality of which he had made, at first, so much. No, the two generations could never see in line; he must not expect that. But he thought of Robin as a boy—as a boy who had made blunders and would make others again, and would at last turn to his father as the only person who could help him. He had fancied once or twice that he had already begun to turn.

Well, he would be there if Robin wanted him. He had decided to speak to Mary about it. Her clear common-sense point of view seemed to drive, like the sun, through the mists of his obscurity; she always saw straight through things—never round them—and her practical mind arrived at a quicker solution than was possible for his rather romantic, quixotic sentiment.

"You are too fond of discerning pleasant motives," she had once said to him. "I daresay they are all right, but it takes such a time to see them."

He had not seen her since the outbreak, and he was rather anxious as to her opinion; but the main thing was to be with her. Since last Sunday he had been, he confessed to himself, absurd. He had behaved more in the manner of a boy of nineteen than a middle-aged widower of forty-five. He had been suddenly afraid of the Bethels—going to tea had seemed such an obvious advance on his part that he had shrunk from it, and he had even avoided Bethel lest that gentleman should imagine that he was on the edge of a proposal for his daughter's hand. He thought that all the world must know of it, and he blushed like a girl at the thought of its being laid bare for Pendragon to laugh and gibe it. It was so precious, so wonderful, that he kept it, like a rich piece of jewellery, deep in a secret drawer, over which he watched delightedly, almost humorously, secure in the delicious knowledge that he alone had the key. He wandered out at night, like a foolish schoolboy, to watch the lamp in her room—that dull circle of golden light against the blind seemed to draw him with it into the intimacy and security of her room.

On one of his solitary afternoon walks he suddenly came upon her. He had gone, as he so often did, over the moor to the Four Stones; he chose that place partly because of the Stones themselves and partly because of the wonderful view. It seemed to him that the whole heart of Cornwall—its mystery, its eternal sameness, its rejection of everything that was modern and ephemeral, the pathos of old deserted altars and past gods searching for their old-time worshippers—was centred there.

The Stones themselves stood on the hill, against the sky, gaunt, grey, menacing, a landmark for all the country-side. The moor ran here into a valley between two lines of hill, a cup bounded on three sides by the hills and on the fourth by the sea. In the spring it flamed, a bowl of fire, with the gorse; now it stood grim and naked to all the winds, blue in the distant hills, a deep red to the right, where the plough had been, brown and grey on the moor itself running down to the sea.

It was full of deserted things, as is ever the way with the true Cornwall. On the hill were the Stones sharp against the sky-line; lower down, in a bend of the valley, stood the ruins of a mine, the shaft and chimney, desolately solitary, looking like the pillars of some ancient temple that had been fashioned by uncouth worshippers. In the valley itself stood the stones of what was once a chapel—built, perhaps, for the men of the desolate mine, inhabited now by rabbits and birds, its windows spaces where the winds that swept the moor could play their eternal, restless games.

On a day of clouds there was no colour on the moor, but when the sun was out great bands of light swept its surface, playing on the Stones and changing them to marble, striking colour from the mine and filling the chapel with gold. But the sun did not reach that valley on many days when the rest of the world was alight—it was as if it respected the loneliness of its monuments and the pathos of them.

Harry sat on the side of the hill, below the Stones, and watched the sea. At times a mist came and hid it; on sunny days, when the sky was intensely blue, there hung a dazzling haze like a golden veil and he could only tell that the sea was there by the sudden gleam of tiny white horses, flashing for a moment on the mirror of blue and shining through the haze; sometimes a gull swerved through the air above his head as though a wave had lost its bounds and, for sheer joy of the beautiful day, had flung itself tossing and wheeling into the air.

But to-day was a day of wind and rapidly sailing clouds, and myriads of white horses curved and tossed and vanished over the shifting colours of the sea; there were wonderful shadows of dark blue and purple and green of such depth that they seemed unfathomable.

Suddenly he saw Mary coming towards him. A scarf—green like the green of the sea—was tied round her hat and under her chin and floated behind her. Her dress was blown against her body, and she walked as though she loved the battling with the wind. Her face was flushed with the struggle, and she had come up to him before she saw that he was there.

"Now, that's luck," she said, laughing, as she sat down beside him; "I've been wanting to see you ever since yesterday afternoon, but you seemed to have hidden yourself. It doesn't sound a very long time, does it? But I've something to tell you—rather important."

"What?" He looked at her and suddenly laughed. "What a splendid place for us to meet—its solitude is almost unreal."

"As to solitude," she said calmly, pointing down the valley. "There's Tracy Corridor; it will be all over the Club to-night—he's been watching us for some time"; a long thin youth, his head turned in their direction, had passed down the footpath towards its ruined chapel, and was rapidly vanishing in the direction of Pendragon.

"Well—let them," said Harry, shrugging his shoulders. "You don't mind, do you?"

"Not a bit," she answered lightly. "They've discussed the Bethel family so frequently and with such vigour that a little more or less makes no difference whatsoever. Pendragon taboo! we won't dishonour the sea by such a discussion in its sacred presence."

"What do you want to tell me?" he asked, watching delightedly the colour of her face, the stray curls that the wind dragged from discipline and played games with, the curve of her wrist as her hand lay idly in her lap.

"Oh, it'll keep," she said quickly. "Never mind just yet. Tell me about yourself—what's happened?"

"How did you know that anything had?" he asked.

"Oh, one can tell," she answered. "Besides, I have felt sure that it would, things couldn't go on just as they were——" she paused a moment and then added seriously, "I hope you don't mind my asking? It seems a little impertinent—but that was part of the compact, wasn't it?"

"Why, of course," he said.

"Because, you know," she went on, "it's really rather absurd. I'm only twenty-six, and you're—oh! I don't know *how* old!—anyhow an elderly widower with a grown-up son; but I'm every bit as old as you are, really. And I'm sure I shall give you lots of good advice, because you've no idea what a truly practical person I am. Only sometimes lately I've wondered whether you've been a little surprised at my—our flinging ourselves into your arms as we have done. It's like father—he always goes the whole way in the first minute; but it isn't, or at any rate it oughtn't to be, like me!"

"You are," he said quietly, "the best friend I have in the world. How much that means to me I will tell you one day."

"That's right," she said gaily, settling herself down with her hands folded behind her head. "Now for the situation. I'm all attention."

"Well," he answered, "the situation is simple enough—it's the next move that's puzzling me. There was, four days ago, an explosion—it was after breakfast—a family council—and I was in a minority of one. I was accused of a good many things—going down to the Cove, paying no attention to the Miss Ponsonbys, and so on. They attacked me as I thought unfairly, and I lost control—on the whole, I am sure, wisely. I wasn't very rude, but I said quite plainly that I should go my own way in the future and would be dictated to by no one. At any rate they understand that."

"And now?"

"Ah, now—well—it's as you would expect. We are quite polite but hostile. Robin and I don't speak. The new game—Father and Son; or how to cut your nearest relations with expedition and security." He laughed bitterly.

"Oh, I should like to shake him!" she cried, sitting up and flinging her arms wide, as though she were saluting the sea. "He doesn't know, he doesn't understand! Neither himself nor any one else. Oh, I will talk to him some day! But, do you know," she said, turning round to him, "it's been largely your fault from the beginning."

"Oh, I know," he answered. "If I had only seen then what I see now. But how could I? How could I tell? But I always have been that kind of man, all my days—finding out things when it's too late and wanting to mend things that are hopelessly broken. And then I have always been impulsive and enthusiastic about people. When I meet them first, I mean, I like them and credit them with all the virtues, and then, of course, there is an awakening. Oh, you don't know," he said, with a little laugh, "how enthusiastic I was when I first came back."

"Yes, I do," she answered; "that was one of the reasons I took to you."

"But it isn't right," he said, shaking his head. "I've always been like that. It's been the same with my friendships. I've rated them too highly. I've expected everything and then cried like a child because I've been disappointed. I can see now not only the folly of it, but the weakness. It is, I suppose, a mistake, caring too much for other people, one loses one's self-respect."

"Yes," she said, staring out to sea, "it's quite true—one does. The world's too hard; it doesn't give one credit for fine feelings—it takes a short cut and thinks one a fool."

"But the worst of it is," he went on ruefully, "that I never feel any older. I have those enthusiasms and that romance in the same way now at forty-five—just as I did at nineteen. I never could bear quarrelling with anybody. I used to go and apologise even when it wasn't my fault—so that, you see, the present situation is difficult."

"Ah, but you must keep your end up," she broke in quickly. "It's the only way—don't give in. Robin is just like that. He is self-centred, all shams now, and when he sees that you are taken in by them, just as he is himself, he despises you. But when he sees you laugh at them or cut them down, then he respects you. I'm the only person, I think, that knows him really here. The others haven't grasped him at all."

"My father grows worse every day," Harry went on, as though pursuing his own train of thought. "He can't last much longer, and when he goes I shall miss him terribly. We have understood each other during this fortnight as we never did in all those early years. Sometimes I funk it utterly—following him with all of them against me."

"Why, no," she cried. "It's splendid. You are in power. They can do nothing, and Robin will come round when he sees how you face it out. Why, I expect that he's coming already. I've faced things out here all these years, and you dare to say that you can't stand a few months of it."

"What have you faced?" he asked. "Tell me exactly. I want to know all about you; you've never told me very much, and it's only fair that I should know."

"Yes," she said gravely, "it is—well, you shall!—at least a part of it. A woman always keeps a little back," she said, looking at him with a smile. "As soon as she ceases to be a puzzle she ceases to interest."

She turned and watched the sea. Then, after a moment's pause, she said:

"What do you want to know? I can only give you bits of things—when, for instance, I ran away from my nurse, aged five, was picked up by an applewoman with a green umbrella who introduced me to three old ladies with black pipes and moustaches—I was found in a coal cellar. Then we lived in Bloomsbury—a little house looking out on to a little green park—all in miniature it seems on looking back. I don't think that I was a very good child, but they didn't look after me very much. Mother was always out, and father in business. Fancy," she said, laughing, "father in business! We were happy then, I think, all of us. Then came the terrible time when father ran away."

"Ah, yes," Harry said, "he told me."

"Poor mother! it was quite dreadful; I was only eight then, and I didn't understand. But she sat up all night waiting for him. She was persuaded that he was killed, and she was very ill. You see he had never left any word as to where he was. And then he suddenly turned up again, and ate an enormous breakfast, as though nothing had happened. I don't think he realised a bit that she had worried.

"It was so like him, the naked selfishness of it and the utter unresponsibility, as of a child.

"Then I went to school—in Bloomsbury somewhere. It was a Miss Pinker, and she was interested in me. Poor thing, her school failed afterwards. I don't know quite why, but she never could manage, and I don't think parents ever paid her. I had great ideas of myself then; I thought that I would be great, an actress or a novelist, but I got rid of all that soon enough. I was happy; we had friends, and luxuries were rare enough to make them valuable. Then—we came down here—this sea, this town, this moor—Oh! how I hate them!"

Her hands were clenched and her face was white. "It isn't fair; they have taken everything from me—leisure, brain, friends. I have had to slave ever since I came here to make both ends meet. Ah! you never knew that, did you? But father has never done a stroke of work since he has been here, and mother has never been the same since that night when he ran away; so I've had it all—and it has been scrape, scrape, scrape all the time. You don't know the tyranny of butter and eggs and vegetables, the perpetual struggle to turn twice two into five, the unending worry about keeping up appearances—although, for us, it mattered precious little, people never came to see if appearances were kept.

"They called at first; I think they meant to be kind, but father was sometimes rude and never seemed to know whether he had met a person before or no. Then he was idle, they thought, and they disliked him for that. We gave some little parties, but they failed miserably, and at last people always refused. And, really, it was rather a good thing, because we hadn't got the money. I suppose I'm a bad manager; at any rate, whatever it is, things have been getting worse and worse, and one day soon there'll be an explosion, and that will be the end. We're up to our eyes in debt. I try to talk to father about it, but he waves it away with his hand. They have, neither of them, the least idea of money. You see, father doesn't need very much himself, except for buying books. He had ten pounds last week—housekeeping money to be given to me; he saw an edition of something that he wanted, and the money was gone. We've been living on cabbages ever since. That's the kind of thing that's always happening. I wanted to talk to him about things this morning, but he said that he had an important engagement. Now he's out on the moor somewhere flying his kite——"

She was leaning forward, her chin on her hand, staring out to sea.

"It takes the beans out of life, doesn't it?" she said, laughing. "You must think me rather a poor thing for complaining like this, only it does some good sometimes to get rid of it, and really at times I'm frightened when I think of the end, the disgrace. If we are proclaimed bankrupts it will kill mother. Father, of course, will soon get over it."

"I say—I'm so sorry." Harry scarcely knew what to say. She was not asking for sympathy; he saw precisely her position—that she was too proud to ask for his help, but that she must speak. No, sympathy was not what she wanted. He suddenly hated Bethel—the selfishness of it, the hopeless egotism. It was, Harry decided, the fools and not the villains who spoilt life.

"I want you to do me a favour," he said. "I want you to promise me that, before the end actually comes, if it is going to come, you will ask me to help you. I won't offer to do anything now—I will stand aside until you want me; but you won't be proud if it comes to the worst, will you? Do you promise? You see," he added, trying to laugh lightly, "we are chums."

"Yes," she answered quietly, "I promise. Here's my hand on it."

As he took her hand in his it was all he could do to hold himself back. A great wave of passion seized him, his body trembled from head to foot, and he grew very white. He was crying, "I love you, I love you, I love you," but he kept the words from his lips—he would not speak yet.

"Thank you," was all that he said, and he stood up to hide his agitation.

For a little they did not speak. They both felt that, in that moment, they had touched on things that were too sacred for speech; he seemed so strong, so splendid in her eyes, as he stood there, facing the sea, that she was suddenly afraid.

"Let us go back," she said. They turned down the crooked path towards the ruined chapel.

"What was the news that you had for me?" he asked suddenly.

"Why, of course," she answered; "I meant to have told you before." Then, more gravely, "It's about Robin——"

"About Robin?"

"Yes. I don't know really whether I ought to tell you, because, after all, it's only chatter and mother never gets stories right—she manages to twist them into the most amazing shapes."

"No. Tell me," he insisted.

"Well—there's a person whom mother knows—Mrs. Feverel. Odious to my mind, but mother sees something of her."

"A lady?"

"No—by no means; a gloomy, forbidding person who would like to get a footing here if she could, and is discontented because people won't know her. You see," she added, "we can only know the people that other people don't know. This Mrs. Feverel has a daughter—rather a pretty girl, about eighteen—I should think she might be rather nice. I am a little sorry for her—there isn't a father.

"Well—these people have, in some way, entangled Robin. I don't quite know the right side of it, but mother was having tea with Mrs. Feverel yesterday afternoon and that good woman hinted a great deal at the power that she now had over your family. For some time she was mysterious, but at last she unburdened herself.

"Apparently, Master Robin had been making advances to the girl in the summer, and now wants to back out of it. He had, I gather, written letters, and it was to these that Mrs. Feverel was referring——"

Harry drew a long breath. "I'm damned," he said.

"Oh, of course, I don't know," she went on; "you see, it may have been garbled. Mrs. Feverel is, I should think, just the person to hint suspicions for which there's no ground at all. Only it won't do if she's going to whisper to every one in Pendragon—I thought you ought to be warned——"

Harry was thinking hard. "The young fool," he said. "But it's just what I've been wanting. This is just where I can come in. I knew something has been worrying him lately. I could see it. I believe he's been in two minds as to telling me—only he's been too proud. But, of course, he will have to tell some one. A youngster like that is no match for a girl and her mother of the class these people seem to be. He will confide in his aunt—" He stopped and burst into uncontrollable laughter. "Oh! The humour of it—don't you see? They'll be terrified—it will threaten the honour of the House. They will all go running round to get the letters back; that girl will have a good time—and that, of course, is just where I come in."

"I don't see," said Mary.

"Why, it's just what I've been watching for. Harry Trojan arrives—Harry Trojan is no good—Harry Trojan is despised—but suddenly he holds the key to the situation. Presto! The family on their knees——"

Mary looked at him in astonishment. It was, she thought, unlike him to exult like this over the misfortunes of his sister; she was a little disappointed. "It is really rather serious," she said, "for your sister, I mean. You know what Pendragon is. If they once get wind of the affair there will be a great deal of talk."

"Ah, yes!" he said gravely. "You mustn't think me a brute for laughing like that. But I'm thinking of Robin. If you knew how I cared for the boy—what this means. Why, it brings him to my feet—if I carry the thing out properly." Then quickly, "You don't think they've got back the letters already?"

"They haven't had time—unless they've gone to-day. Besides, the girl's not likely to give them up easily. But, of course, I don't really know if that's how the case lies—mother's account was very confused. Only I am certain that Mrs. Feverel thinks she has a pull somewhere; and she said something about letters."

"I will go at once," Harry said, walking quickly. "I can never be grateful enough to you. Where do they live?"

"10 Seaview Terrace," she answered. "A little dingy street past the church and Breadwater Place—it faces the sea."

"And the girl—what is she like?"

"I've only seen her about twice. I should say tall, thin, dark—rather wonderful eyes in a very pale face; dresses rather well in an aesthetic kind of way."

He said very little more, and she did not interrupt his thoughts. She was surprised to find that she was a little jealous of Robin, the interest in her own affairs had been very sweet to her, the remembrance of it now sent the blood to her cheeks, but this news seemed to have driven his thought for her entirely out of his head.

Suddenly, at the bend of the little lane leading up to the town, they came upon her father, flying a huge blue kite. The kite soared above his head; he watched it, his body bent back, his arm straining at the cord. He saw them and pulled it in.

"Hullo! Trojan, how are you? You ought to do this. It's the most splendid fun—you've no idea. This wind is glorious. I shan't be home till dark, Mary——" and they left him, laughing like a boy. She gave him further directions as to the house, and they parted. She felt a little lonely as she watched him hurrying down the street. He seemed to have forgotten her completely. "Mary Bethel, you're a selfish pig," she said, as she climbed the stairs to her room. "Of course, he cares more about his son—why not?" But nevertheless she sighed, and then went down to make tea for her mother, who was tired and on the verge of tears.

CHAPTER X

As he passed through the town all his thoughts were of his splendid fortune. This was the very thing for which he had been hoping, the key to all his difficulties.

The dusk was creeping down the streets. A silver star hung over the roofs silhouetted black against the faint blue of the night sky. The lamps seemed to wage war with the departing daylight; the after-glow of the setting sun fluttered valiantly for a little, and then, yielding its place to the stronger golden circles stretching like hanging moons down the street, vanished.

The shops were closing. Worthley's Hosiery was putting up the shutters and a boy stood in the doorway, yawning; there had been a sale and the shop was tired. Midgett's Bookshop at the corner of the High Street was still open and an old man with spectacles and a flowing beard stood poring over the odd-lot box at 2d. a volume by the door.

The young man who advised ladies as to the purchase of six-shilling novels waited impatiently. He had hoped to be off by six to-night. He had an appointment at seven—and now this old man.... "We close at six, sir," he said. But the old gentleman did not hear. He bent lower and lower until his beard almost swept the pavement. Harry passed on.

All these things passed like shadows before Harry; he noticed them, but they fitted into the pattern of his thoughts, forming a frame round his great central idea—that at last he had his chance.

There was no fear in his mind that he would not get the letters. There was, of course, the chance that Clare had been before him, but then, as Mary had said, she had scarcely had time, and it was not likely that the girl would give them up easily. It was just possible, too, that the whole affair was a mistake, that Mrs. Feverel had merely boasted for the sake of impressing old Mrs. Bethel, that there was little or nothing behind it, but that was unlikely.

He had formed no definite decision as to the method of his attack; he must wait and see how the land lay. A great deal depended on the presence of the mother—the girl, too, might be so many different things; he was not even certain of her age. If there was nothing in it, he would look a fool, but he must risk that. A wild idea came into his head that he might, perhaps, find Clare there—that would be amusing. He imagined them bidding for the letters, and that brought him to the point that money would be necessary—well, he was ready to pay a good deal, for it was Robin for whom he was bidding.

He found the street without any difficulty. Its dinginess was obvious, and now, with a little wind whistling round its corners and whirling eddies of dust in the road, its three lamps at long distances down the street, the monotonous beat of the sea beyond the walls, it was depressing and sad.

It reminded him of the street in Auckland where he had heard the strange voice; it was just such another moment now—the silence bred expectancy and the sea was menacing.

"I shall get the shivers if I don't move," he said, and rang the bell.

The slatternly servant that he had expected to see answered the bell, and the tap-tap of her down-at-heels slippers sounded along the passage as she departed to see if Mrs. Feverel would see him.

He waited in the draughty hall; it was so dark that coats and hats loomed, ghostly shapes, by the farther wall. A door opened, there was sound of voices—a moment's pause, then the door closed and the maid appeared at the head of the stairs.

"The missis says you can come up," she said ungraciously.

She eyed him curiously as he passed her, and scented drama in the set of his shoulders and the twitch of his fingers.

"A military!" she concluded, and tap-tapped down again into the kitchen.

A low fire was burning in the grate and the blind napped against the window. The draught blew the everlastings on the mantelpiece together with a little dry, dusty sound like the rustle of a breeze in dried twigs.

Mrs. Feverel sat bending over the fire, and he thought as he saw her that it would need a very great fire indeed to put any warmth into her. Her black hair, parted in the middle, was bound back tightly over her head and confined by a net.

She shook hands with him solemnly, and then waited as though she expected an explanation.

Harry smiled. "I'm afraid, Mrs. Feverel," he said, "that you may think this extraordinary. I can only offer as apology your acquaintance with my son."

"Ah yes—Mr. Robert Trojan."

Her mouth closed with a snap and she waited, with her hands folded on her lap, for him to say something further.

"You knew him, I think, at Cambridge in the summer?"

"Yes, my daughter and I were there in the summer."

Harry paused. It would be harder than he expected, and where was the daughter?

"Cambridge is very pleasant in the summer?" he asked, his resolution weakening rapidly before her impassivity.

"My daughter and I found it so. But, of course, it depends——"

It depended, he reflected, on such people as his son—boys whom they could cheat at their ease. He had no doubt at all now that the mother was an adventuress of the common, melodrama type. He suspected the girl of being the same. It made things in some ways much simpler, because money would, probably, settle everything; there would be no question of fine feelings. He knew exactly how to deal with such women, he had known them in New Zealand; but he was amused as he contemplated Clare's certain failure—such a woman was entirely outside her experience.

He came to the point at once.

"My being here is easily explained. I learn, Mrs. Feverel, that my son formed an attachment for your daughter during last summer. He wrote some letters now in your daughter's possession. His family are naturally anxious that those letters should be returned. I have come to see what can be done about the matter." He paused—but she said nothing, and remained motionless by the fire.

"Perhaps," he said slowly, "you would prefer, Mrs. Feverel, to name a possible price yourself?"

Afterwards, on looking back, he felt that his expectations had been perfectly justified; she had, up to that point, given him every reason to take the line that he adopted. She had listened to the first part of his speech without remark; she must, he reflected afterwards, have known what was coming, yet she had given no sign that she heard.

And so the change in her was startling and took him utterly by surprise.

She looked up at him from her chair, and the thin ghost of a smile that crept round the corners of her mouth, faced him for a moment, and then vanished suddenly, was the strangest thing that he had ever seen.

"Don't you think, Mr. Trojan, that that is a little insulting?"

It made him feel utterly ashamed. In her own house, in her drawing-room, he had offered her money.

"I beg your pardon," he stammered.

"Yes," she answered slowly. "You had rather misconceived the situation."

Harry felt that her silences were the most eloquent that he had ever known. He began to be very frightened, and, for the first time, conceived the possibility of not securing the letters at all. The thought that his hopes might be dashed to the ground, that he might be no nearer his goal at the end of the interview than before, sharpened his wits. It was to be a deal in subtlety rather than the obvious thing that he had expected—well, he would play it to the end.

"I beg your pardon," he said again. "I have been extremely rude. I am only recently returned from abroad, and my knowledge of the whole affair is necessarily very limited. I came here with a very vague idea both as to yourself and your intentions. In drawing the conclusions that I did I have done both you and your daughter a grave injustice, for which I humbly apologise. I may say that, before coming here, I had had no interview with my son. I am, therefore, quite ignorant as regards facts."

He did not feel that his apology had done much good. He felt that she had accepted both his insult and apology quite calmly, as though she had regarded them inevitably.

"The facts," she said, looking down again at the fire, "are quite simple. My daughter and your son became acquainted at Cambridge in May last. They saw a great deal of each other during the next few months. At the end of that time they were engaged. Mr. Robert Trojan gave us to understand that he was about to acquaint his family with the fact. They corresponded continually during the summer—letters, I believe, of the kind common to young people in love. Mr. Robert Trojan spoke continually of the marriage and suggested dates. We then came down here, and, soon after our arrival, I perceived a change in your son's attitude. He came to see us very rarely, and at last ceased his visits altogether. My daughter was naturally extremely upset, and there were several rather painful interviews. He then wrote returning her letters and demanding the return of his own. This she definitely refused. Those are the facts, Mr. Trojan."

She had spoken without any emotion, and evidently expected that he should do the same.

"I have come," he said, "on behalf of my son to demand the return of those letters."

"Demand?"

"Naturally. Letters, Mrs. Feverel, of that kind are dangerous things to leave about."

"Yes?" She smiled. "Dangerous for whom? I think you forget a little, Mr. Trojan, in your anxiety for your son's welfare, my daughter's side of the question. She naturally treasures what represents to her the happiest months of her existence. You must remember that your son's conduct—shall I call it desertion?—was a terrible blow. She loved him, Mr. Trojan, with all her heart. Is it not right that he should suffer a little as well?"

"I refuse to believe," he answered sharply, "that this is all a matter of sentiment. I regret extremely that my son should have behaved in such a cowardly and dastardly manner—it has hurt and surprised me more than I can say—but, were that all, it were surely better to bury the whole affair as soon as may be. I cannot believe that you are keeping the letters with no intention of making public use of them."

"Ah," said Mrs. Feverel, "I wonder."

"Hadn't we better come to a clear understanding, Mrs. Feverel?" he asked. "We are neither of us children, and this beating about the bush serves no purpose whatever. If you refuse to return the letters, I have at least the right to ask what you mean to do with them."

"Here is my daughter," she answered, "she shall speak for herself."

He turned round at the sound of the opening door, and watched her as she came in. She was very much as he had imagined—thin and tall, walking straight from the hips, giving a little the impression that she was standing on her toes. Her eyes seemed amazingly dark in the whiteness of her face. She seemed a little older than he had expected—perhaps twenty-five or twenty-six.

She looked at him sharply as she entered and then came forward to her mother. He could see that she was agitated—her breath came quickly, and her hands folded and unfolded as though she were tearing something to pieces.

"This," said Mrs. Feverel, "is my daughter, Mr. Trojan. My dear, Mr. Henry Trojan."

She bowed and sat down opposite her mother. He thought she looked rather pathetic as she faced him; here was no adventuress, no schemer. He began to feel that his son had behaved brutally, outrageously.

Mrs. Feverel rose. "I will leave you, my dear. Mr. Trojan will tell you for what he has come."

She moved slowly from the room and Harry drew a breath of relief at her absence. There was a moment's pause. "I hope you will forgive me, Miss Feverel," he said gently. "I'm afraid that both your mother and yourself must regard this as impertinent, but, at the same time, I think you will understand."

She seemed to have regained her composure. "It is about Robin, I suppose?"

"Yes. Could you tell me exactly what the relations between you were?"

"We were engaged," she answered simply, "last summer at Cambridge. He broke off the engagement."

"Yes—but I understand that you intend to keep his letters?"

"That is quite true."

"I have come to ask you to restore them."

"I am sorry. I am afraid that it is a waste of time. I shall not go back on my word."

He could not understand what her game was—he was not sure that she had a game at all; she seemed very helpless, and, at the same time, he felt that there was strength behind her answers. He was at a loss; his experience was of no value to him at all.

"I am going to beg you to alter your decision. I am pleading with you in a matter that is of the utmost importance to me. Robin is my only son. He has behaved abominably, and you can understand that it has been rather a blow to me to return after twenty years' absence and find him engaged in such an affair. But he is very young, and—pardon me—so are you. I am an older man and my experience of the world is greater than yours; believe me when I say that you will regret persistence in your refusal most bitterly in later years. It seems to me a crisis—a crisis, perhaps, for all of us. Take an older man's word for it; there is only one possible course for you to adopt."

"Really, Mr. Trojan," she said, laughing, "you are intensely serious. Last week I thought that my heart was broken; but now—well, it takes a lot to break a heart. I am sure that you will be glad to hear that my appetite has returned. As to the letters—why, think how pleasant it will be for me to sentimentalise over them in my old age! Surely, that is sufficient motive."

She was trying to speak lightly, but her lip quivered.

"You are running a serious risk, Miss Feverel," he answered gravely. "Your intention is, I imagine, to punish Robin. I can assure you that in a few years' time he will be punished enough. He scarcely realises as yet what he has done. That knowledge will come to him later."

"Poor Robin!" she said. "Yes, he ought to feel rather a worm now; he has written me several very agitated letters. But really I cannot help it. The affair is over—done with. I regard the letters as my personal property. I cannot see that it is any one else's business at all."

"Of course it is our business," he answered seriously. "Those letters must be destroyed. I do not accuse you of any deliberate malicious intentions, but there is, as far as I can see, only one motive in your keeping them. I have not seen them, but from what I have heard I gather that they contain definite promise of marriage. Your case is a strong one."

"Yes," she laughed. "Poor Robin's enthusiasm led him to some very violent expressions of affection. But, Mr. Trojan, revenge is sweet. Every woman, I think, likes it, and I am no exception to my sex. Aren't you a little unfair in claiming all the pleasure and none of the pain?"

"No," he answered firmly. "I am not. It is as much for your own sake as for his that I am making my claim. You cannot see things in fair proportion now; you will bitterly regret the step you contemplate taking."

"Well, I am sure," she replied, "it is very good of you to think of me like that. I am deeply touched—you seem to take quite a fatherly interest." She lay back in her chair and watched him with eyes half closed.

He was beginning to believe that it was no pose after all, and his anger rose.

"Come, Miss Feverel," he said, "let's have done with playing—let us come to terms. It is a matter of vital importance that I should receive the letters. I am ready to go some lengths to obtain them. What are your terms?"

She flushed a little.

"Isn't that a little rude, Mr. Trojan?" she said. "It is of course the melodramatic attitude. It was not long ago that I saw a play in which letters figured. Pistols were fired, and the heroine wore red plush. Is that to be our style now? I am sorry that I cannot oblige you. There are no pistols, but I will tell you frankly that it is no question of terms. I refuse, under any circumstances whatever, to return the letters."

"That is your absolute decision?"

"My absolute decision."

He got up and stood, for a moment, by her chair.

"My dear," he said, "you do not know what you are doing. You are disappointed, you are insulted—you think that you will have your revenge at all costs. You do not know now, but you will discover later, that it has been no revenge at all. It will be the most regretted action of your life. You have a great chance; you are going to throw it away. I am sorry, because you are not, I think, at all that sort of girl." He paused a moment. "Well, there is no more to be said. I am sorry as much for your sake as my own. Good-bye."

He moved to the door. The disappointment was almost more than he could bear. He did not know how strong his hopes had been; and now he must return with things as they were before, with the added knowledge that his son had behaved like a cad, and that the world would soon know.

"Good-bye," he said again and turned round towards her.

She rose from her chair and tried to smile. She said something that he could not catch, and then, suddenly, to his intense astonishment, she flung herself back into her chair again, hid her face in her hands, and burst into uncontrollable tears. He stood irresolute, and then came back and waited by the fireplace. He thought it was the most desolate thing that he had ever known—the flapping of the blind against the window, the dry rustling of the leaves on the mantel-piece, only accentuated the sound of her sobbing. He let her cry and then, at last—"I am a brute," he said. "I am sorry—I will go away."

"No." She sat up and began to dry her eyes with her handkerchief. "Don't go—it was absurd of me to give way like that; I thought that I had got over all that, but one is so silly—one never can tell——"

He sat down again and waited.

"You see," she went on, "I had liked you, always, from the first moment that I saw you. You were different from the others—quite different—and after

Robin had behaved—as he did—I distrusted every one. I thought they were all like that, except you. You do not know what people have done to us here. We have had no friends; they have all despised us, especially your family. And Robin said—well, lots of things that hurt. That I was not good enough and that his aunt would not like me. And then, of course, when I saw that, if I kept the letters, I could make them all unhappy—why, of course, I kept them. It was natural, wasn't it? But I didn't want to hurt you—I felt that all the time; and when I saw you here when I came in, I was afraid, because I hardly knew what to do. I thought I would show you that I wasn't weak and foolish as you thought me—the kind of girl that Robin could throw over so easily without thinking twice about it—and so I meant to hold out. There—and now, of course, you think me hateful."

He sat down by her and took her hand. "It's all rather ridiculous, isn't it?" he said. "I'm old enough to be your father, but I'm just where you are, really. We've all been learning this last fortnight—you and Robin, and I—and all learning the same thing. It's been a case," he hesitated for a word, "of calf-love, for all three of us. Don't regret Robin; he's not worth it. Why, you are worth twenty of him, and he'll know that later on. I'm afraid that sounds patronising," he added, laughing. "But I'm humble really. Never mind the letters. You shall do what you like with them and I will trust you. You are not," he repeated, "that sort of girl. Why, dash it!" he suddenly added, "Robin doesn't know what he has lost."

"Ah!" she said, blushing, "it wouldn't have done. I can see that now—but I can see so many things that I couldn't see before. I wish I had known a man like you—then I might have learnt earlier; but I had nobody, nobody at all, and I nearly made a mess of things. But it isn't too late!"

"Too late! Why, no!" he answered. "I'm only beginning now, and I'm forty-five. I, too, have learned a lot in this fortnight."

She looked at him anxiously for a moment. "They don't like you, do they? Robin and the others?"

"No," he answered; "I don't think they do."

"I know," she said quickly; "I heard from Robin, and I'm sorry. You must have had a bad time. But why, if they have been like that, do you want the letters? They have treated us both in the same way."

"Why, yes," he answered. "Only Robin is my son. That, you see, is my great affair. I care for him more than for anything in the world, and if I had the letters——"

"Why, of course," she cried, "I see—it gives you the pull. Why, how blind I've been! It's splendid!" She sprang up, and went to a small writing-desk by the window; she unlocked a drawer and returned with a small packet in her hand. "There," she said, "there they are. They are not many, are they, for such a big fuss? But I think that I meant you to have them all the time—from the first moment that I saw you. I had hoped that you would ask for them——"

He took the letters, held them in his hand for a moment, and then slipped them into his pocket.

"Thank you," he said, "I shall not forget."

"Nor I," she answered. "We are, I suppose, ships that pass in the night. We have just shared for a moment an experience, and it has changed both of us a little. But sometimes remember me, will you? Perhaps you would write?"

"Why, of course," he answered, "I shall want to know how things turn out. What will you do?"

"I don't know. We will go away from here, of course. Go back to London, I expect—and I will get some work. There are lots of things to do, and I shall be happy."

"I hope," he said, "that the real thing is just beginning for both of us."

She stood by the window looking out into the street. "It makes things different if you believe in me," she said. "It will give one courage. I had begun to think that there was no one in the world who cared."

"Be plucky," he said. "Work's the only thing. It is because we've both been idle here that we're worried. Don't think any more of Robin. He isn't good enough for you yet; he'll learn, like the rest of us; but he'll have to go through something first. You'll find a better man."

"Poor Robin," she said. "Be kind to him!"

He took her hand for a moment, smiled, and was gone. She watched him from the window.

He looked back at her and smiled again. Then he passed the corner of the street.

"So that's the end!" She turned back from the window. "Now for a beginning!"

CHAPTER XI

Garrett Trojan had considered the matter for two days and had come to no conclusion. His manner of considering anything was peculiar. He loved procrastination and coloured future events with such beautiful radiancy that, when they actually came, the shock of finding them only drab was so terrible that he avoided them altogether. He was, however, saved from any lasting pain and disappointment because he had been given, from early childhood, that splendid gift of discovering himself to be the continual hero of a continual play. It was not only that he could make no move in life at all without being its hero—that, of course, was pleasant enough; but that it was always a fresh discovery was truly the amazing thing. He was able to wake up, as it were, and discover afresh, every day of his life, what a hero he was; this was never monotonous, never wearisome. He played the game anew from day to day—and the best part of the game was not knowing that it was a game at all.

It must be admitted that he only maintained the illusion by keeping somewhat apart from his fellow-men—too frequent contact must have destroyed his dreams. But his aloofness was termed preserving his individuality, and in the well-curtained library, in carpet-slippers and a smoking-jacket, he built his own monument with infinite care before an imaginary crowd in an imaginary city of dreams.

There were times, of course, when he was a little uneasy. He had heard men titter at the Club: Clare had, occasionally, spoken plain words as to his true position in the House, and he had even, at times, doubts as to the permanent value of the book on which he was engaged. During these awful moments he gazed through the rent curtain into a valley of dead men's bones ruled by a dreary god who had no knowledge of Garrett Trojan and cared very little for the fortunes of the Trojan House.

But a diligent application to the storehouses of his memory produced testimonials dragged, for the most part, from reluctant adherents which served to prove that Garrett Trojan was a great man and the head of a great family.

He would, however, like some definite act to prove conclusively that he was head. He had, at times, the unhappy suspicion that an outsider, regarding the matter superficially, might be led to conclude that Clare held command. He found that if he interfered at all in family matters this suspicion was immediately strengthened, and so he confined himself to his room and watered diligently the somewhat stinted crop of Illusions.

Nevertheless he felt the necessity of some prominent action that would still for ever his suspicions of incompetence, and would afford him a sure foundation on which to build his palace of self-complacency and personal appreciation. During his latter years he had regarded himself as his father's probable successor. Harry had seemed a very long way off in New Zealand, and became, eventually, an improbable myth, for Garrett had that happy quality bestowed on the ostrich of sticking his head into the sand of imagination and boastfully concluding that facts were not there. Harry was a fact, but by continuously asserting that New Zealand was a long way off and that Harry would never come back, Harry's existence became a very pleasant fairy-story, like nautical tales of the sea-serpent and the Bewitching Mermaid. They might be there, and it was very pleasant to listen to stories about them, but they had no real bearing on life as he knew it.

Harry's return had, of course, shattered this bubble, and Garrett had had to yield all hopes of eventual succession. He had, on the whole, borne it very well, and had come to the conclusion that succeeding his father would have entailed the performance of many wearisome duties; but that future being denied him, it was more than ever necessary to seize some opportunity of personal distinction.

The discussion as to the destruction of the Cove had seemed to offer him every chance of attaining a prominent position. The matter had grown in importance every day. Pendragon had divided into two separate and sharply-distinguished camps, one standing valiantly by its standard of picturesque tradition and its hatred of modern noise and materialism, the other asserting loudly its love of utility and progress, derisively pointing the finger of scorn at old-world Conservatism run mad and an incredible affection for defective drainage. Garrett had flung himself heart and soul (as he said) into the latter of these parties, and, feeling that this was a chance of distinction that fortune was not likely to offer him again in the near future, appeared frequently at discussions and even on one occasion in the Town Hall spoke.

But he was surprised and disappointed; he found that he had nothing to say, the truth being that he was much more interested in Garrett than in the Cove, and that his audience had come to listen to the second of these two subjects rather than the first. He found himself shelved; he was most politely told that he was not wanted, and he retired into his carpet-slippers again after one of those terrible quarters of an hour when he peeped past the curtain and saw a miserable, naked puppet shivering in a grey world, and that puppet was Garrett Trojan.

Then suddenly a second opportunity presented itself. Robin's trouble was unexpectedly reassuring. This, he told himself, was the very thing. If he could only prove to the world that he had dealt successfully with practical matters in a practical way, he need never worry again. Let him deal with this affair promptly and resourcefully, as a man of the world and a true Trojan, and his position was assured. He must obtain the letters and at once. He spent several pleasant hours picturing the scene in which he returned the letters to Robin. He knew precisely the moment, the room, the audience that he would choose—he had decided on the words that he would speak, but he was not sure yet as to how he would obtain the letters.

He thought over it for three days and came to no conclusion. It ought not to be difficult; the girl was probably one of those common adventuresses of whom one heard so often. He had never actually met one—they did not suit carpet-slippers—but one knew how to deal with them. It was merely a matter of tact and *savoir-faire*.

Yes, it would be fun when he flourished the letters in the face of the family; how amazed Clare would be and how it would please Robin!—and then he suddenly awoke to the fact that time was getting on, and that he had done nothing. And, after all, there were only two possible lines of action—to write or to seek a personal interview. Of these he infinitely preferred the first. He need not leave his room, he could direct operations from his arm-chair, and he could preserve that courtesy and decorum that truly befitted a Trojan. But he had grave fears that the letter would not be accepted; Robin's had been scorned and his own might suffer the same fate—no, he was afraid that it must be a personal interview.

He had come to this conclusion reluctantly, and now he hesitated to act on it; she might be violent, and he felt that he could not deal with melodrama. But the thought of ultimate victory supported him. The delicious surprise of it, the gratitude, the security of his authority from all attack for the rest of his days! Ah yes, it was worth it.

He dressed carefully in a suit of delicate grey, wearing, as he did on all public occasions, an eyeglass. He took some time over his preparations and drank a whisky and soda before starting; he had secured the address from Robin, without, he flattered himself, any discovery as to the reason of his request. 10 Seaview Terrace! Ah yes, he knew where that was—a gloomy back street, quite a fitting place for such an affair.

He was still uncertain as to the plan of campaign, but he could not conceive it credible that any young woman in any part of the British Empire would stand up long against a Trojan—it would, he felt certain, prove easy.

He noticed with pleasure the attention paid to him by the down-at-heels servant—it was good augury for the success of the interview. He lowered his voice to a deep bass whilst asking for Miss Feverel, and he fixed his eyeglass at a more strikingly impressive angle. He looked at women from four points of view, and he had, as it were, a sliding scale of manners on which he might mark delicately his perception of their position. There was firstly the Countess, or Titled Nobility. Here his manner was slightly deferential, and at the same time a little familiar—proof of his own good breeding.

Secondly, there was the Trojan, or the lady of Assured Position. Here he was quite familiar, and at the same time just a little patronising—proof of his sense of Trojan superiority.

Thirdly, there was the Governess, or Poor Gentility Position. To members of this class he was affably kind, conveying his sense of their merits and sympathy with their struggle against poverty, but nevertheless marking quite plainly the gulf fixed between him and them.

Fourthly, there were the Impossibles, or the Rest—ranging from the wives of successful Brewers to that class known as Unfortunate. Here there was no alteration in his manner; he was stern, and short, and stiff with all of them, and the reason of their existence was one of the unsolved problems that had always puzzled him. This woman would, of course, belong to this latter class—he drew himself up haughtily as he entered the drawing-room.

Dahlia Feverel was alone, seated working in the window. Life was beginning to offer attractions to her again. The thought of work was pleasing; she had decided to train as a nurse, and she began to see Robin in a clear, true light; she was even beginning to admit that he had been right, that their marriage would have been a great mistake. The announcement of Garrett Trojan took her by surprise—she gathered her work together and rose, her brain refusing to act consecutively. He wanted, of course, the letters—well, she had not got them.... It promised to be rather amusing.

And he on his side was surprised. He had expected a woman with frizzled hair and a dress of violent colours; he saw a slender, pale girl in black, and she looked rather more of a lady than he had supposed. He was, in spite of himself, confused. He began hurriedly—

"I am Mr. Garrett Trojan—I dare say you have heard of me from my nephew—Robin—Robert—with whom, I believe, you are acquainted, Miss—ah—Feverel. I have come on his behalf to request the return of some letters that he wrote to you during the summer."

He drew a breath and paused. Well, that was all right anyhow, and quite sufficiently business-like.

"Won't you sit down, Mr. Trojan?" she said, smiling at him. "It is good of you to have taken so much trouble simply about a few letters—and you really might have written, mightn't you, and saved yourself a personal visit?"

He refused to sit down and drew himself up. "Now I warn you, Miss Feverel," he said, "that this is no laughing matter. You are doing a very foolish thing in keeping the letters—very foolish—ah! um! You must, of course, see that—exceedingly foolish!"

He came to a pause. It was really rather difficult to know what to say next.

"Ah, Mr. Trojan," she answered, "you must leave me to judge about the foolishness of it. After all, they are my letters."

"Pure waste of time," he answered, his voice getting a little shrill. "After all, there can be no question about it. We *must* have the letters—we are ready to go to some lengths to obtain them—even—ah, um—money——"

"Now, Mr. Trojan," she said quickly, "you are scarcely polite. But I am sure that you will see no reason for prolonging this interview when I say that, under no circumstances whatever, can I return the letters. That is my unchanging decision."

He had no words; he stared at her, dumb with astonishment. This open defiance was the very last thing that he had expected. Then, at last—

"You refuse?" he said with a little gasp.

"Yes," she answered lightly, "and I cannot see anything very astonishing in my refusal. They are my property, and it is nobody else's business at all."

"But it is," he almost screamed. "Business! Why, I should think it was! Do you think we want to have a scandal throughout the kingdom? Do you imagine that it would be pleasant for us to have our name in all the papers—our name that has never known disgrace since the days of William the Conqueror? You can have," he added solemnly, "very little idea of the value of a name if you imagine that we are going to tolerate its abuse in this fashion. Dear me, no!"

He was growing quite red at the thought of his possible failure. The things in the room annoyed him—the everlasting rustling on the mantelpiece—a staring photograph of Mr. Feverel, deceased, that seemed to follow him, protestingly, round and round the room—a corner of a dusty grey road seen dimly through dirty window-panes; why did people live in such a place—or, rather, why did such people live at all?—and to think that it was people like that who dared to threaten Trojan honour! How could Robin have been such a fool!

So, feeling that the situation was so absurd that argument was out of place, he began to bluster—

"Come now, Miss Feverel—this won't do, you know! it won't really. It's too absurd—quite ridiculous. Why, you forget altogether who the Trojans are! Why, we've been years and years—hundreds of years! You can't intend to oppose institutions of that kind! Why—it's impossible—you don't realise what you're doing. Dear me, no! Why, the whole thing's fantastic—" and then rather lamely, "You'll be sorry, you know."

She had been listening to him with amusement. It was pleasant to have the family on its knees like this after its treatment of her. He was saying, too, very many of the things that his brother had said, but how different it was!

"You know, Mr. Trojan," she said, "that I can't help feeling that you are making rather a lot of it. After all, I haven't said that I'm going to do anything with the letters, have I?—simply keep them, and that, I think, I am quite entitled to do. And really my mind won't change about that—I cannot give them to you."

"Cannot!" he retorted eagerly. "Why, it's easy enough. You know, Miss Feverel, it won't do to play with me. I'm a man of the world and fencing won't do, you know—not a bit of it. When I say I mean to have the letters, I mean to have them, and—ah, um—that's all about it. It won't do to fence, you know," he said again.

"But I'm not fencing, Mr. Trojan, I'm saying quite plainly what is perfectly true, that I cannot let you have the letters—nothing that you can say will change my mind."

And he really didn't know what to say. He didn't want to have a scene—he shrunk timidly from violence of any kind; but he really must secure the letters. How they would laugh at the Club! Why, he could hear the guffaws of all Pendragon! London would be one enormous scream of laughter!—all Europe would be amused! and to his excited fancy Asia and Africa seemed to join the chorus! A Trojan and a common girl in a breach of promise case! A Trojan!

"I say," he stammered, "you don't know how serious it is. People will laugh, you know, if you bring the case on. Of course it was silly of him—Robin, I mean. I can't conceive myself how he ever came to do such a thing. Boys will be boys, and you're rather pretty, my dear. But, bless me, if we were to take all these little things seriously, why, where would some of us be?" He paused, and hinted impressively at a hideous past. "You *are* attractive, you know." He looked at her in his most flattering manner—"Quite a nice girl, only you shouldn't take it seriously—really you shouldn't."

This manner of speech was a great deal more offensive than the other, and Dahlia got up, her cheeks flushed—

"That is enough, Mr. Trojan. I think this had better come to an end. I can only repeat what I have said already, that I cannot give you the letters—and, indeed, if I had ever intended to do so, your last speech, at least, would have changed my mind—I am sorry that I cannot oblige you, but there is really nothing further to be said."

He tried to stammer something; he faced her for a moment and endeavoured to be indignant, and then, to his own intense astonishment, found that he was walking down the stairs with the drawing-room door closed behind him. How amazing!—but he had done his best, and, if he had failed, why, after all, no other man could have succeeded any better. And she really was rather bewitching—he had not expected anything quite like that. What had he expected? He did not know, but he thought of his softly-carpeted, nicely-cushioned room with pleasurable anticipation. He would fling himself into his book when he got back ... he had several rather neat ideas.... He noticed, with pleasure, that the young man standing by the door of Mead's Groceries touched his hat very respectfully, and Twitchett, his tailor, bowed. Come, come! There were a few people left who had some sense of Trojan supremacy. It wasn't such a bad world! He would have tea in his room—not with Clare—and crumpets—yes, he liked crumpets.

Dahlia went back to her work with a sigh. What, she wondered, would be the next move? It had not been quite so amusing as she had expected, but it had been a little more exciting. For she had a curious feeling in it all, that she was fighting Harry Trojan's battles. These were the people that had insulted him just as they had insulted her, and now they would have to pay for it, they would have to go to him as they had gone to her and crawl on their knees. But what a funny situation! That she should play the son for the father, and that she should be able to look at her own love affair so calmly! Poor Robin—he had taught her a great deal, and now it was time for him to learn his own lesson. For her the episode was closed and she was looking forward to the future. She would work and win her way and have done with sentiment. Friendship was the right thing—the thing that the world was meant for—but *Love*—Ah! that wounded so much more than it blessed!

But she was to have further experiences—the Trojan family had not done with her yet. Garrett had been absent barely more than half an hour when the servant again appeared at the door with, "Miss Trojan, Miss Dahlia, would like to see yer and is waiting in the 'all." Her hand twitching at her apron and mouth gaping with astonishment testified to her curiosity. For weeks the house had been unvisited and now, in a single day—!

"Show her up, Annie!"

She was a little agitated; Garrett had been simple enough and even rather amusing, but Clare Trojan was quite another thing. She was, Dahlia knew, the head of the family and a woman of the world. But Dahlia clenched her teeth; it was this person who was responsible for the whole affair—for the father's unhappiness, for the son's disloyalty. It was she who had been, as it were, behind Robin's halting speeches concerning inequality and one's duty to the family. Here was the head of the House, and Dahlia held the cards.

But Clare was very calm and collected as she entered the room. She had decided that a personal interview was necessary, but had rather regretted that it could not be conducted by letter. But still if you had to deal with that kind of person you must put up with their methods, and having once made up her mind about a thing she never turned back.

She hated the young person more bitterly than she had ever hated any one, and she would have heard of her death with no shadow of pity but rather a great rejoicing. In the first place, the woman had come between Clare and Robin; secondly, she threatened the good name of the family; thirdly, she was forcing Clare to do several things that she very much disliked doing. For all these reasons the young person was too bad to live—but she had no intention of being uncivil. Although this was her first experience of diplomacy, she had very definite ideas as to how such things ought to be conducted, and civility would hide a multitude of subtleties. Clare meant to be very subtle, very kind, and, once the letters were in her hand, very unrelenting.

She was wearing a very handsome dress of grey silk with a large picture hat with grey feathers: she entered the room with a rustle, and the sweep of the skirts spoke of infinite condescension.

"Miss Feverel, I believe—" she held out her hand—"I am afraid this is a most unceremonious hour for a call, and if I have interrupted you in your work, pray go on. I wouldn't for the world. What a day, hasn't it been? I always think that these sort of grey depressing days are so much worse than the downright pouring ones, don't you? You are always expecting, you know, and then nothing ever comes."

Dahlia looked rather nervous in the window, and on her face there fluttered a rather uncertain smile.

"Yes," she said, a little timidly; "but I think that most of the days here are grey."

"Ah, you find that, do you? Well, now, that's strange, because I must say that I haven't found that my own experience—and Cornwall, you know, is said to be the land of colour—the English Riviera some, rather prettily, call it—and St. Ives, you know, along the coast is quite a place for painters because of the colour that they get there."

Dahlia said "Yes," and there was a pause. Then Clare made her plunge.

"You must wonder a little, Miss Feverel, what I have come about. I really must apologise again about the hour. But I won't keep you more than a moment; and it is all quite a trivial matter—so trivial that I am ashamed to disturb you about it. I would have written, but I happened to be passing and—so—I came in."

"Yes?" said Dahlia.

"Well, it's about some letters. Perhaps you have forgotten that my nephew, Robert Trojan, wrote to you last summer. He tells me that you met last summer at Cambridge and became rather well acquainted, and that after that he wrote to you for several months. He tells me that he wrote to you asking you to return his letters, and that you, doubtless through forgetfulness, failed to reply. He is naturally a little nervous about writing to you again, and so I thought that—as I was passing—I would just come and see you about the matter. But I am really ashamed to bother you about anything so trivial."

"No," answered Dahlia, "I didn't forget—I wrote—answered Robin's letter."

"Ah! you did? Then he must have misunderstood you. He certainly gave me to understand——"

"Yes, I wrote to Robin saying that I was sorry—but I intended to keep the letters."

Clare paused and looked at her sharply. This was the kind of thing that she had expected; of course the young person would bluff and stand out for a tall price, which must, if necessary, be paid to her.

"But, Miss Feverel, surely"—she smiled deprecatingly—"that can't be your definite answer to him. Poor Robin!—surely he is entitled to letters that he himself has written."

"Might I ask, Miss Trojan, why you are anxious that they should be returned?"

"Oh, merely a whim—nothing of any importance. But Robin feels, as I am sure you must, that the whole episode—pleasant enough at the time, no doubt—is over, and he feels that it would be more completely closed if the letters were destroyed."

"Ah! but there we differ!" said Dahlia sharply. "That's just what I don't feel about it. I value those letters, Miss Trojan, highly."

Now what, thought Clare, exactly was she? Number One, the intriguing adventuress? Number Two, the outraged woman? Number Three, the helpless girl clinging to her one support? Now, of Numbers One and Two Clare had had no experience. Such persons had never come her way, and indeed of Number Three she could know very little; so she escaped from generalities and fixed her mind on the actual girl in front of her. This was most certainly no intriguing adventuress. Clare had quite definite ideas about that class of person; but she very possibly was the outraged female. At any rate, she would act on that conclusion.

"My dear young lady," she said softly, "you must not think that I do not sympathise. I do indeed, from the bottom of my heart. Robin has behaved abominably, and any possible reparation we, as a family, will gladly pay. I think, however, that you are a little hard on him. He was young, so were you; and it is very easy for us—we women especially—to mistake the reality of our affection. Robin at any rate made a mistake and saw it—and frankly told you so. It was wrong—very; but I cannot help feeling—forgive me if I speak rather plainly—that it would be equally wrong on your part if you were to indulge any feeling of revenge."

"There is not," said Dahlia, "any question of revenge."

"Ah," said Clare brightly, "you will let me have the letters, then?"

"I cannot," Dahlia answered gravely. "Really, Miss Trojan, I'm afraid that we can gain nothing by further discussion. I have looked at the matter from every point of view, and I'm afraid that I can come to no other decision."

Clare stared in front of her. What was to be her next move? Like Garrett, she had been brought to a standstill by Dahlia's direct refusal. Viewing the matter indefinitely, from the security of her own room, it had seemed to her that the girl would be certain to give way at the very mention of the Trojan name. She would face Robin—yes, that was natural enough, because, after all, he was only a boy and had no knowledge of the world and the proper treatment of such a case—but when it came to the head of the family with all the influence of the family behind her, then instant submission seemed inevitable.

Clare was forced to realise that instant submission was very far away indeed, and that the girl sitting quietly in the window showed little sign of yielding. She sat up a little straighter in her chair and her voice was a little sharper.

"It seems then, Miss Feverel, that it is a question of terms. But why did you not say so before? I would have told you at once that we are willing to pay a very considerable sum for the return of the letters."

Dahlia's face flushed, and after a moment's pause she rose from her chair and walked towards Clare.

"Miss Trojan," she said quietly, "I have no intention of taking money for them—or, indeed, of taking anything."

"I'm sure," broke in Clare, flushing slightly, "*I* had no intention of——"

"Ah—no, I know," went on Dahlia. "But it is not, I assure you, a case for melodrama—but a very plain, simple little affair that is happening everywhere all the time. You say that you cannot understand why I should wish to keep the letters. Let me try and explain, and also let me try and urge on you that it is really no good at all trying to change my mind. It is now several days since I had my last talk with Robin, and I have, of course, thought a good deal about it—it is scarcely likely that half-an-hour's conversation with you will change a determination that I have arrived at after ten days' hard thinking. And surely it is not hard to understand. Six months ago I was happy and inexperienced. I had never been in love, and, indeed, I had no idea of its meaning. Then your nephew came: he made love to me, and I loved him in return."

She paused for a moment. Clare looked sympathetic. Then Dahlia continued: "He meant no harm, no doubt, and perhaps for the time he was quite serious in what he said. He was, as you say, very young. But it was a game to him—it was everything to me. I treasured his letters, I thought of them day and night. I—but, of course, you know the kind of thing that a girl goes through when she is in love for the first time. Then I came here and went through some bad weeks whilst he was making up his mind to tell me that he loved me no longer. Of course, I saw well enough what was happening—and I knew why it was—it was the family at his back."

A murmur from Clare. "I assure you, Miss Feverel."

"Oh yes, Miss Trojan, you don't suppose that I cared for you very much during those weeks. I suffered a little, too, and it changed me from a girl into a woman—rather too quickly to be altogether healthy, perhaps. And then he came and told me in so many words. I thought at first that it had broken my heart; a girl does, you know, when it happens the first time, but you needn't be afraid—my heart's all right—and I wouldn't marry Robin now if he begged me to. But it had hurt, all of it, and perhaps one's pride had suffered most of all—and so, of course, I kept the letters. It was the one way that I could hurt you. I'm frank, am I not?—but every woman would do the same. You see you are so very proud, you Trojans!

"It is not only that you thank God that you are not as other men, but you are so bent on making the rest of us call out 'Miserable sinner!' very loudly and humbly. And we don't believe it. Why should we? Everybody has their own little bits o' things that they treasure, and they don't like being told that they're of no value at all. Why, Miss Trojan, I'm quite a proud person really—you'd be surprised if you knew."

She laughed, and then sat down on the sofa opposite Clare, with her chin resting on her hand.

"So you see, Miss Trojan, it's natural, after all, that I kept the letters."

Clare had listened to the last part of her speech in silence, her lips firmly closed, her hands folded on her lap. As she listened to her she knew that it was quite hopeless, that nothing that she could ever say would change the young person's mind. She was horribly disappointed, of course, and it would be terrible to be forced to return to Robin, and tell him that she had failed: for the first time she would have to confess failure—but really she could not humble herself any longer: she was not sure that, even now, she had not unbent a little more than was necessary. If the young person refused to consider the question of terms there was no more to be said—and how dare she talk about the Trojans in that way?

"Really, Miss Feverel, I scarcely think that it is necessary for us to enter into a discussion of that kind, is it? I daresay you have every reason for personal pride—but really that is scarcely my affair, is it? If no offer of money can tempt you—well, really, there the matter must rest, mustn't it? Of course I am sorry, but you know your own mind. But that you should think yourself insulted by such an offer is, it seems to me, a little absurd. It is quite obvious what you mean to do with them."

Dahlia smiled.

"Is it?" she said. "That is very clever of you, Miss Trojan. I am sorry that you should have so much trouble for such a little result."

"There is no more to be said," answered Clare, moving to the door. "Good morning," and she was gone.

"Oh dear," said Dahlia, as she went back to the window, "how unpleasant she is. Poor Robin! What a time he will have!"

For her the pathos was over, but for them—well—it had not begun.

CHAPTER XII

The question of the Cove was greatly agitating the mind of Pendragon. Meetings had been held, a scheme had been drawn up, and it would appear that the thing was settled. It had been conclusively proved that two rows of lodging-houses where the Cove now stood would be an excellent thing. The town was over-crowded—it must spread out in some direction, and the Cove-end was practically the only possible place for spreading.

The fishery had been declining year by year, and it was hinted at the Club that it would be rather a good thing if it declined until it vanished altogether; the Cove was in no sense of the word useful, and by its lack of suitable drainage and defective protection from weather, it was really something of a scandal,—it formed, as Mr. Grayseed, pork butcher and mayor of the town, pointed out, the most striking contrast with the upward development so marked in Pendragon of late years. He called the Cove an "eyesore" and nearly proclaimed it an "anomaly"—but was restrained by the presence of his wife, a nervous woman who followed her husband with difficulty in his successful career, and checked his language when the length of his words threatened their accuracy.

The town might be said to be at one on these points, and there was no very obvious reason why the destruction of the Cove should not be proceeded with—but, still, nothing was done. It was said by a few that the Cove was picturesque and undoubtedly attracted strangers by the reason of its dirty, crooked streets and bulging doorways—an odd taste, they admitted, but nevertheless undoubted and of commercial importance. On posters Pendragon was described as "the picturesque abode of old-time manners and customs," and Baedeker had a word about "charming old-time byways and an old Inn, the haunt, in earlier times, of smugglers and freebooters." Now this was undoubtedly valuable, and it would be rather a pity were it swept away altogether. Perhaps you might keep the Inn—it might even be made into a Museum for relics of old Pendragon—bits of Cornish crosses, stones, some quaint drawings of the old town, now in the possession of Mr. Quilter, the lawyer.

The matter was much discussed at the Club, and there was no doubt as to the feeling of the majority; let the Cove go—let them replace it with a smart row of red-brick villas, each with its neat strip of garden and handsome wooden paling.

Harry had learnt to listen in silence. He knew, for one thing, that no one would pay very much attention if he did speak, and then, of late, he had been flung very much into himself and his reserve had grown from day to day. People did not want to listen to him—well, he would not trouble them. He felt, too, as Newsome had once said to him, that he belonged properly to "down-along," and he knew that he was out of touch with the whole of that modern movement that was going on around him. But sometimes, as he listened, his cheeks burned when they talked of the Cove, and he longed to jump up and plead its defence; but he knew that it would be worse than useless and he held himself in—but they didn't know, they didn't know. It enraged him most when they spoke of it as some lifeless, abstract thing, some old rubbish-heap that offended their sight, and then he thought of its beauties, of the golden sand and the huddling red and grey cottages clustering over the sea as though for protection. You might fancy that the waves slapped them on the back for good-fellowship when they dashed up against the walls, or kissed them for love when they ran in golden ripples and softly lapped the stones.

On the second night after his visit to Dahlia Feverel, Harry went down, after dinner, to the Cove. He found those evening hours, before going to bed, intolerable at the House. The others departed to their several rooms and he was suffered to go to his, but the loneliness and dreariness made reading impossible and his thoughts drove him out. He had lately been often at the Inn, for this was the hour when it was full, and he could sit in a corner and listen without being forced to take any part himself. To-night a pedlar and a girl—apparently his daughter—were entertaining the company, and even the melancholy sailor with one eye seemed to share the feeling of gaiety and chuckled solemnly at long intervals. It was a scene full of colour; the lamps in the window shone golden through the haze of smoke on to the black beams of the ceiling, the dust-red brick of the walls and floor, and the cavernous depths of the great fireplace. Sitting cross-legged on the table in the centre of the room was the pedlar, a little, dark, beetle-browed man, and at his side were his wares, his pack flung open, and cloths of green and gold and blue and red flung pell-mell at his side. Leaning against the table, her hands on her hips, was the girl, dark like her father, tall and flat-chested, with a mass of black hair flung back from her forehead. No one knew from what place they had come nor whither they intended to go—such a visit was rare enough in these days of trains—and the little man's reticence was attacked again and again, but ever unsuccessfully. There were perhaps twenty sailors in the room, and they sat or stood by the fireplace watching and listening.

Harry slipped in and took his place by Newsome in the corner.

"I will sing," said the girl.

She stood away from the table and flung up her head—she looked straight into the fire and swayed her body to the time of her tune. Her voice was low, so that men bent forward in order that they might hear, and the tune was almost a monotone, her voice rising and falling like the beating of the sea, with the character of her words. She sang of a Cornish pirate, Coppinger, "Cruel Coppinger," and of his deeds by land and sea, of his daring and his cleverness and his brutality, and the terror that he inspired, and at last of his pursuit by the king's cutter and his utter vanishing "no man knew where." But gradually as her song advanced Coppinger was forgotten and her theme became the sea—she spoke like one possessed, and her voice rose and fell like the wind—all Time and Place were lost. Harry felt that he was unbounded by tradition of birth or breeding, and he knew that he was absolutely as one of these others with him in the room—that he felt that call of those old gods just as they did. The girl ceased and the room was silent. Through the walls came the sound of the sea—in the fire was the crackling of the coals, and down the great chimney came a little whistle of the wind. "A mighty fine pome 'tis fur sure," said the white-bearded sailor solemnly, "and mostly wonderful true." He sighed. "They'm changed times," he said.

The girl sat on the table at her father's side, watching them seriously. She flung her arms behind her head and then suddenly—

"I can dance too," she said.

They pulled the table back and watched her.

It was something quite simple and unaffected—not, perhaps, in any way great dancing, but having that quality, so rarely met with, of being exactly right and suited to time and place. Her arms moved in ripples like the waves of the sea—every part of her body seemed to join in the same motion, but quietly, with perfect tranquillity, without any sense of strain or effort. The golden lamps, the coloured clothes, the red-brick floor, made a background of dazzling colour, and her black hair escaped and fell in coils over her neck and shoulders.

Suddenly she stopped. "There, that's all," she said, binding her hair up again with quick fingers. She walked over to the sailors and talked to them with perfect freedom and ease; at last she stayed by the handsomest of them—a dark, well-built young fellow, who put his arm round her waist and shared his drink with her.

Harry, as he watched them, felt strangely that it was for him a scene of farewell—that it was for the last time that the place was to offer him such equality or that he himself would be in a position to accept it. He did not know why he had this feeling—perhaps it was the talk of the Club about the Cove, or his own certain conviction that matters at the House were rapidly approaching a crisis. Yes, his own protests were of no avail—things must move, and perhaps, after all, it were better that they should.

Bethel came in, and as usual joined the group at the fire without a word; he looked at the pedlar curiously and then seemed to recognise him—then he went up to him and soon they were in earnest conversation. It grew late, and at the stroke of midnight Newsome rose to shut up the house.

"I will go back with you," Bethel said to Harry, and they walked to the door together. For a moment Harry turned back. The girl was bending over the sailor—her arms were round his neck, and his head was tilted back to meet her mouth; the pedlar was putting his wares into his pack again, but some pieces of yellow and blue silk had escaped him and lay on the floor at his feet; down the street three of the sailors were tramping home, and the chorus of a chanty died away as they turned the corner.

The girl, the pedlar, the colours of the room, the vanishing song, remained with Harry to the end of his life—for that moment marked a period.

As he walked up the hill he questioned Bethel about the pedlar.

"Oh, I had met him," he said vaguely. "One knows them all, you know. But it is difficult to remember where. He is one of the last of his kind and an amusing fellow enough——" But he sighed—"I am out of sorts to-night—my kite broke. Do you know, Trojan, there are times when one thinks that one has at last got right back—to the power, I mean, of understanding the meaning and truth of things—and then, suddenly, it has all gone and one is just where one was years ago and it seems wasted. I tell you, man, last night I was on the moor and it was alive with something. I can't tell you what—but I waited and watched—I could feel them growing nearer and nearer, the air was clearer—their voices were louder—and then suddenly it was all gone. But of course you won't understand—none of you—why should you? You think that I am flying a kite—why, I am scaling the universe!"

"Whatever you are doing," said Harry seriously, "you are not keeping your family. Look here, Bethel, you asked me once if I would be a friend of yours. Well, I accepted that, and we have been good friends ever since. But it really won't do—this kind of thing, I mean. Scaling the universe is all very well, if you are a single man—then it is your own look-out; but you are married—you have people depending on you, and they will soon be starving."

Bethel burst out laughing.

"They've got you, Trojan! They've got you!" he cried. "I knew it would come sooner or later, and it hasn't taken long. Three weeks and you're like the rest of them. No, you mustn't talk like that, really. Tell me I'm a damned fool—no good—an absolutely rotten type of fellow—and it's all true enough. But you must accept it at that. At least I'm true to my type, which is more than the rest of them are, the hypocrites!—and as to my family, well, of course I'm sorry, but they're happy enough and know me too well to have any hope of ever changing me——"

"No—of course, I don't want to preach. I'm the last man to tell any one what they should do, seeing the mess that I've made of things myself. But look here, Bethel, I like you—I count myself a friend, and what are friends for if they're not to speak their minds?"

"Oh! That's all right enough. Go on—I'll listen." He resigned himself with a humorous submission as though he were indulging the opinions of a child.

"Well, it isn't right, you know—it isn't really. I don't want to tell you that you're a fool or a rotter, because you aren't, but that's just what makes it so disappointing for any one who cares about you. You're letting all your finer self go. You're becoming, what they say you are, a waster. Of course, finding yourself's all right—every man ought to do that. But you have no right to throw off all claims as completely as you have done. Life isn't like that. We've all got our Land of Promise, and, just in order that it may remain, we are never allowed to reach it. Whilst you are lying on your back on the moor, your wife and daughter are killing themselves in order to keep the home together—I say that it is not fair."

"Oh, come, Trojan," Bethel protested, "is that quite fair on your side? Things are all right, you know. They like it better, they do really. Why, if I were to stay at home and try to work they'd think I was going to be ill. Besides, I couldn't—not at an office or anything like that. It isn't my fault, really—but it would kill me now if I couldn't get away when I want to—not having liberty would be worse than death."

"Ah, that's yourself," said Harry. "That's selfish. Why don't you think of them? You can't let things go on as they are, man. You must get something to do."

"I'm damned if I will." Bethel stopped short and stretched his arms wide over the moor. "It isn't as if it would do them any good, and it would kill me. Why, one is deaf and blind and dumb as soon as one has work to do. I'm a child, you know. I've never grown up, and of course I hadn't any right to marry. I don't know now why I did. And all you people—you grown-ups—with your businesses and difficult pleasures and noisy feasts—of course you can't understand what these things mean. Only a few of you who sit with folded hands and listen can know what it is. I saw a picture once—some people feasting in a forest, and suddenly a little faun jumped from a tree on to their table and waited for them to play with him. But some were eating and some drinking and some talking scandal, and they did not see him. Only a little boy and an old man—they were doing nothing—just dreaming—and they saw him. Oh! I tell you, the dreamer has his philosophy and creed like the rest of you!"

"That's all very well," cried Harry. "But it's a case of bread and butter. You will be bankrupt if you go on as you are!"

"Oh no!" Bethel laughed. "Providence looks after the dreamers. Something always happens—I know something will happen now. We are on the edge of some good fortune. I can feel it."

The man was incorrigible—there was no doubt of it—but Harry had something further to say.

"Well, I want you to let me take a deeper interest in your affairs. May I ask your daughter to marry me?"

"What? Mary?" Bethel stopped and shouted—"Why! That's splendid! Of course, that's what Providence has been intending all this time. The very thing, my dear fellow——" and he put his arm on Harry's shoulder—"there's no one I'd rather give my girl to. But it's nothing to do with me, really. She'll know her mind and tell you what she feels about it. Dear me! Just to think of it!"

He broke out into continuous chuckles all the way home, and seemed to regard the whole affair as a great joke. Harry left him shouting at the moon. He had scarcely meant to speak of it so soon, but the thought of her struggle and the knowledge of her father's utter indifference decided matters. He went back to the house, determining on an interview in the morning.

Mary meanwhile had been spending an evening that was anything but pleasant—she had been going through her accounts and was horrified at what she saw. They were badly overdrawn, most of the shops had refused them further credit, and the little income that came to them could not hope to cover one-half of their expenses. What was to be done? Ruin and disgrace stared them in the face. They might borrow, but there was no one to whom she could go. They must, of course, give up their little house and go into rooms, but that would make very little difference. She looked at it from every point of view and could think of no easier alternative. She puzzled until her head ached, and the room, misty with figures, seemed to swim round her. She felt cruelly lonely, and her whole soul cried out for Harry—he would help her, he would tell her what to do. She knew now that she loved him with all the strength that was in her, that she had always loved him, from the first moment that she had known him. She remembered her promise to him that she would come and ask for his help if she really needed it—well, perhaps she would, in the end, but now, at least, she must fight it out alone. The first obvious thing was that her parents must know; that they would be of any use was not to be expected, but at least they must realise on what quicksands their house was built. They were like two children, with no sense whatever of serious consequences and penalties, and they would not, of course, realise that they were face to face with a brick wall of debts and difficulties and that there was no way over—but they must be told.

On the next morning, after breakfast, Mary penned her mother into the little drawing-room and broached the subject. Mrs. Bethel knew that something serious was to follow, and sat on the edge of her chair, looking exactly like a naughty child convicted of a fault. She was wearing a rather faded dress of bright yellow silk and little yellow shoes, which she poked out from under her dress every now and again and regarded with a complacent air.

"They are really not so shabby, Mary, my dear—not nearly so shabby as the blue ones, and a good deal more handsome—don't you think so, my dear? But you say you want to talk about something, so I'll be quiet—only if you wouldn't mind being just a little quick because there are, really, so many things to be done this morning, that it puzzles me how——"

"Yes, mother, I know. But there is something I want to say. I won't be long, only it's rather important."

"Yes, dear—only don't scold. You look as if you were going to scold. I can always tell by that horrid line you have, dear, in your forehead. I know I've done something I oughtn't to, but what it is unless it's those red silks I bought at Dixon's on Friday, and they were so cheap, only——"

"No, mother, it's nothing you've done. It's rather what I've done, or all of us. We are all in the same boat. It's my managing, I suppose; anyhow, I've made a mess of it and we're very near the end of the rope. There doesn't seem any outlook anywhere. We're overdrawn at the bank; they won't give us credit in the town, and I don't see where any's to come from."

"Oh, it's money! Well, my dear, of course it is provoking—such a horrid thing to have to worry about; but really I'm quite relieved. I thought it was something I'd done. You quite frightened me; and I'm glad you don't mind about the red silks, because it really was tempting with——"

"No, dear, that's all right. But this is serious. I've come to the end and I want you to help me. Will you just go through the books with me and see if anything can be done? I'm so tired and worried. I've been going at them so long that I daresay I've muddled it. It mayn't be quite so hopeless as I've made out."

"The books! My dear Mary——" Mrs. Bethel looked at her daughter pathetically. "You know that I've no head for figures. Why, when mother died at home—we were in Chertsey then, Frank and Doris and I—and I tried to manage things, you know, it was really too absurd. I used to make the most ridiculous mistakes and Frank said that the village people did just what they liked with me, and I remember old Mrs. Blenkinsop charging me for eggs after the first month at quite an outrageous rate because——"

"Yes, mother, I know. But two heads are better than one, and I am really hopelessly puzzled to know what to do." Mary got up and went over to her mother and put her arm round her. "You see, dear, it is serious. There's no money at all—less than none; and I don't know where we are to turn. There's no outlook at all. I'm afraid that it's no use appealing to father—no use—and so it's simply left for us two to do what we can. It's frightening always doing it alone, and I thought you would help me."

"Well, of course, Mary dear, I'll do what I can. No, I'm afraid that it would be no good appealing to your father. It's strange how very little sense he's ever had of money—of the value of it. I remember in the first week that we were married he bought some book or other and we had to go without quite a lot of things. I was angry then, but I've learnt since. It was our first quarrel."

She sighed. It was always Mrs. Bethel's method of dealing with any present problem to flee into the happy land of reminiscence and to stay there until the matter had, comfortably or otherwise, settled itself.

"But I shouldn't worry," she said, looking up at her daughter. "Things always turn up, and besides," she added, "you might marry, dear."

"Marry!" Mary looked up at her mother sharply. Mrs. Bethel looked a little frightened.

"Well, you will, you know, dear, probably—and perhaps—well, if he had money——"

"Mother!" She sprang up from her chair and faced her with flaming cheeks. "Do you mean to say that they are talking about it?"

"They? Who? It was only Mrs. Morrison the other day, at tea-time, said—that she thought——"

"Mrs. Morrison? That hateful woman discussing me? Mother, how could you let her? What did she say?"

"Why, only—I wish you wouldn't look so cross, dear. It was nothing really—only that Mr. Trojan obviously cared a good deal—and it would be so nice if——"

"How dare she?" Mary cried again. "And you think it too, mother—that I would go on my knees to him to take us out of our trouble—that I would sweep his floors if he would help the family! Oh! It's hateful! Hateful!"

She flung herself into a chair by the window and burst into tears. Mrs. Bethel stared at her in amazement. "Well, upon my word, my dear, one never knows how to take you! Why, it wasn't as if she'd said anything, only that it would be rather nice." She paused in utter bewilderment and seemed herself a little inclined to cry.

At this moment the door opened—Mary sprang up. "Who is it?" she asked.

"Mr. Henry Trojan, miss, would like to come up if it wouldn't——"

"No. Tell him, Jane, that——"

But he had followed the servant and appeared in the doorway smiling.

"I knew you wouldn't mind my coming unconventionally like this," he said; "it's a terrible hour in the morning—but I felt sure that I would catch you."

He had seen at once that there was something wrong, and he stopped confusedly in the doorway.

But Mrs. Bethel came forward, smiling nervously.

"Oh, please, Mr. Trojan, do come in. We always love to see you—you know we do—you're one of our real friends—one of our best—and it's only too good of you to spare time to come round and see us. But I am busy—it's quite true—one is, you know, in the morning; but I don't think that Mary has anything very important immediately. I think she might stop and talk to you," and in a confusion of tittered apologies she vanished away.

But he stood in the doorway, waiting for Mary to speak. She sat with her head turned to the window and struggled to regain her self-command; they had been talked about in the town. She could imagine how it had gone. "Oh! the Bethel girl! Yes, after the Trojan money and doing it cleverly too; she'll hook him all right—he's just the kind of man." Oh! the hatefulness of it!

"What's up?" He came forward a little, twisting his hat in his hands.

"Nothing!" She turned round and tried to smile. Indeed she almost laughed, for he looked so ridiculous standing there—like a great schoolboy before the headmaster, his hat turning in his hands; or rather, like a collie plunging out of the water and ready to shake himself on all and sundry. As she looked at him she knew that she loved him and that she could never marry him because Pendragon thought that she had hooked him for his money.

"Yes—there is something. What is it?" He had come forward and taken her hands.

But she drew them away slowly and sat down on the sofa. "I'm tired," she said a little defiantly, "that's all—you know if you will come and call at such dreadfully unconventional hours you mustn't expect to find people with all the paint on. I never put mine on till lunch——"

"No—it's no good," he answered gravely. "You're worried, and it's wrong of you not to tell me. You are breaking your promise——"

"I made no promise," she said quickly.

"You did—that day on the moor. We were to tell each other always if anything went wrong. It was a bargain."

"Well, nothing's wrong. I'm tired—bothered a bit—the old thing—there's more to be bought than we're able to pay for."

"I've come with a proposition," he answered gravely. "Just a suggestion, which I don't suppose you'll consider—but you might—it is that you should marry me."

It had come so suddenly that it took her by surprise. The colour flew into her cheeks and then ebbed away again, leaving her whiter than ever. That he should have actually said the words made her heart beat furiously, and there was a singing in her ears so that she scarcely heard what he said. He paused a moment and then went on. "Oh! I know it's absurd when we've only known each other such a little time, and I've been telling myself that again and again—but it's no good. I've tried to keep it back, but I simply couldn't help it—it's been too strong for me."

He paused again, but she said nothing and he went on. "I ought to tell you about myself, so that you should know, because I'm really a very rotten type of person. I've never done anything yet, and I don't suppose I ever shall; I've been a failure at most things, and I'm stupid. I never read the right sort of books, or look at the right sort of pictures, or like the right sort of music, and even at the sort of things that most men are good at I'm nothing unusual. I can't write, you know, a bit, and in my letters I express myself like a boy of fifteen. And then I'm old—quite middle-aged—although I feel young enough. So that all these things are against me, and it's really a shame to ask you."

He paused again, and then he said timidly, bending towards her—

"Could you ever, do you think, give me just a little hope—I wouldn't want you to right away at once—but, any time, after you'd thought about it?"

She looked up at him and saw that he was shaking from head to foot. Her pride was nearly overcome and she wanted to fling herself at his feet, and kiss his hands, and never let him go, but she remembered that Pendragon had said that she was catching him for his money; so, by a great effort, she stayed where she was, and answered quietly, even coldly—

"I am more honoured, Mr. Trojan, than I can tell you by your asking me. It is much, very much more than I deserve, and, indeed, I'm not in the least worthy of it. I'm sorry, but I'm afraid it's no good. You see I'm such a stupid sort of girl—I muddle things so. It would never do for me to attempt to manage a big place like 'The Flutes'—and then I don't think I shall ever marry. I don't think I am that sort of girl. You have been an awfully good friend to me, and

I'm more grateful to you than I can say. I can't tell you how much you have helped us all during these last weeks. But I'm afraid I must say no."

The light from the window fell on her hair and the blue of her dress—a little gold pin at her throat flashed and sparkled; his eye caught it, and was fixed there.

"No—don't say actually no." He was stammering. "Please—please. Think about it after I have gone away. I will come again another day when you have thought about it. I'm so stupid in saying things—I can't express myself; but, Miss Bethel—Mary—I love you—I love you. There isn't much to say about it—I can't express it any better—but, please—you mustn't say no like that. I would be as good a husband to you as I could, dear, always. I'm not the sort of fellow to change."

"No"—she was speaking quickly as though she meant it to be final—"no, really, I mean it. I can't, I can't. You see one has to feel certain about it, hasn't one?—and I don't—not quite like that. But you are the very best friend that I have ever had; don't let it spoil that."

"Perhaps," he said slowly, "it's my age. You don't feel that you could with a man old enough to be your father. But I'm young—younger than Robin. But I won't bother you about it. Of course, if you are certain——"

He rose and stumbled a moment over the chair as he passed to the door.

"Oh! I'm so sorry!" she cried. "I——" and then she had to turn to hide her face. In her heart there was a struggle such as she had never faced before. Her love called her a fool and told her that she was flinging her life away—that the ship of her good fortune was sailing from her, and it would be soon beyond the horizon; but her pride reminded her of what they had said—that she had laid traps for him, for his money.

"I am sorry," she said again. "But it must be only friendship."

But she had forgotten that although her back was turned he was towards the mirror. He could see her—her white face and quivering lips.

He sprang towards her.

"Mary, try me. I will love you better than any man in God's world, always. I will live for you, and work for you, and die for you."

It was more than she could bear. She could not reason now. She was only resolved that she would not give way, and she pushed past him blindly, her head hanging.

The drawing-room door closed. He stared dully in front of him. Then he picked up his hat and left the house.

She had flung herself on her bed and lay there motionless. She heard the door close, his steps on the stairs, and then the outer door.

She sprang to the window, and then, moved by some blind impulse, rushed to the head of the stairs. There were steps, and Mrs. Bethel's voice penetrated the gloom. "Mary, Mary, where are you?"

She crept back to her room.

He walked back to "The Flutes" with the one fact ever before him—that she had refused him. He realised now that it had been his love for her that had kept him during these weeks sane and brave. Without it, he could not have faced his recent troubles and all the desolate sense of outlawry and desolation that had weighed on him so terribly. Now he must face it, alone, with the knowledge that she did not love him—that she had told him so. It was his second rejection—the second flinging to the ground of all his defences and walls of protection. Robin had rejected him, Mary had rejected him, and he was absolutely, horribly alone. He thought for a moment of Dahlia Feverel and of her desertion. Well, she had faced it pluckily; he would do the same. Life could be hard, but he would not be beaten. His methods of consolation, his pulling of himself together—it was all extremely commonplace, but then he was an essentially commonplace man, and saw things unconfusedly, one at a time, with no entanglement of motives or complicated searching for origins. He had accepted the fact of his rejection by his family with the same clear-headed indifference to side-issues as he accepted now his rejection by Mary. He could not understand "those artist fellows with their complications"—life for him was perfectly straight-forward.

But the gods had not done with his day. On the way up to his room he was met by Clare.

"Father is worse," she said quickly. "He took a turn this morning, and now, perhaps, he will not live through the night. Dr. Turner and Dr. Craile are both with him. He asked for you a little while ago."

She passed down the stairs—the quiet, self-composed woman of every day. It was characteristic of a Trojan that the more agitated outside circumstances became the quieter he or she became. Harry was Trojan in this, and, as was customary with him, he put aside his own worries and dealt entirely with the matter in hand.

Already, over the house, a change was evident. In the absolute stillness there could be felt the presence of a crisis, and the monotonous flap of a blind against some distant window sounded clearly down the passages.

In Sir Jeremy's room there was perfect stillness. The two doctors had gone downstairs and the nurse was alone. "He asked for you, sir," she whispered; "he is unconscious again now."

Harry sat down by the bed and waited. The air was heavy with scents of medicine, and the drawn blinds flung grey, ghost-like shadows over the bed. The old man seemed scarcely changed. The light had gone from his eyes and his hand lay motionless on the sheets, and his lips moved continually in a never-ceasing murmur.

Suddenly he turned and his eyes opened. The nurse moved forward. "Where's Harry?" He waved his arm feebly in the air.

"I'm here, father," Harry said quietly.

"Ah, that's good"—he sank back on the pillows again. "I'm going to die, you know, and I'm lonely. It's damned gloomy—got to die—don't want to—but got to."

He felt for his son's hand, found it, and held it. Then he passed off again into half-conscious sleep, and Harry watched, his hand in his father's and his thoughts with the girl and the boy who had rejected him rather than with the old man who had accepted him.

CHAPTER XIII

Meanwhile there was Robin—and he had been spending several very unhappy days. In the gloom of his room, alone and depressed, he had been passing things in review. He had never hitherto felt any very burning desire to know how he stood with the world; at school and Cambridge he had not thought at all—he had just, as it were, slid into things; his surroundings had grouped themselves of their own accord, making a delicately appreciative circle with no disturbing element. His friends had been of his own kind, the things that he had wished to do he had done, his thoughts had been dictated by set forms and customs. This had seemed to him, hitherto, an extraordinarily broad outlook; he had never doubted for a moment its splendid infallibility. He applied the tests of his set to the world at large, and the world conformed. Life was very easy on such terms, and he had been happy and contented.

His meeting with Dahlia had merely lent a little colour to his pleasant complacency, and then, when it had threatened to become something more, he had ruthlessly cut it out. This should have been simple enough, and he had been at a loss to understand why the affair had left any traces. Friends of his at college had had such episodes, and had been mildly amused at their rapid conclusion. He had tried to be mildly amused at the conclusion of his own affair, but had failed miserably. Why? ... he did not know. He must be sensitive, he supposed; then, in that case, he had failed to reach the proper standard.... Randal was never sensitive. But there had been other things.

During the last week everything had seemed to be topsy-turvy. He dated it definitely from the arrival of his father. He recalled the day; his tie was badly made, he remembered, and he had been rather concerned about it. How curious it all was; he must have changed since then, because now—well, ties seemed scarcely to matter at all. He saw his father standing at the open window watching the lighted town.... "Robin, old boy, we'll have a good time, you and I..."—and then Aunt Clare with her little cry of horror, and his father's hurried apology. That had been the beginning of things; one could see how it would go from the first. Had it, after all, been so greatly his father's fault? He was surprised to find that he was regarding his uncle and aunt critically.... It had been their fault to a great extent—they had never given him a chance. Then he remembered the next morning and his own curt refusal to his father's invitation—"He had books to pack for Randal!" How absurd it was, and he wondered why he should have considered Randal so important. He could have waited for the books.

But these things depended entirely on his own sudden discovery that he had failed in a crisis—failed, and failed lamentably. He did not believe that Randal would have failed. Randal would not have worried about it for a moment. What, then, was precisely the difference? He had acted throughout according to the old set formula—he had applied all the rules of the game as he had learnt them, and nevertheless he had been beaten. And so there had crept over him gradually, slowly, and at last overwhelmingly, the knowledge that the world that he had imagined was not the world as it is, that the people he had admired were not the only admirable people in it, and that the laws that had governed him were only a small fragment of the laws that rule the world.

When this discovery first comes to a man the effect is deadening; like a ship that has lost its bearings he plunges in a sea of entangled, confused ideas with no assurances as to his own ability to reach any safe port whatever. It is this crisis that marks the change from youth to manhood.

Three weeks ago Robin had been absolutely confident, not only in himself, but in his relations, his House and his future; now he trusted in nothing. But he had not yet arrived at the point when he could regard his own shortcomings as the cause of his unhappiness; he pointed to circumstances, his aunt, his uncle, Dahlia, even Randal, and he began a search for something more reliable.

Of course, his aunt and uncle might have solved the problem for him; he had not dared to question them and they had never mentioned the subject themselves, but they did not look as though they had succeeded—he fancied that they had avoided him during the last few days.

The serious illness of his grandfather still further complicated matters; he was not expected to live through the week. Robin was sorry, but he had never seen very much of his grandfather; and it was, after all, only fitting that such a very old man should die some time; no, the point really was that his father would in a week's time be Sir Henry Trojan and head of the House—that was what mattered.

Now his father was the one person whom he could find no excuse whatever for blaming. He had stood entirely outside the affair from the beginning, and, as far as Robin could tell, knew nothing whatever about it. Robin, indeed, had taken care that he should not interfere; he had been kept outside from the first.

No, Robin could not blame his father for the state of things; perhaps, even, it might have been better if his advice had been asked.

But everything drove him back to the ultimate fact from which, indeed, there was no escaping—that there was every prospect of his finding himself, within a few weeks' time, the interesting centre of a common affair in the

Courts for Breach of Promise; and as this ultimate issue shone clearer and clearer Robin's terror increased in volume. To his excited fancy, living and dead seemed to turn upon him. Country cousins—the Rev. George Trojan of West Taunton, a clergyman whose evangelical tendencies had been the mock of the House; Colonel Trojan of Cheltenham, a Port-and-Pepper Indian, as Robin had scornfully called him; the Misses Trojan of Southsea, ladies of advanced years and slender purses, who always sent him a card at Christmas; Mrs. Adeline Trojan of Teignmouth, who had spent her life in beating at the doors of London Society and had retired at last, defeated, to the provincial gentility of a seaside town—Oh! Robin had laughed at them all and scorned them again and again—and behold how the tables would be turned! And the Dead! Their scorn would be harder still to bear. He had thought of them often enough and had long ago known their histories by heart. He had gazed at their portraits in the Long Gallery until he knew every line of their faces: old Lady Trojan of 1640, a little like Rembrandt's "Lady with the Ruff," with her stern mouth and eyes and stiff white collar—she must have been a lady of character! Sir Charles Trojan, her son, who plotted for William of Orange and was rewarded royally after the glorious Revolution; Lady Gossiter Trojan, a woman who had taken active part in the '45, and used "The Flutes" as a refuge for intriguing Jacobites; and, best of all, a dim black picture of a man in armour that hung over the mantel-piece, a portrait of a certain Sir Robert Trojan who had fought in the Barons' Wars and been a giant of his times; he had always been Robin's hero and had formed the centre of many an imaginary tapestry worked by Robin's brain—and now his descendant must pay costs in a Breach of Promise Case!

They had all had their faults, those Trojans; some of them had robbed and murdered with little compunction, but they had always had their pride, they had never done anything really low—what they had done they had done with a high hand; Robin would be the first of the family to let them down. And it was rather curious to think that, three weeks ago, it had been his father who was going to let them down. Robin remembered with what indignation he had heard of his father's visits to the Cove, his friendship with Bethel and the rest—but surely it was they who had driven him out! It was their own doing from the first—or rather his aunt and uncle's. He was beginning to be annoyed with his aunt and uncle. He felt vaguely that they had got him into the mess and were quite unable to pull him out again; which reflection brought him back to the original main business, namely, that there was a mess, and a bad one.

It was one of his qualities of youth that he could not wait; patience was an utterly unlearned virtue, and this desperate uncertainty, this sitting like Damocles under a sword suspended by a hair, was hard to bear. What was Dahlia doing? Had she already taken steps? He watched every post with terror lest it should contain a lawyer's writ. He had the vaguest ideas about such things ... perhaps they would put him in prison. To his excited fancy the letters seemed enormous—horrible, black, menacing, large for all the world to see. What had Aunt Clare done? His uncle? And then, last of all, had his father any suspicions?

Whether it was the London tailor, or simply the reassuring hand of custom, his father was certainly not the uncouth person he had seemed three weeks ago; in fact, Robin was beginning to think him rather handsome—such muscles and such a chest!—and he really carried himself very well, and indeed, loose, badly-made clothes suited him rather well. And then he had changed so in other ways; there was none of that overwhelming cheerfulness, that terrible hail-fellow-well-met kind of manner now; he was brief and to the point, he seldom smiled, and surely it wasn't to be wondered at after the way in which they had treated him at the family council a week ago.

There had been several occasions lately on which Robin would have liked to have spoken to his father. He had begun, once, after breakfast, a halting conversation, but he had only received monosyllables as a reply—the thing had broken down painfully. And so he went down to his aunt.

It was her room again, and she was having tea with Uncle Garrett. Robin remembered the last occasion, only a week ago, when he had made his confession. He had been afraid of hurting his aunt then, he remembered. He did not mind very much now ... he saw his aunt and uncle as two people suddenly grown effete, purposeless, incapable. They seemed to have changed altogether, which only meant that he was, at last, finding himself.

There hung a gloom over Clare's tea-table, partly, no doubt, because of Sir Jeremy—the old man with the wrinkled hands and parchment face seemed to follow one, noiselessly, remorselessly, through every passage and into every room ... but there was also something else—that tension always noticeable in a room where people whose recent action towards some common goal is undeclared are gathered together; they were waiting for some one else to make the next move.

And it was Robin who made it, asking at once, as he dropped the sugar into his cup and balanced for a moment the tongs in the air: "Well, Aunt Clare, what have you done?"

She noticed at once that he asked it a little scornfully, as though assured beforehand that she had done very little. There was a note of antagonism in the way that he had spoken, a hint, even, of challenge. She knew at once that he had changed during the last week, and again, knowing as she did of her failure with the girl, and guessing perhaps at its probable sequence, she hated Harry from the bottom of her heart.

"Done? Why, how, Robin dear? I don't advise those tea-cakes—they're heavy. I must speak to Wilson—she's been a little careless lately; those biscuits are quite nice. Done, dear?"

"Yes, aunt—about Miss Feverel. No, I don't want anything to eat, thanks—it seems only an hour or so since lunch—yes—about—well, those letters?"

Clare looked up at him pleadingly. He was speaking a little like Harry; she had noticed during the last week that he had several things in common with his father—little things, the way that he wrinkled his forehead, pushed back his hair with his hand; she was not sure that it was not conscious imitation, and indeed it had seemed to her during the last week that every day drew him further from herself and nearer to Harry. She had counted on this affair as a means of reclaiming him, and now she must confess failure—Oh! it was hard!

"Well, Robin, I have tried——" She paused.

"Well?" he said drily, waiting.

"I'm afraid it wasn't much of a success," she said, trying to laugh. "I suppose that really I'm not good at that sort of thing."

"At what sort of thing?"

He stood over her like a judge, the certainty of her failure the only thing that he could grasp. He did not recognise her own love for him, her fear lest he should be angry; he was merciless as he had been three weeks ago with his father, as he had been with Dahlia Feverel, and for the same reason—because each had taken from him some of that armour of self-confidence in which he had so greatly trusted; the winds of the heath were blowing about him and he stood, stripped, shivering, before the world.

"She was not good at that sort of thing"—that was exactly it, exactly the summary of his new feeling about his aunt and uncle; they were not able to cope with that hard, new world into which he had been so suddenly flung—they were, he scornfully considered, "tea-table" persons, and in so judging them he condemned himself.

"I'm so very sorry, dear. I did my very best. I went to see the—um—Miss Feverel, and we talked about them. But I'm afraid that I couldn't persuade her—she seemed determined——"

"What did she say?"

"Oh, very little—only that she considered that the letters were hers and that therefore she had every right to keep them if she liked. She seemed to attach some especial, rather sentimental value to them, and considered, apparently, that it would be quite impossible to give them up."

"How was she looking—ill?" It had been one of Robin's consolations during these weeks to imagine her pale, wretched, broken down.

"Oh no, extremely well. She seemed rather amused at the whole affair. I was not there very long."

"And is that all you have done? Have you, I mean, taken any other steps?"

"Yes—I wrote yesterday morning. I got an answer this morning."

"What was it?" Robin spoke eagerly. Perhaps his aunt had some surprise in store and would produce the letters suddenly; surely Dahlia would not have written unless she had relented.

Clare went to her writing-table and returned with the letter, held gingerly between finger and thumb.

"I'm afraid it's not very long," she said, laughing nervously, and again looking at Robin appealingly. "I had written asking her to think over what she had said to me the day before. She says:

"'DEAR Miss TROJAN—Surely the matter is closed after what happened the other day? I am extremely sorry that you should be troubled by my decision; but it is, I am afraid, unalterable.—Yours truly,

D. FEVEREL.'"

"Her decision?" cried Robin quickly. "Had she told you anything? Had she decided anything?"

"Only that she would keep the letters," answered Clare slowly. "You couldn't expect me, Robin dear, to argue with her about it. One had, after all, one's dignity."

"Oh! it's no use!" cried Robin. "She means to use them—of course, it's all plain enough; we've just got to face it, I suppose"; and then, as a forlorn hope, turning to his uncle—

"You've done nothing, I suppose, Uncle Garrett?"

His uncle had hitherto taken no part in the discussion, but sat intent on the book that he was reading. Now he answered, without looking up—

"Yes—I saw the girl."

"You saw her?" from Clare.

"What! Dahlia!" from Robin.

"Yes, I called." He laid the book down on his knee and enjoyed the effect of his announcement. He could be important for a moment at any rate, although he must, with his next words, confess failure, so he prolonged the situation. "Some more tea, Clare, please, and not quite so strong this time—you might speak about the tea—why not make it yourself?"

She took his cup and went over to the tea-table. She knew how to play the game as well as he did, and she showed no astonishment or vulgar curiosity, but if he had succeeded where she had failed she must change her hand. She had never thought very much about Garrett; he was a thorough Trojan—for that she was very grateful, but he had always been more of an emblem to her than a man. Now if he had got the letters she was humiliated indeed. Robin would despise her for having failed where his uncle had succeeded.

"Well, have you got them?"

Robin bent forward eagerly.

"No, not precisely," Garrett answered deliberately. "But I went to see her——"

"With what result?"

"With no precise result—that is to say, she did not promise to surrender them—not immediately. But I have every hope——" He paused mysteriously.

"Of what?" If his uncle had really a chance of getting them, he was not such a fool after all. Perhaps he was a cleverer man than one gave him credit for being.

"Well, of course, one has very little ground for any real assertion, but we discussed the matter at some length. I think I convinced her that it would be her

136

wisest course to deliver up the letters as soon as might be, and I assured her that we would let the matter rest there and take no further steps. I think she was impressed," and he sipped his tea slowly and solemnly.

"Impressed! Yes, but what has she promised?" Robin cried impatiently. He knew Dahlia better than they did, and he did not feel somehow that she was very likely to be impressed with Uncle Garrett. He was not the kind of man.

"Promised? No, not a precise promise—but she was quite pleasant and seemed to be open to argument—quite a nice young person."

"Ah! you have done nothing!" There was a note of relief in Clare's exclamation. "Why not say so at once, Garrett, instead of beating about the bush? There is an end of it. We have failed, Robin, both of us; we are where we were before, and what to do next I really don't know."

It was rather a comfort to drag Garrett into it as well. She was glad that he had tried; it made her own failure less noticeable.

Robin looked at both of them, gloomily, from the fireplace. Aunt Clare, handsome, aristocratic, perfectly well fitted to pour out tea in any society, but useless, useless, useless when it came to the real thing; Uncle Garrett and his eyeglass, trying to make the most of a situation in which he had most obviously failed—no, they were no good either of them, and three weeks ago they had seemed the ultimate standard by which his own life was to be tested. How quickly one learnt!

"Well, what is to be done?" he said desperately. "It's plain enough that she means to stick to the things; and, after all, there can only be one reason for her doing it—she means to use them. I can see no way out of it at all—one must just stand up to it."

"We'll think, dear, we'll think," said Clare eagerly. "Ideas are sure to come if we only wait."

"Wait! But we can't wait!" cried Robin. "She'll move at once. Probably the letters are in the lawyer's hands already."

"Then there's nothing to be done," said Garrett comfortably, settling back again into his book—he was, he flattered himself, a man of most excellent practical sense.

"No, it really seems, Robin, as if we had better wait," said Clare. "We must have patience. Perhaps after all she has taken no steps."

But Robin was angry. He had long ago forgotten his share in the business; he had adopted so successfully the rôle of injured sufferer that his own actions seemed to him almost meritorious. But he was very angry with them. Here they were, in the face of a family crisis, deliberately adopting a policy of *laissez-faire*; he had done his best and had failed, but he was young and ignorant of the world (that at least he now admitted), but they were old, experienced, wise—or, at least, they had always seemed to him to stand for experience and wisdom, and yet they could do nothing—nay, worse—they seemed to wish to do nothing—Oh! he was angry with them!

The whole room with its silver and knick-knacks—its beautifully worked cushions and charming water-colours, its shining rows of complete editions and dainty china stood to him now for incapacity. Three weeks ago it had seemed his Holy of Holies.

"But we can't wait," he repeated—"we can't! Don't you see, Aunt Clare, she isn't the sort of girl that waiting does for? She'd never dream of waiting herself." Dahlia seemed, by contrast with their complacent acquiescence, almost admirable.

"Well, dear," Clare answered, "your uncle and I have both tried—I think that we may be alarming ourselves unnecessarily. I must say she didn't seem to me to bear any grudge against you. I daresay she will leave things as they are——"

"Then why keep the letters?"

"Oh, sentiment. It would remind her, you see——"

But Robin could only repeat—"No, she's not that kind of girl," and marvel, perplexedly, at their short-sightedness.

And then he approached the point—

"There is, of course," he said slowly, "one other person who might help us——" He paused.

Garrett put his book down and looked up. Clare leaned towards him.

"Yes?" Clare looked slightly incredulous of any suggested remedy—but apparently composed and a little tired of all this argument. But, in reality, her heart was beating furiously. Had it come at last?—that first mention of his father that she had dreaded for so many days.

"I really cannot think——" from Garrett.

"Why not my father?"

Again it seemed to Clare that she and Harry were struggling for Robin ... since that first moment of his entry they had struggled—she with her twenty years of faithful service, he with nothing—Oh! it was unfair!

"But, Robin," she said gently—"you can't—not, at least, after what has happened. This is an affair for ourselves—for the family."

"But *he* is the family!"

"Well, in a sense, yes. But his long absence—his different way of looking at things—make it rather hard. It would be better, wouldn't it, to settle it here, without its going further."

"To *settle* it, yes—but we can't—we don't—we are leaving things quite alone—waiting—when we ought to do something."

Robin knew that she was showing him that his father was still outside the circle—that for herself and Uncle Garrett recent events had made no difference.

But was he outside the circle? Why should he be? At any rate he would soon be head of the House, and then it would matter very little——

"Also," Clare added, "he will scarcely have time just now. He is with father all day—and I don't see what he could do, after all."

"He could see her," said Robin slowly. He suddenly remembered that Dahlia had once expressed great admiration for his father—she was the very woman to like that kind of man. A hurried mental comparison between his father and Uncle Garrett favoured the idea.

"He could see her," he said again. "I think she might like him."

"My dear boy," said Garrett, "take it from me that what a man could do I've done. I assure you it's useless. Your father is a very excellent man, but, I must confess, in my opinion scarcely a diplomat——"

"Well, at any rate it's worth trying," cried Robin impatiently. "We must, I suppose, eat humble pie after the things you said to him, Aunt Clare, the other day, but I must confess it's the only chance. He will be decent about it, I'm sure—I think you scarcely realise how nasty it promises to be."

"Who is to ask?" said Garrett.

"I will ask him," said Clare suddenly. "Perhaps after all Robin is right—he might do something."

It might, she thought, be the best thing. Unless he tried, Robin would always consider him capable of succeeding—but he should try and fail—fail! Why, of course he would fail.

"Thank you, Aunt Clare." Robin walked to the door and then turned: "Soon would be best"—then he closed the door behind him.

His father was coming down the stairs as he passed through the hall. He saw him against the light of the window and he half turned as though to speak to him—but his father gave no sign; he looked very stern—perhaps his grandfather was dead.

The sudden fear—the terror of death brought very close to him for the first time—caught him by the throat.

"He is not dead?" he whispered.

"He is asleep," Harry said, stopping for a moment on the last step of the stairs and looking at him across the hall—"I am afraid that he won't live through the night."

They had both spoken softly, and the utter silence of the house, the heaviness of the air so that it seemed to hang in thick clouds above one's head, drove Robin out. He looked as though he would speak, and then, with bent head, passed into the garden.

He felt most miserably lonely and depressed—if he hadn't been so old and proud he would have hidden in one of the bushes and cried. It was all so terrible—his grandfather, that weighty, eerie impression of Death felt for the first time, the dreadful uncertainty of the Feverel affair, all things were quite enough for misery, but this feeling of loneliness was new to him.

He had always had friends, but even when they had failed him there had been behind them the House—its traditions, its records, its history—his aunt and uncle, and, most reassuring of all, himself.

But now all these had failed him. His friends were vaguely unattractive; Randal was terribly superficial, he was betraying the House; his aunt and uncle were unsatisfactory, and for himself—well, he wasn't quite so splendid as he had once thought. He was wretchedly dissatisfied with it all and felt that he would give all the polish and culture in the world for a simple, unaffected friendship in which he could trust.

"Some one," he said angrily, "that would do something"—and his thoughts were of his father.

It was dark now, and he went down to the sea, because he liked the white flash of the waves as they broke on the beach—this sudden appearing and disappearing and the rustle of the pebbles as they turned slowly back and vanished into the night again.

He liked, too, the myriad lights of the town: the rows of lamps, rising tier on tier into the night sky, like people in some great amphitheatre waiting in silence for the rising of a mighty curtain. He always thought on these nights of Germany—Germany, Worms, the little bookseller, the distant gleam of candles in the Cathedrals, the flash of the sun through the trees over the Rhine, the crooked, cobbled streets at night with the moon like a lamp and the gabled roofs flinging wild shadows over the stones ... the night-sea brought it very close and carried Randal and Cambridge and Dahlia Feverel very far away, although he did not know why.

He watched the light of the town and the waves and the great flashing eye of the lighthouse and then turned back. As he climbed the steps up the cliff he heard some one behind him, and, turning, saw that it was Mary Bethel. She said "Good-night" quickly and was going to pass him, but he stopped her.

"I haven't seen you for ages, Mary," he said. He resolved to speak to her. She knew his father and had always been a good sort—perhaps she would help him.

"Are you coming back, Robin?" she said, stopping and smiling. There was a lamp at the top of the cliff where the road ran past the steps, and by the light of it he saw that she had been crying. But he was too much occupied with his own affairs to consider the matter very deeply, and then girls cried so easily.

"Yes," he said, "let us go round by the road and the Chapel—it's a splendid night; besides, we don't seem to have met recently. We've both been busy, I suppose, and I've a good deal to talk about."

"If you like," she said, rather listlessly. It would, at least, save her from her own thoughts and protect her perhaps from the ceaseless repetition of that scene of three days ago when she had turned the man that she loved more than all the world away and had lied to him because she was proud.

And so at first she scarcely listened to him. They walked down the road that ran along the top of the cliff and the great eye of the lighthouse wheeled upon them, flashed and vanished; she saw the room with its dingy carpet and wide-open window, and she heard his voice again and saw his hands clenched—oh! she had been a fine fool! So it was little wonder that she did not hear his son.

But Robin had at last an audience and he knew no mercy. All the agitation of the last week came pouring forth—he lost all sense of time and place; he was at the end of the world addressing infinity on the subject of his woes, and it says a good deal for his vanity and not much for his sense of humour that he did not feel the lack of proportion in such a position.

"It was a girl, you know—perhaps you've met her—a Miss Feverel—Dahlia Feverel. I met her at Cambridge and we got rather thick, and then I wrote to her—rot, you know, like one does—and when I wanted to get back the letters she wouldn't let me have them, and she's going to use them, I'm afraid, for—well—Breach of Promise!"

He paused and waited for the effect of the announcement, but it never came; she was walking quickly, with her head lifted to catch the wind that blew from the sea—he could not be certain that she had heard.

"Breach of Promise!" he repeated impressively. "It would be rather an awful thing for people in our position if it really came to that—it would be beastly for me. Of course, I meant nothing by it—the letters, I mean—a chap never does. Everybody at Cambridge talks to girls—the girls like it—but she took it seriously, and now she may bring it down on our heads at any time, and you can't think how beastly it is waiting for it to come. We've done all we could—all of us—and now I can tell you it's been worrying me like anything wondering what she's done. My uncle and aunt both tried and failed; I was rather disappointed, because after all one would have thought that they would be able to deal with a thing like that, wouldn't one?"

He paused again, but she only said "Yes" and hurried on.

"So now I'm at my wits' end and I thought that you might help me."

"Why not your father?" she said suddenly.

"Ah! that's just it," he answered eagerly. "That's where I wanted you to give me your advice. You see—well, it's a little hard to explain—we weren't very nice to the governor when he came back first—the first day or two, I mean. He was—well, different—didn't look at things as we did; liked different things and had strong views about knocking down the Cove. So we went on our way and didn't pay much attention to him—I daresay he's told you all about it—and I'm sorry enough now, although it really was largely his own fault! I don't think he seemed to want us to have much to do with him, and then one day Clare spoke to him about things and asked him to consider us a little and he flared up.

"Well, I've a sort of idea that he could help us now—at any rate, there's no one else. Aunt Clare said that she would ask him, but you know him better than any of us, and, of course, it is a little difficult for us, after the way that we've spoken to him; you might help us, I thought."

He couldn't be sure, even now, that Mary had been listening—she looked so strange this evening that he was afraid of her, and half wished that he had kept his affairs to himself. She was silent for a moment, because she was wondering what it was that Harry had really done about the letters. It was amusing, because they obviously didn't know that she had told him—but what had he done?

"Do you want me to help you, Robin?" she asked.

"Yes, of course," he answered eagerly. "You know him so well and could get him to do things that he would never do for us. I'm afraid of him, or rather have been just lately. I don't know what there is about him exactly."

"You want me to help you?" she asked again. "Well then, you've got to put up with a bit of my mind—you've caught me in a bad mood, and I don't care whether it hurts you or not—you're in for a bit of plain speaking."

He looked up at her with surprise, but said nothing.

"Oh, I know I'm no very great person myself," she went on quickly—almost fiercely. "I've only known in the last few weeks how rotten one can really be, but at least I have known—I do know—and that's just what you don't. We've been friends for some time, you and I—but if you don't look out, we shan't be friends much longer."

"Why?" he asked quietly.

"You were never very much good," she went on, paying no attention to his question, "and always conceited, but that was your aunt's fault as much as any one's, and she gave you that idea of your family—that you were God's own chosen people and that no one could come within speaking distance of you—you had that when you were quite a little boy, and you seem to have thought that that was enough, that you need never do anything all your life just because you were a Trojan. Eton helped the idea, and when you went up to Cambridge you were a snob of the first order. I thought Cambridge would knock it out of you, but it didn't; it encouraged you, and you were always with people who thought as you did, and you fancied that your own little corner of the earth—your own little potato-patch—was better than every one else's gardens; I thought you were a pretty poor thing when you came back from Cambridge last year, but now you've beaten my expectations by a good deal——"

"I say——" he broke in—"really I——" but she went on unheeding—

"Instead of working and doing something like any decent man would, you loafed along with your friends learning to tie your tie and choosing your waistcoat-buttons; you go and make love to a decent girl and then when you've tired of her tell her so, and seem surprised at her hitting back.

"Then at last when there is a chance of your seeing what a man is like—that he isn't only a man who dresses decently like a tailor's model—when your father comes back and asks you to spend a few of your idle hours with him, you laugh at him, his manners, his habits, his friends, his way of thinking; you insult him and cut him dead—your father, one of the finest men in the world. Why, you aren't fit to brush his clothes!—but that isn't the worst! Now—when you find you're in a hole and you want some one to help you out of it and you don't know where to turn, you suddenly think of your father. He wasn't any good before—he was rough and stupid, almost vulgar, but now that he can help you, you'll turn and play the dutiful son!

"That's you as you are, Robin Trojan—you asked me for it and you've got it; it's just as well that you should see yourself as you are for once in your life—you'll forget it all again soon enough. I'm not saying it's only you—it's the lot of you—idle, worthless, snobbish, empty, useless. Help you? No! You can go to your father yourself and think yourself lucky if he will speak to you."

Mary stopped for lack of breath. Of course, he couldn't know that she'd been attacking herself as much as him, that, had it not been for that scene three days ago, she would never have spoken at all.

"I say!" he said quietly, "is it really as bad as that? Am I that sort of chap?"

"Yes. You know it now at least."

"It's not quite fair. I am only like the rest. I——"

"Yes, but why should you be? Fancy being proud that you are like the rest! One of a crowd!"

They turned up the road to her house, and she began to relent when she saw that he was not angry.

"No," he said, nodding his head slowly, "I expect you're about right, Mary. Things have been happening lately that have made everything different—I've been thinking ... I see my father differently...."

Then, "How could you?" she cried. "*You* to cut him and turn him out? Oh! Robin! you weren't always that sort——"

"No," he answered. "I wasn't once. In Germany I was different—when I got away from things—but it's harder here"—and then again slowly—"But am I really as bad as that, Mary?"

Sudden compunction seized her. What right had she to speak to him? After all, he was only a boy, and she was every bit as bad herself.

"Oh! I don't know!" she said wearily. "I'm all out of sorts to-night, Robin. We're neither of us fit to speak to him, and you've treated him badly, all of you—I oughtn't to have spoken as I did, perhaps; but here we are! You'd better forget it, and another day I'll tell you some of the nice things about you——"

"Am I that sort of chap?" he said again, staring in front of him with his hand on the gate. She said good-night and left him standing in the road. He turned up the hill, with his head bent. He was scarcely surprised and not at all angry. It only seemed the climax to so many things that had happened lately—"a snob"—"a pretty poor thing"—"You don't work, you learn to choose your waistcoat-buttons"—that was the kind of chap he was. And his father: "One of the finest men there is——" He'd missed his chance, perhaps, he would never get it again! But he would try!

He passed into the garden and fumbled for his latch-key. He would speak to his father to-morrow!

Mary was quite right ... he *was* a "pretty poor thing!"

CHAPTER XIV

That night was never forgotten by any one at "The Flutes." Down in the servants' hall they prolonged their departure for bed to a very late hour, and then crept, timorously, to their rooms; they were extravagant with the electric light, and dared Benham's anger in order to secure a little respite from terrible darkness. Stories were recalled of Sir Jeremy's kindness and good nature, and much speculation was indulged in as to his successor—the cook recalled her early youth and an engagement with a soldier that aroused such sympathy in her hearers that she fraternised, unexpectedly, with Clare's maid—a girl who had formerly been considered "haughty," but was now found to be agreeable and pleasant.

Above stairs there was the same restlessness and sense of uneasy expectancy. Clare went to bed, but not to sleep. Her mind was not with her father—she had been waiting for his death during many long weeks, and now that the time had arrived she could scarcely think of it otherwise than calmly. If one had lived like a Trojan one would die like one—quietly, becomingly, in accordance with the best traditions. She was sure that there would be something ready for Trojans in the next world a little different from other folks' destiny—something select and refined—so why worry at going to meet it?

No, it was not Sir Jeremy, but Robin. Throughout the night she heard the clocks striking the quarters; the first light of dawn crept timidly through the shuttered blinds, the full blaze of the sun streamed on to her bed—and she could not sleep. The conversation of the day before recalled itself syllable for syllable; she read into it things that had never been there and tortured herself with suspicion and doubt. Robin was different—utterly different. He was different even from a week ago when he had first told them of the affair. She could hear his voice as he had bent over her asking her to forgive him; that had seemed to her then the hour of her triumph—but now she saw that it was the premonition of defeat. How she had worked for him, loved him, spoilt him; and now, in these weeks, her lifework was utterly undone. And then, in the terrible loneliness of her room, with the darkness on the world and round her bed and at her heart, she wept—terrible, tearless sobbing that left her in the morning weak, unstrung, utterly unequal to the day.

This conversation with Robin had also worried Garrett. The consolation that he had frequently found in the reassuring comforts of his study seemed utterly wanting to-night. The stillness irritated him; it seemed stuffy, close, and he had an overmastering desire for a companion. This desire he conquered, because he felt that it would be scarcely dignified to search the byways of the house for a friend; but he listened for steps, and fancied over and over again that he heard the eagerly anticipated knock. But no one came, and he sat far into the night, fancying strange sounds and trembling at the dark; and at last fell asleep in his chair, and was discovered in an undignified position on the floor in the early morning by the politely astonished Benham.

But it was for Harry that the night most truly marked a crisis. He spent it in vigil by the side of his father, and watched the heavy passing of the hours, like grey solemn figures through the darkened room. The faint glimmer of the electric light, heavily shaded, assumed fantastic and portentous shapes and fleecy enormous shadows on the white surface of the staring walls. Strange blue shadows glimmered through the black caverns of the windows, and faint lights came from beneath the door, and hovered on the ceiling like mysteriously moving figures.

Sir Jeremy was perfectly still. Death had come to him very gently and had laid its hand quietly upon him, with no violence or harshness. It was only old age that had greeted him as a friend, and then with a smile had persuaded him to go. He was unconscious now, but at any moment his senses might return, and then he would ask for Harry. The crisis might come at any time, and Harry must be there.

He felt no weariness; his brain was extraordinarily active and he passed every incident since his return in review. It all seemed so clear to him now; the inevitability of it all; and his own blindness in escaping the meaning of it. It seemed now that he had known nothing of the world at all three weeks ago. Then he had judged it from his own knowledge—now he saw it in many lights; the point of view of Robin, of Dahlia Feverel, of Clare, of Sir Jeremy, of Bethel, of Mary—he had arrived at the great knowledge that Life could be absolutely right for many different sorts of people—that the same life, like a globe of flashing colours, could shine into every corner of obscurity, gleaming differently in every different place and yet be unchangeable. Murderer, robber, violator, saint, priest, king, beggar—they were all parts of a wonderful, inevitable world, and, he saw it now, were all of them essential. He had been tolerant before from a wide-embracing charity; he was tolerant now from a wide-embracing knowledge: "Er liebte jeden Hund, und wünschte von jedem Hund geliebt zu sein."

They had all learnt in that last three weeks. Dahlia Feverel would pass into the world with that struggle at her heart and the strength of her victory—his father would solve the greatest question of all—Robin! Mary! Clare!—they had all been learning too, but what it was that they had learnt he could not yet tell; the conclusion of the matter was to come. But it had all been, for him at least, only a prelude; he was to stand for the world as head of the House, he had his life before him and his work to do, he had only, like Robin, just "come of age."

He did not know why, but he had no longer any doubt. He knew that he would win Robin, he knew that he would win Mary; up to that day he had been uncertain, vacillating, miserable—but now he had no longer any hesitation. The work of his life was to fit Robin for his due succession, and, please God, he would do it with all his heart and soul and strength; there was to be no false sentiment, no shifting of difficult questions, no hiding from danger, no sheltering blindly under unquestioned creeds, no false bids for popularity.

Robin was to be clean, straight, and sane, with all the sturdy cleanliness and strength and sanity that his father's love and knowledge could give him.

Oh! he loved his son!—but no longer blindly, as he had loved him three weeks ago ... and so he faced his future.

And of Mary, too, he was sure. He knew that she loved him; he had seen her face in the mirror as her lips had said "No," and he saw that her heart had said "Yes." With the new strength that had come to him he vowed to force her defences and carry her away.... Oh! he could be any knight and fight for any lady.

But as he sat by the bed, watching the dawn struggle through the blinds and listening to the faint, clear twittering of birds in the grey, dew-swept garden—he wished that he could tell his father of his engagement. He wondered if there would be time. That it would please the old man he knew, and it would seal the compact, and place a secret blessing on their married life together. Yes, he would like to tell him.

The clocks struck five—he heard their voices echo through the house; and, at the last, the tiny voice of the cuckoo clock sounded and the little wild flap of his wings came quite clearly through the silence; his voice was answered by a chorus from the garden, the voices of the birds seemed to grow ever louder and louder; in that strange dark room, with its shaded lights and heavy airs, it was clear and fresh like the falling of water on cold, shining stone.

Harry went softly to the window and drew back a corner of the blind. The dawn was gradually revealing the forms and colours of the garden, and in the grey, misty light things were mysterious and uncertain; like white lights in a dusky room the two white statues shone through the mist. At that strange hour they seemed in their right atmosphere; they seemed to move and turn and bend—he could have fancied that they sailed on the mist—that, for a moment, they had vanished and then that they had grown enormous, monstrous. He watched them eagerly, and as the light grew clearer he made them out more plainly—the straight, eager beauty of the man, the dim, mysterious grace of the woman. Perhaps they talked in those early hours when they were alone in the garden; perhaps they might speak to him if he were to join them then. Then he fancied that the mist formed into figures of men and women; to his excited fancy the garden seemed peopled with shapes that increased and dwindled and vanished. Round the statues many shapes gathered; one in especial seemed to walk to and fro with its face turned to the house. It was a woman—her grey dress floated in the air, and he saw her form outlined against the statue. Then the mist seemed to sweep down again and catch the statues in its eddies and hide them from his gaze. The dawn was breaking very slowly. From the window the sweep of the sea was, in daylight, perfectly visible: now in the dim grey of the sky it was hidden—but Harry knew where it must be and watched for its appearance. The first lights were creeping over the sky, breaking in delicate tints and ripples of silver and curving, arc-shaped, from the west to the east.

Where sky and sea divided a faint pale line of grey hovered and broke, turning into other paler lights of the most delicate blue. The dawn had come.

He turned back again to the garden and started with surprise: in the more certain light there was no doubt that it was a woman who stood there by the statues, guarding the first early beauties of the garden. Everything was pearl-grey, save where, high above the water of the fountain that stood in the centre of the lawn, the sky had broken into a little lake of the palest blue and this was reflected in the still mirror of the fountain—but it *was* a woman. He could see the outline of her form—the bend of her neck as she turned with her face to the house, the straight line of her arms as they tell at her sides. And, as he looked, his heart began to beat thickly. He seemed to recognise that carriage of the body from the hips, the fling-back of the head as she stared towards the windows.

The light of the dawn was breaking over the garden, the chorus of the birds was loud in the trees, and he knew that it was no dream.

He glanced for a moment at his father, and then crept softly from the room. He found one of the nurses making tea over a spirit-lamp in the dressing-room and asked her to take his place.

The house was perfectly silent as he opened the French window of the drawing-room and stepped on to the lawn. The grass was heavy with dew and the fresh air beat about his face; he had never known anything quite so fresh—the air, the grass, the trees, the birds' song like the sound of hidden waters tumbling on to some unseen rock.

Her face was turned away from him and his feet made no sound on the grass. He came perfectly silently towards her, and then when he saw that it had indeed been no imagination but that it was reality, and when he knew all that her coming there meant and what it implied, for moment his limbs shook so that he could scarcely stand. Then he laughed a little and said "Mary!"

She turned with a little cry, and when she saw who it was the crimson flooded her face, changing it as the rising sun was soon to change the grey of the sea and the garden.

"Oh!" she cried, "I didn't know—I didn't mean. I——"

"It is going to be a lovely day," he said quietly, "the sun will be up in a moment. I have been watching you from my father's window."

"Oh! You mustn't!" she cried eagerly. "I thought that I was safe—absolutely; I was here quite by chance—really I was—I couldn't sleep, and I thought that I would watch the sunrise over the sea—and I went down to the beach—and then—well, there was the little wood by your garden, and it was so wonderfully still and silent, and I saw those statues gleaming through the trees, and they looked so beautiful that I came nearer. I meant to come only for a moment and then go away again—but—I—stayed——"

But he could scarcely hear what she said; he only saw her standing there with her dress trembling a little in the breeze.

"Mary," he said, "you did not mean what you told me the other day?"

She looked at him for a moment and then suddenly flung out her hands and touched his coat. "No," she answered.

For a moment they were utterly silent. Then he took her into his arms.

"I love you! How I love you!"

Her hair was about his face, for a moment her face was buried in his coat, then she lifted it and their lips met.

He shook from head to foot, he crushed her to him, then he released her.

She glanced up at him with her hand still touching his coat and looked into his eyes.

"I will love you and serve you and honour you always," she said. She took his arm and they passed down the lawn and watched the light breaking over the sea. The sky was broken into thousands of fleecy clouds of mother-of-pearl—the sea was trembling as though the sun had whispered that it was near at hand, and, on the horizon, the first bars of pale gold heralded its coming.

"I have loved you," he said, "since the first moment that I saw you—I gave you tea and muffins; I deserted the Miss Ponsonbys in order to serve you."

"And I too!" she answered, laughing. "I could not eat the muffin for love of you, and I was jealous of the Miss Ponsonbys!"

"Why did you turn me out the other day?"

"They had been talking—mother and the others; and I was hurt terribly, and I thought that you would hear what they had said and would think, perhaps, that it was true and would despise me. And then after you had gone, I knew that nothing in the world could make any difference—that they could say what they pleased, but that I could not live without you—you see I am very young!"

"Oh, and I am so old, dear! You mustn't forget that! Do you think that you could ever put up with any one as old as I am?"

She laughed. "You are just the same age as myself," she cried. "You will always be the same age, and I am not sure but I think that you are younger——"

And suddenly the sun had risen—a great ball of fire changing all the blue of the sky to red and gold, and they watched as the gods had watched the flaming ruin of Valhalla.

But the daylight drove them to other thoughts.

"I must go back," she said. "I will go down to the shore and perhaps will meet father. Oh! you don't know what I have suffered during these last few days. I thought that perhaps I had driven you away and that you would never come back—and then I had a silly idea that I would watch your windows—and so I came——"

"Why! I have watched yours!" he cried—"often! Oh! we will have some times!"

"But you must remember that there will be three of us," she answered. "There is Robin!"

"Robin! Why, it will be splendid! You and Robin and I!"

"Poor Robin——" She laughed. "You don't know how I scolded him last night. It was about you and I was unhappy. He is changing fast, and it is because of you. He has come round——"

"We have all come round!" cried Harry. "He and you and I! Oh! this is the beginning of the world for all of us—and I am forty-five! Will you write to me later in the day? I cannot get down until to-night. My father is very ill—I must be here. But write to me—a long letter—it will be as though you were talking."

She laughed. "Yes, I'll write," she cried; then she looked at him again—"I love you," she said, as though she were reciting her faith, "because you are good, because you are strong, because—oh! for no reason at all—just because you are you."

For a moment they watched the sea, and then again he took her in his arms and held her as though he would never let her go—then she vanished through the trees.

The house was waking into life as he re-entered it; servants were astir at an early hour: he had been away such a little time, but the world was another place. Every detail of the house—the stairs, the hall, the windows, the clocks, the pot-pourri scent from the bowls of dried roses, the dance of the dust in the light of the rising sun, was presented to him now with a new meaning. He was glad that she had stayed with him such a little while—it made it more precious, her coming with the shadows in that grey of breaking skies and a mysterious plunging sea, and then vanishing with the rising sun. Oh! they would come down to earth soon enough!—let him keep that kiss, those few words, her last smile as she vanished into the wood, like the visible signs of the other world that had, at last, been allowed to him. The vision of the Grail had passed from his eyes, but the memory of it was to be his most sacred possession.

He went to his room, had a bath, and then returned to his father; of course, he could not sleep.

Clare, Garrett, and Robin met at breakfast with the sense of approaching calamity heavy upon them. As far as Sir Jeremy himself was concerned there was little real regret—how could there be? Of course, there was the sentiment of separation, the breaking of a great many ties that had been strong and traditional; but it was better that the old man should go—of that there was no question. Sir Jeremy himself would rather. No, "Le roi est mort" was easy enough to say, but how "Vive le roi" stuck in their throats.

Garrett hinted at a wretched night, and quoted Benham on the dangers of an arm-chair at night-time.

"Of course, one had been thinking," he said vaguely, after a melancholy survey of eggs and bacon that developed into resignation over dry toast—"there was a good deal to think about. But I certainly had intended to go to bed—I can't imagine what——"

Robin said nothing. His mind was busy with Mary's speech of the night before; his world lay crumbled about him, and, like Cato, he was finding a certain melancholy satisfaction in its ruins. His thoughts were scarcely with his grandfather; he felt vaguely that there was Death in the house and that its immediate presence was one of the things that had helped to bring his self-content about his ears. But it was of his father that he was thinking, and of a certain morning when he had refused a walk. If he got a chance again!

Clare looked wretched. Robin thought that she had never seemed so ill before; there was, for the first time, an air of carelessness about her, as though she had flung on her clothes anyhow—something utterly unlike her.

"I am going to speak to Harry this morning," she said.

Garrett looked up peevishly. "Scarcely the time, Clare. I should say that it were better for us to wait until—well, afterwards. There is, perhaps, something a little indecent——"

"I have considered the matter carefully," interrupted Clare decisively. "This is the best time——"

"Oh, well, of course. Only I should have thought that I might have had just a little say in the matter. I was, after all, originally consulted as well as yourself. I saw the girl, and was even, I might venture to suggest, with her for some time. But, of course, a mere man's opinion——"

"Oh, don't be absurd, Garrett. It is I that have to ask him—it is pretty obvious that I have every right to choose my own time."

"Oh! Please, don't let me interfere—only I should scarcely have thought that this was quite the moment when Harry would be most inclined to listen to you."

"If we don't ask him now," she answered, "there's no knowing when we shall have the opportunity. When poor father is gone he will have a great deal to settle and decide; he will have no time for anything at all for months ahead. This morning is our last chance."

But she had another thought. Her great desire now was that he should try and fail; that he would fail she was sure. She was eagerly impatient for that day when he must come to them and admit his failure. She looked ahead and fashioned that scene for herself—that scene when Robin should know and confess that his father was only as the rest of them; that their failure was his failure, their incapacity his incapacity—and then the balance would be restored and Robin would see as he had seen before.

"Coffee, Robin? It's quite hot still. I saw Dr. Brady just now. He says that there is no change, nor is there likely to be one for some hours. You're looking tired, Robin, old boy. Have you been sleeping on the floor, too?"

"No!" He looked up and smiled. "But I was awake a good bit. The house is different somehow, when——"

"Oh yes, I know. One feels it, of course. But eating's much the best thing for keeping one's spirits up. I suppose Harry is coming down. Just find out from Benham, will you, Wilder, whether Mr. Henry is coming down?"

The footman left the room, returning in a moment with the answer that Mr. Henry was about to come down.

Garrett moved to the door, but Clare stopped him.

"I want you, Garrett—you can bear me out!"

"I thought that my opinion was of so little importance," he answered sulkily, "that I might as well go."

But he sat down again and buried himself in his paper.

They waited, and Robin made mental comparisons with a similar scene a week before; there were still the silver teapot, the toast, the ham—they were all there, and it was only he himself who had altered. Only a week, and what a difference! What a cad he had been! a howling cad! Not only to his father, but to Dahlia, to every one with whom he had had to do. He did not spare himself; he had at least the pluck to go through with it—*that* was Trojan.

At Harry's entrance there was an involuntary raising of eyebrows to see, if possible, how *he* took it; *it* being his own immediate succession rather than his father's death. He was grave, of course, but there was a light in his eyes that Clare could not understand. Had he some premonition of her request? He apologised for being late.

"I have been up most of the night. There is no immediate danger of a change, but we ought, I think, to be ready. Yes, the toast, Robin, please—I hope you've slept all right, Clare?"

How quickly he had picked up the manner, she reflected, as she watched him! But of course that was natural enough; once a Trojan, always a Trojan, and no amount of colonies will do away with it. But three weeks was a short time for so vast a change.

"No, Harry, not very well—of course, it weighs on one rather."

She sighed and rose from the breakfast-table; she looked terribly tired and Harry was suddenly sorry for her, and, for the first time since the night of his return, felt that they were brother and sister; but after the adventure of the early morning it was as though he were related to the whole world—Love and Death had drawn close to him, and, with the sound of the beating of their wings, the world had revealed things to him that had, in other days, been secrets. Love and Death were such big things that his personal relations with Clare, with Garrett, even with Robin, had assumed their true proportion.

"Clare, you're tired!" he said. "I should go and lie down again. You shall be told if anything happens."

"No, thanks, Harry. I wanted to ask you something—but, perhaps, first I ought to apologise for some of the things that I said the other day. I said more than I meant to. I am sorry—but one forgets at times that one has no right to meddle in other people's affairs. But now I—we—all of us—want to ask you a favour——"

"Yes?" he said, looking up.

"Well, of course, this is scarcely the time. But it is something that can hardly wait, and you can decide about acting yourself——"

She paused. It was the very hardest thing that she had ever had to do, and she would never forget it to the day of her death. But it was harder for Robin;

he sat there with flaming cheeks and his head hanging—he could not look at his father.

"It is to do with Robin—" Clare went on; "he was rather afraid to ask you about it himself, because, of course, it is not a business of which he is very proud, and so he has asked me to do it for him. It is a girl—a Miss Feverel—whom he met at Cambridge and to whom he had written letters, letters that gave the young woman some reasons to suppose that he was offering her marriage. He saw the matter more wisely after a time and naturally wished Miss Feverel to restore the letters, but this she refused to do. Both Garrett and myself have done what we could and have, I am afraid, failed. Miss Feverel is quite resolute—most obstinately so. We are afraid that she may take steps that would be unpleasant to all of us—it is rather worrying us, and we thought—it seemed—in short, I determined to ask you to help us. With your wider experience you will probably know the best way in which to deal with such a person."

Clare paused. She had put it as drily as possible, but it was, nevertheless, humiliating.

There was a pause.

"I am scarcely surprised," said Harry, "that Robin is ashamed of the affair."

"Of course he is," answered Clare eagerly, "bitterly ashamed."

"I suppose you made love to—ah—Miss Feverel?" he said, turning directly to Robin.

"Yes," said Robin, lifting his head and facing his father. As their eyes met the colour rushed to his cheeks.

"It was a rotten thing to do," said Harry.

"I have been very much ashamed of myself," answered Robin. "I would make Miss Feverel any apology that is in my power, but there seems to be little that I can do."

Harry said no more.

"I am really sorry," said Clare at last, "to speak about a business like this just now—but really there is no time to lose. I am sure that you will do something to prevent trouble in the Courts, and that is what Miss Feverel seems to threaten."

"What do you want me to do?" he asked.

"To see her—to see her and try and arrange some compromise——"

"I should have thought that Robin was the proper person——"

"He has tried and failed; she would not listen to him."

"Then I am afraid that she will not listen to me—a perfect stranger with no claims on her interest."

"It is precisely that. You will be able to put it on a business footing, because sentiment does not enter into the question at all."

"Do you want me to help you, Robin?"

At the direct question Robin looked up again. His father looked very stern and judicial. It was the schoolmaster rather than the parent, but, after all, what else could he expect? So he said, quite simply—"Yes, father."

But at this moment there was an interruption. With the hurried opening of the door there came the sounds of agitated voices and steps in the passage—then Benham appeared.

"Sir Jeremy is worse, Mr. Henry. The doctor thinks that, perhaps——"

Harry hurriedly left the room. Absolute silence reigned. The sudden arrival of the long-expected crisis was terrifying. They sat like statues, staring in front of them, and listening eagerly to every sound. The monotonous ticking of the clock on the mantelpiece was terrifying—the clock on the wall by the door seemed to run a race. The "tick-tock" grew faster and faster—at last it was as if both clocks were screaming aloud.

The room was filled with the clamour, and through it all they sat motionless and silent.

In a moment Harry had returned. "All of you," he said quickly—"he would like to see you—I am afraid——"

After that Robin was confused and saw nothing clearly. As he crept tremblingly up the stairs everything assumed gigantic and menacing shapes—the clock, the pot-pourri bowls, the window-curtains, and the brass rods on the stairs. In the room there was that grey half-light that seemed so terrible, and the spurt and crackle of the fire seemed to fill the place with sounds. He scarcely saw his grandfather. In the centre of the bed, something was lying; the eyes gleamed for a moment in the light of the fire, the lips seemed to move. But he did not realise that those things were his grandfather whom he had known for so many years—in another hour he would be dead.

But the things that he saw were the shadows of the fire on the wall, the dancing in the air of the only lock of hair that Dr. Brady possessed, the way that Clare's hands were folded as she stood silently by the bed, Uncle Garrett's waistcoat-buttons that shot little sparks of light into the room as he turned, ever so slightly, from side to side.

At a motion of the doctor's, he came forward to bid Sir Jeremy farewell. As he bent over the bed panic seized him—he did not see Sir Jeremy but something horrible, terrible, ghoulish—Death. Then he saw the old man's eyes, and they were twinkling; then he knew that he was speaking to him. The words came with difficulty, they were quite clear—

"You'll be a good man, Robin—but listen to your father—he knows—he'll show you how to be a Trojan."

For a moment he held the wrinkled, shrivelled hand in his own, and then he stepped back. Clare bent down and kissed her father, and then kneeled down by the bed; Robin had a mad longing to laugh as he saw his uncle and aunt kneeling there, their heads made enormous shadows on the wall.

Harry also bent down and kissed his father; the old man held his hand and kept it—

"I've tried to be a fair man and a gentleman—I've not been a good one. But I've had some fun and seen life—thank God, I was born a Trojan—so will the rest of you. Harry, my boy, you're all right—you'll do. I'm going, but I don't regret anything—your sins are experience—and the greatest sin of all is not having any."

His lips closed—as the fire flashed with the falling of a cavern of blazing coal his head rolled back on to the pillow.

Suddenly he smiled—

"Dear old Harry!" he said, and then he died.

The shadows from the fire leapt and danced on the wall, and the kneeling figures by the bed flung grotesque shapes over the dead man.

CHAPTER XV

It was five o'clock of the same day and Harry was asleep in front of his fire. In the early hours of the afternoon the strain under which he had been during the past week began to assert itself, and every part of his body seemed to cry out for sleep.

His head was throbbing, his legs trembled, and strange lights and figures danced before his eyes; he flung himself into a chair in his small study at the top of the West Tower and fell asleep.

He had grown to love that room very dearly: the great stretch of the sea and the shining sand with the grey bending hills hemming it in; that view was never the same, but with the passing of every cloud held new colours like a bowl of shining glass.

The room was bare and simple—that had been his own wish; a photograph of his first wife hung over the mantelpiece, a small sketch of Auckland Harbour, a rough drawing of the Terraces before their destruction—these were all his pictures.

He had been trying to read since his return, and copies of "The Egoist" and some of Swinburne's poetry lay on the table; but the first had seemed incomprehensible to him and the second indecent, and he had abandoned them; but he *had* made one discovery, thanks to Bethel, Walt Whitman's "Leaves of Grass"—it seemed to him the greatest book that he had ever read, the very voicing of all his hopes and ideals and faith. Ah! that man knew!

Benham came in and drew the curtains. He watched the sleeping man for a moment and nodded his head. He was the right sort, Mr. Harry! He would do!—and the Watcher of the House stole out again.

Harry slept on, a great, dreamless sleep, grey and formless as sleep of utter exhaustion always is; then he suddenly woke to the dim twilight of the room, the orange glow of the dying fire, and the distant striking of the hour—it was six o'clock!

As he lay back in his chair, dreamily, lazily watching the fire, his thoughts were of his father. He had not known that he would regret him so intensely, but he saw now that the old man had meant everything to him during those first weeks of his return. He thought of him very tenderly—his prejudices, his weaknesses, his traditions. It was strange how alike they all were in reality, the Trojans! Sir Jeremy, Clare, Garrett, Robin, himself, the same bedrock of traditional pride was there, it was only that circumstances had altered them superficially. Three weeks ago Clare and he had seemed worlds apart, now he saw how near they were! But for that very reason, they would never get on—he saw that quite clearly. They knew too well the weak spots in each other's armour, and their pride would be for ever at war.

He did not want to turn her out—she had been there for all those years and it was her home; but he thought that she herself would prefer to go. There was a charming place in Norfolk, Wrexhall Pogis, that had been let for years, and there was quite a pleasant little place in town, 3 Southwick Crescent—yes, she would probably prefer to go, even had he not meant to marry Mary. The announcement of that little affair would be something in the nature of a thunderbolt.

It was impossible for him to go—the head of the House must always live at "The Flutes." But he knew already how much that House was going to mean to him, and so he guessed how much it must mean to Clare.

And to Robin? What would Robin do? Three weeks ago there could have been but one answer to that question—he would have followed his aunt. Now Harry was not so sure. There was this affair of Miss Feverel; probably Robin would come to him about it and then they would be able to talk. He had had that very day a letter from Dahlia Feverel. He looked at it again now; it said:—

"DEAR MR. TROJAN—Mother and I are leaving Pendragon to-morrow—for ever, I suppose—but before I go I thought that I should like to send you a little line to thank you for your kindness to me. That sounds terribly formal, doesn't it? but the gratitude is really there, and indeed I am no letter-writer.

"You met a girl at the crisis in her life when there were two roads in front of her and you helped her to choose the right one. I daresay that you thought that you did very little—it cannot have seemed very much, that short meeting that we had; but it made just the difference to me and will, I know, be to me a white stone from which I shall date my new life. I am not a strong woman—I never shall be a strong woman—and it was partly because I thought that love for Robin was going to give me that strength that it hurt so terribly when I found that the love wasn't there. The going of my love hurt every bit as much as the going of his—it had been something to be proud of.

"I relied on sentiment and now I am going to rely on work; those are the only two alternatives offered to women, and the latter is so often denied to them.

"I hope that it may, one day, give you pleasure to think that you once helped a girl to do the strong thing instead of the weak one. Of course, my love for

Robin has died, and I see him clearly now without exaggeration. What happened was largely my fault—I spoilt him, I think, and helped his self-pride. I know that he has been passing through a bad time lately, and I am sure that he will come to you to help him out of it. He is a lucky fellow to have some one to help him like that—and then he will suddenly see that he has done a rather cruel thing. Poor Robin! he will make a fine man one day.

"I have got a little secretaryship in London—nothing very big, but it will give me the work that I want; and, because you once said that you believed in me, I will try to justify your belief. There! that is sentiment, isn't it!—and I have flung sentiment away. Well, it is the last time!

"Good-bye—I shall never forget. Thank you.—

Yours sincerely,

DAHLIA FEVEREL."

So perhaps, after all, Robin's mistakes had been for the good of all of them. Mistake was, indeed, a slight word for what he had done, and, thinking of it even now, Harry's anger rose.

And she had been a nice girl, too, and a plucky one.

He had answered her:—

"MY DEAR MISS FEVEREL—I was extremely pleased to get your letter. It is very good of you to speak as you have done about myself, but I assure you that what I did was of the smallest importance. It was because you had pluck yourself that you pulled through. You are quite right to fling away sentiment. I came back to England three weeks ago longing to call every man my brother. I thought that by a mere smile, a bending of the finger, the world was my friend for life. I soon found my mistake. Friendship is a very slow and gradual affair, and I distrust the mushroom growth profoundly. Life isn't easy in that kind of way; you and I have found that out together.

"I wish you every success in your new life; I have no doubt whatever that you will get on, and I hope that you will let me hear sometimes from you.

"Things have been happening quickly during the last few days. My father died this morning; he was himself glad to go, but I shall miss him terribly—he has been a most splendid friend to me during these weeks. Then I know that you will be interested to hear that I am engaged to Miss Bethel—you know her, do you not? I hope and believe that we shall be very happy.

"As to Robin, he has, as you say, been having a bad time. To do him justice it has not been only the fear of the letters that has hung over him—he has also discovered a good many things about himself that have hurt and surprised him.

"Well, good-bye—I am sure that you will look back on the Robin episode with gratitude. It has done a great deal for all of us. Good luck to you!—Always your friend,

HENRY TROJAN."

He turned on the lights in his room and tried to read, but he found that that was impossible. His eyes wandered off the page and he listened: he caught himself again and again straining his ears for a sound. He pictured the coming of steps up the stairs and then sharp and loud along the passage—then a pause and a knock on his door. Often he fancied that he heard it, but it was only fancy and he turned away disappointed; but he was sure that Robin would come.

They had decided not to dine downstairs together on that evening—they were, all of them, overwrought and the situation was strained; they were wondering what he was going to do. There were, of course, a thousand things to be done, but he was glad that they had left him alone for that night at any rate. He wanted to be quiet.

He had written a letter of enormous length to Mary, explaining to her what had happened and telling her that he would come to her in the morning. It was very hard, even then, not to rush down to her, but he felt that he must keep that day at least sacred to his father.

Would Robin come? It was quarter to seven and that terrible sleep was beginning to overcome him again. The fire, the walls, the pictures, danced before his eyes ... the stories of the fishermen in the Cove came back to him ... the Four Stones and the man who had lost his way ... the red tiles and the black rafters of "The Bended Thumb" ... and then Mary's beauty above it all. Mary on the moors with the wind blowing through her hair; Mary in the house with the firelight on her face, Mary ... and then he suddenly started up, wide awake, for he heard steps on the stair.

He knew them at once—he never doubted that they were Robin's. The last two steps were taken slowly and with hesitation.

Then he hurried down the passage as though he had suddenly made up his mind; then, again, there was a long pause before the door. At last came the knock, timidly, and then another loudly and almost violently.

Harry shouted "Come in," and Robin entered, his face pale and his hands twisting and untwisting.

"Ah, Robin—do you want anything? Come in—sit down. I've been asleep."

"Oh, I'm sorry, did I wake you up? No, thanks, I won't sit down. I've got some things I want to say. I'd rather say them standing up."

There was a long pause. Harry said nothing and stared into the fire.

"I've got a good lot to say altogether." Robin cleared his throat. "It's rather hard. Perhaps this doesn't seem quite the time—after grandfather—and—everything—but I couldn't wait very well. I've been a bit uncomfortable."

"Out with it," said Harry. "This time will do excellently—there's a pause just now, but to-morrow everything will begin again and there's a terrible lot to do. What is it?"

Was it, he wondered, Robin's fault or his own that there was that barrier so strangely defined between them even now? He could feel it there in the room with them now. He wondered whether Robin felt it as well.

"It is about what my aunt said to you this morning—and other things—other things right from the beginning, ever since you came back. I'm not much of a chap at talking, and probably I shan't say what I mean, but I will try. I've been thinking about it all lately, but what made me come and speak to you was this morning—having to ask you a favour after being so rude to you. A chap doesn't like doing that, and it made me think—besides there being other things."

"Oh, there's no need to thank me about this morning," Harry said drily; "I shall be very pleased to do what I can."

"Oh, it isn't that," Robin said quickly. "It isn't about that somehow that I mind at all now; I have been worrying about it a good bit, but that isn't what I want to speak about. I'll go through with it—Breach of Promise—or whatever it is—if only you wouldn't think me—well, quite an utter rotter."

"I wish," said Harry quietly, "that you would sit down. I'm sure that you would find it easier to talk."

Robin looked at him for a moment and then at the chair—then he sat down.

"You see, somehow grandfather's dying has made things seem different to one—it has made one younger somehow. I used to think that I was really very old and knew a lot; but his death has shown me that I know nothing at all—really nothing. But there have been a lot of things all happening together—your coming back, that business with Dahlia—Miss Feverel, you know—a dressing down that I got from Miss Bethel the other evening, and then grandfather's dying——"

He paused again and cleared his throat. He looked straight into the fire, and, every now and again, he gave a little choke and a gasp which showed that he was moved.

"A chap doesn't like talking about himself," he went on at last; "no decent chap does; but unless I tell you everything from the beginning it will never be clear—I must tell you everything——"

"Please—I want to hear."

"Well, you see, before you came back, I suppose that I had really lots of side. I never used to think that I had, but I see now that what Mary said the other night was perfectly right—it wasn't only that I 'sided' about myself, but about my set and my people and everything. And then you came back. You see we didn't any of us very much think that we wanted you. To begin with, you weren't exactly like my governor; not having seen you all my life I hadn't thought much about you at all, and your letters were so unlike anything that I knew that I hadn't believed them exactly. We were very happy as we were. I thought that I had everything I wanted. And then you didn't do things as we did; you didn't like the same books and pictures or anything, and I was angry because I thought that I must know about those things and I couldn't understand you. And then you know you made things worse by trying to force my liking out of me, and chaps of my sort are awfully afraid of showing their feelings to any one, least of all to a man——" Robin paused.

"Yes," said Harry, "I know."

"But all this isn't an excuse really; I was a most awful cad, and there's no getting away from it. But I think I began to see almost from the very beginning that I hadn't any right to behave like that, but I was obstinate.

"And then I began to get in a fright about Miss Feverel. She wouldn't give my letters back, although I went to her and Uncle Garrett and Aunt Clare—all of us—but it was no good—she meant to keep them and of course we knew why. And then, too, I saw at last that I'd behaved like an utter cad—it was funny I didn't see it at the time. But I'd seen other chaps do the same sort of thing and the girls didn't mind, and I'd thought that she ought to be jolly pleased at getting to know a Trojan—and all that sort of thing.

"But when I saw that she wasn't going to give the letters back but meant to use them I was terribly frightened. It wasn't myself so much, although I hated the idea of my friends knowing about it all and laughing at me—but it was the House too—my letting it down so.

"I'd been thinking about you a good bit already. You see you changed after Aunt Clare spoke to you that morning and I began to be rather afraid of you—and when a chap begins to be afraid of some one he begins to like him. I got Aunt Clare and Uncle Garrett to go and speak to Dahlia, and they couldn't get anything out of her at all; so, then, I began to wonder whether you could do anything, and as soon as I began to wonder that I began to want to talk to you. But I never got much chance; you were always in grandfather's room, and you didn't give me much encouragement, did you? and then—I began to be awfully miserable. I don't want to whine—I deserved it all right enough—but I didn't seem to have a friend anywhere and all my things that I'd believed in seemed to be worth nothing at all. Then I wanted to talk to you awfully, and when grandfather was worse and was dying I began to see things straight—and then I saw Mary and she told me right out what I was, and I saw it all as clear as daylight.

"And so; well, I've come—not to ask you to help me about Dahlia—but whether you'll help me to play the game better. I wasn't always slack and rotten like I am now. When I was in Germany I thought I was going to do all sorts of things ... but anyhow I can't say exactly all that I mean. Only I'm awfully lonely and terribly ashamed; and I want you to forgive me for being so beastly to you——"

He looked wretched enough as he sat there facing the fire with his lip quivering. He made a strong effort to control himself, but in a moment he had broken down altogether and hid his head in the arm of the chair, sobbing as if his heart would break.

Harry waited. The moment for which he had longed so passionately had come at last; all those weary weeks had now received their reward. But he was very tired and he could not remember anything except that his boy was there and that he was crying and wanted some one to help him—which was very sentimental.

He got up from his chair and put his hand on Robin's shoulder.

"Robin, old boy—don't; it's all right really. I've been waiting for you to come and speak to me; of course, I knew that you would come. Never mind about those other things—we're going to have a splendid time, you and I."

He put his arm round him. There was a moment's silence, then the boy turned round and gripped his father's coat—then he buried his head in his father's knees.

Benham entered half an hour later with Harry's evening meal.

"I will have mine here, too, Benham," said Robin, "with my father."

"There is one thing, Robin," said Harry a little later, laughing—"what about the letters?"

"Oh, I know!" Robin looked up at his father appealingly. "I don't know what you must think of me over that business. But I suppose I believed for a time in it all, and then when I saw that it wouldn't do I just wanted to get out of it as quickly as I could. I never seem to have thought about it at all—and now I'm more ashamed than I can say. But I think I'll go through with it; I don't see that there's anything else very much for me to do, any other way of making up—I think I'd rather face it."

"Would you?" said Harry. "What about your friends and the House?"

Robin flinched for a moment; then he said resolutely, "Yes, it would be better for them too. You see they know already—the House, I mean. All the chaps in the dining-hall and the picture-gallery, they've known about it all day, and I know that they'd rather I didn't back out of it. Besides—" he hesitated a moment. "There's another thing—I have the kind of feeling that I can't have hurt Dahlia so very much if she's the kind of girl to carry that sort of thing through; if, I mean, she takes it like that she isn't the sort of girl that would mind very much what I had done——"

"Is she," said Harry, "that sort of girl?"

"No, I don't think she is. That's what's puzzled me about it all. She was worth twenty of me really. But any decent sort of girl would have given them back——"

"She has——"

"What?"

"Given them back."

"The letters?"

Harry went to his writing-table and produced the bundle. They lay in his hand with the blue ribbon and the neat handwriting, "For Robert Trojan," outside.

Robin stared. "Not *the* letters?"

"Yes—the letters; I have had them some days."

But still he did not move. "*You've* had them?—several days?"

"Yes. I went to see Miss Feverel on my own account and she gave me them——"

"You had them when we asked you to help us!"

"Yes—of course. It was a little secret of my own and Miss Feverel's—our—if you like—revenge."

"And we've been laughing at you, scorning you; and we tried—all of us—and could do nothing! I say, you're the cleverest man in England! Score! Why I should think you have!" and then he added, "But I'm ashamed—terribly. You have known all these days and said nothing—and I! I wonder what you've thought of me——"

He took the letters into his hand and undid the ribbon slowly. "I'm jolly glad you've known—it's as if you'd been looking after the family all this time, while we were plunging around in the dark. What a score! That we should have failed and you so absolutely succeeded—" Then again, "But I'm jolly ashamed—I'll tell you everything—always. We'll work together——"

He looked them through and then flung them into the fire.

"I've grown up," he suddenly cried; "come of age at last—at last I know."

"Not too fast," said Harry, smiling; "it's only a stage. There's plenty to learn—and we'll learn it together." Then, after a pause, "There's another thing, though, that will astonish you a bit—I'm engaged——"

"Engaged!" Robin stared. Quickly before his eyes passed visions of terrible Colonial women—some entanglement that his father had contracted abroad and had been afraid to announce before. Well, whatever it might be, he would stand by him! It was they two against the world whatever happened!—and Robin felt already the anticipatory glow of self-sacrificing heroism.

Harry smiled. "Yes—Mary Bethel!"

"Mary! Hurrah!"

He rushed at his father and seized his hand—"You and Mary! Why, it's simply splendid! The very thing—I'd rather it were she than any one!—she told me what she thought of me the other night, I can tell you—fairly went for me. By Jove! I'm glad—we'll have some times, three of us here together. When was it?"

"Oh! only this morning! I had asked her before, but it was only settled this morning."

Then Robin was suddenly grave. "Oh! but, I say, there's Aunt Clare—and Uncle Garrett!" He had utterly forgotten them. What would they say? The Bethels of all people!

"Yes. I've thought about it. I'm very sorry, but I'm afraid Aunt Clare won't want to stay. I don't see what's to be done. I haven't told her yet——"

Robin saw at once that he must choose his future; it was to be his aunt or his father. His aunt with all those twenty years of faithful service behind her, his aunt who had done everything for him—or his father whom he had known for three weeks. But he had no hesitation; there was now no question it was his father for ever against the world!

"I'm sorry," he said slowly. "Perhaps there will be some arrangement. Poor Aunt Clare! Did you—tell grandfather?"

"No. I wanted to, but I had no opportunity. But he knows—I am sure that he knows."

Their thoughts passed to the old man. It was almost as if he had been there in the room with them, and they felt, curiously, as though he had at that moment handed over the keys of the House. For an instant they saw him; his eyes like diamonds, his wrinkled cheeks, his crooked fingers—and then his laugh. "Harry, my boy, you'll do."

"It's almost as if he was here," said Robin. He turned round and put his hand in his father's.

"I know he's pleased," he said.

And so it was during the next week, through the funeral, and the gathering of relatives and the gradual dispersing of them again, and the final inevitable seclusion when the world and the relations and the dead had all joined in leaving the family alone. The gathering of Trojans had shown, beyond a doubt, that Harry was quite fitted to take his place at the head of the family. He had acted throughout with perfect tact and everything had gone without a hitch. Many a Trojan had arrived for the funeral—mournful, red-eyed Trojans, with black crape and an air of deferential resignation that hinted, also, at curiosity as regards the successor. They watched Harry, ready for anything that might gratify their longing for sensational failure; a man from the backwoods was certain to fail, and their chagrined disappointment was only solaced by their certainty of some little sensation in the announcement of his surprising success.

Of course, Clare had been useful; it was on such an occasion that she appeared at her best. She was kind to them all, but at the same time impressed the dignity of her position upon them, so that they went away declaring that Clare Trojan knew how to carry herself and was young for her years.

The funeral was an occasion of great ceremony, and the town attended in crowds. Harry realised in their altered demeanour to himself their appreciation of the value of his succession, and he knew that Sir Henry Trojan was something very different from the plain Harry. But he had, from the beginning, taken matters very quietly. Now that he was assured of the affection of the only two people who were of importance to him he could afford to treat with easy acquiescence anything else that Fate might have in store for him. His diffidence, had, to some extent, left him, and he took everything that came with an ease that had been entirely foreign to him three weeks before.

Clare might indeed wonder at the change in him, for she had not the key that unlocked the mystery. The week seemed to draw father and son very closely together. Years seemed to have made little difference in their outlook on things, and in some ways Robin was the elder of the two. They said nothing about Mary—that was to wait until after the funeral; but the consciousness of their secret added to the bond between them.

Clare herself regarded the future complacently. She was, she felt, absolutely essential to the right ruling of the House, and she intended, gradually but surely, to restore her command above and below stairs. The only possible lion in her path was Harry's marrying, but of that there seemed no fear at all.

She admired him a little for his conduct during their father's funeral; he was not such an oaf as she had thought—but she would bide her time.

At last, however, the thunderbolt fell. It was a week after the funeral, and they had reached dessert. Clare sometimes stayed with them while they smoked, and, as a rule, conversation was not very general. To-night, however, she rose to go. Her black suited her; her dark hair, her dark eyes, the dark trailing clouds of her dress—it was magnificently sombre against the firelight and the shine of the electric lamps on the silver. But Harry's "Wait a moment, Clare, I want to talk," called her back, and she stood by the door looking over her shoulder at him.

Then when she saw from his glance that it was a matter of importance, she came back slowly again towards him.

"Another family council?" said Garrett rather impatiently. "We have had a generous supply lately."

"I'm afraid this is imperative," said Harry. "I am sorry to bother you, Clare, but this seems to me the best time."

"Oh, any time suits me," she said indifferently, sitting down reluctantly. "But if it's household affairs, I should think that we need hardly keep Garrett and Robin."

"It is something that concerns us all four," said Harry. "I am going to be married!"

It had been from the beginning of things a Trojan dictum that the revealing of emotion was the worst of gaucheries—Clare, Garrett, and Robin himself had been schooled in this matter from their respective cradles; and now the lesson must be put into practice.

For Robin, of course, it was no revelation at all, but he dared not look at his aunt; he understood a little what it must mean to her. To those that watched her, however, nothing was revealed. She stood by the fire, her hands at her side, her head slightly turned towards her brother.

"Might I ask," she said quietly, "the name of the fortunate lady?"

"Miss Bethel!"

"Miss Bethel!" Garrett sprang to his feet. "Harry, you must be joking! You can't mean it! Not the daughter of Bethel at the Point—the madman!—the——"

"Please, Garrett," said Harry, "remember that she has promised to be my wife. I am sorry, Clare——"

He turned round to his sister.

But she had said nothing. She pulled a chair from the table and sat down, quietly, without obvious emotion.

"It is a little unexpected," she said. "But really if we had considered things it was obvious enough. It is all of a piece. Robin tried for Breach of Promise, the Bethels in the house before father has been buried for three days—the policy and traditions of the last three hundred years upset in three weeks."

"Of course," said Harry, "I could scarcely expect you to welcome the change. You do not know Miss Bethel. I am afraid you are a little prejudiced against her. And, indeed, please—please, believe me that it has been my very last wish to go counter in any way to your own plans. But it has seemed almost unavoidable; we have found that one thing after another has arisen about which we could not agree. Is it too late now to reconsider the position? Couldn't we pull together from this moment?"

But she interrupted him. "Come, Harry," she said, "whatever we are, let us avoid hypocrisy. You have beaten me at every point and I must retire. I have seen in three weeks everything that I had cared for and loved destroyed. You come back a stranger, and without knowing or caring for the proper dignity of the House, you have done what you pleased. Finally, you are bringing a woman into the House whose parents are beggars, whose social position makes her unworthy of such a marriage. You cannot expect me to love you for it. From this moment we cease to exist for each other. I hope that I may never see you again or hear from you. I shall not indulge in heroics or melodrama, but I will never forgive you. I suppose that the house at Norfolk is at my disposal?"

"Certainly," he answered. Then he turned to his brother. "I hope, Garrett," he said, "that you do not feel as strongly about the matter as Clare. I should be very glad if you found it possible to remain."

That gentleman was in a difficult position; he changed colour and tried to avoid his sister's eyes. After a rapid survey of the position, he had come to the conclusion that he would not be nearly as comfortable in Norfolk—he could not write his book as easily, and the house had scarcely the same position of importance. He had grown fond of the place. Harry, after all, was not a bad chap—he seemed very anxious to be pleasant; and even Mary Bethel mightn't turn out so badly.

"You see, Clare," he said slowly, "there is the book—and—well, on the whole, I think it would be almost better if I remained; it is not, of course, that——"

Clare's lip curled scornfully.

"I understand, Garrett, you could scarcely be expected to leave such comforts for so slight a reason. And you, Robin?"

She held the chair with her hand as she spoke. The fury at her heart was such that she could scarcely breathe; she was quite calm, but she had a mad desire to seize Harry as he sat there at the table and strangle him with her hands. And Garrett!—the contemptible coward! But if only Robin would come with her, then the rest mattered little. After all, it had only been a fortnight ago when he had stood at her side and rejected his father. The scene now was parallel—her voice grew soft and trembled a little as she spoke to him.

"Robin, dear, what will you do? Will you come with me?"

For a moment father and son looked at each other, then Robin answered—

"I shall be very glad to come and stay sometimes, Aunt Clare—often—whenever you care to have me. But I think that I must stay here. I have been talking to father and I am going up to London to try, I think, for the Diplomatic. We thought——"

But the "we" was too much for her.

"I congratulate you," she said, turning to Harry. "You have done a great deal in three weeks. It looks," she said, looking round the room, "almost like a conspiracy. I——" Then she suddenly broke down. She bent down over Robin and caught his head between her hands—

"Robin—Robin dear—you must come, you must, dear. I brought you up—I have loved you—always—always. You can't leave me now, old boy, after all that I have done—all, everything. Why, he has done nothing—he——"

She kissed him again and again, and caught his hands: "Robin, I love you—you—only in all the world; you are all that I have got——"

But he put her hands gently aside. "Please—please—Aunt Clare, I am dreadfully sorry——"

And then her pride returned to her. She walked to the door with her head high.

"I will go to the Darcy's in London until that other house is ready. I will go to-morrow——"

She opened the door, but Harry sprang up—

"Please, Clare—don't go like that. Think over it—perhaps to-morrow——"

"Oh, let me go," she answered wearily; "I'm tired."

She walked up the stairs to her room. She could scarcely see—Robin had denied her!

She shut the door of her bedroom behind her and fell at the foot of her bed, her face buried in her hands. Then at last she burst into a storm of tears—

"Robin! Robin!" she cried.

CHAPTER XVI

It was Christmas Eve and the Cove lay buried in snow. The sea was grey like steel, and made no sound as it ebbed and flowed up the little creek. The sky was grey and snowflakes fell lazily, idly, as though half afraid to let themselves go; a tiny orange moon glittered over the chimneys of "The Bended Thumb."

Harry came out of the Inn and stood for a moment to turn up the collar of his coat. The perfect stillness of the scene pleased him; the world was like the breathless moment before some great event: the opening of Pandora's box, the leaping of armed men from the belly of the wooden horse, the flashing of Excalibur over the mere, the birth of some little child.

He sighed as he passed down the street. He had read in his morning paper that the Cove was doomed. The word had gone forth, the Town Council had decided; the Cove was to be pulled down and a street of lodging-houses was to take its place. Pendragon would be no longer a place of contrasts; it would be all of a piece, a completely popular watering-place.

The vision of its passing hurt him—so much must go with it; and gradually he saw the beauty and the superstition and the wonder being driven from the world—the Old World—and a hard Iron and Steel Materialism relentlessly taking its place.

But he himself had changed; the place had had its influence on him, and he was beginning to see the beauty of these improvements, these manufactures, these hard straight lines and gaunt ugly squares. Progress? Progress? Inevitable?—yes! Useful?—why, yes, too! But beautiful?—Well, perhaps ... he did not know.

At the top of the hill he turned and saluted the cold grey sky and sea and moor. The Four Stones were in harmony to-day: white, and pearl-grey, with hints of purple in their shadows—oh beautiful and mysterious world!

He went into the Bethels' to call for Mary. Bethel appeared for a moment at the door of his study and shouted—

"Hullo! Harry, my boy! Frightfully busy cataloguing! Going out for a run in a minute!"—the door closed.

His daughter's engagement seemed to have made little difference to him. He was pleased, of course, but Harry wondered sometimes whether he realised it at all.

Not so Mrs. Bethel. Arrayed in gorgeous colours, she was blissfully happy. She was at the head of the stairs now.

"Just a minute, Harry—Mary's nearly ready. Oh! my dear, you haven't been out in that thin waistcoat ... but you'll catch your death—just a minute, my dear, and let me get something warmer? Oh do! Now you're an obstinate, bad man! Yes, a bad, bad man"—but at this moment arrived Mary, and they said good-bye and were away.

During the few weeks that they had been together there had been no cloud. Pendragon had talked, but they had not listened to it; they had been perfectly, ideally happy. They seemed to have known each other completely so long ago—not only their virtues but their faults and failures.

With her arm in his they passed through the gate and found Robin waiting for them.

"Hullo! you two! I've just heard from Macfadden. He suggests Catis in Dover Street for six months and then abroad. He thinks I ought to pass easily enough in a year's time—and then it will mean Germany!"

His face was lighted with excitement.

"Right you are!" cried Harry. "Anything that Macfadden suggests is sure to be pretty right. What do you say, Mary?"

"Oh, I don't know anything about men's businesses," she said, laughing. "Only don't be too long away, Robin."

They passed down the garden, the three of them, together.

In Norfolk a woman sat at her window and watched the snow tumbling softly against the panes. The garden was a white sea—the hills loomed whitely beyond—the sky was grey with small white clouds, hanging like pillows heavily in mid-air.

The snow whirled and tossed and danced.

Clare turned slowly from the windows and drew down the blinds.

THE END

Made in the USA
Las Vegas, NV
23 September 2024

95674376R00095